German-American Genealogical Research

Monograph No. 7

NINETEENTH-CENTURY EMIGRATION OF "OLD LUTHERANS" FROM EASTERN GERMANY (MAINLY POMERANIA AND LOWER SILESIA) TO AUSTRALIA, CANADA, AND THE UNITED STATES

Clifford Neal Smith

CLEARFIELD

Reprint, 1984
Reprint, 1985 September   ±√
Reprint, 1986 March   ±√
Reprint, 1988 May   qz
Reprint, February 1989   qz
Reprint, November 1989   qz
Reprint, August 1990   qz
Reprint, April 1991   qz
Reprint, June 1993   qz
Reprint, July 1993   qz
Reprint, January 1994   rz
Reprint, February 1994   qz
Reprint, November 1994   ru
Reprint, April 1995   qz
Reprint, July 1995   rz
Reprint, June 1996   qz
Reprint, November 1996   rz
Reprint, January 1997   u
Reprint, February 1997   ru
Reprint, May 1997   u
Reprint, August 1997   u

Reprinted for
Clearfield Company, Inc. by
Genealogical Publishing Co., Inc.
Baltimore, Maryland
2004

International Standard Book Number: 0-8063-5228-0

Made in the United States of America

CONTENTS

INTRODUCTION

In 1943 Wilhelm Iwan published a two-volume study in German, entitled *Die altlutherische Auswanderung um die Mitte des 19. Jahrhunderts* (The Old Lutheran Emigration Around the Middle of the Nineteenth Century).[1] The work contains large amounts of material of genealogical value from state archives in eastern Germany and western Poland.[2] His work is valuable not only because of the detailed information on immigrants to Australia and the United States, but also because it records a relatively recent case of migration for religious motives. Eighteenth-century religious migrations to America are poorly documented; the exact manner in which the migrations occurred can only be superficially reconstructed. The migration of nineteenth-century Old Lutherans, on the other hand, is voluminously documented and may serve, perhaps, as a model from which to inquire into the mechanisms of previous migrations of closed social groups.[3]

This monograph summarizes most of the material of genealogical importance in Herr Iwan's study. Omitted herein are textual passages mentioning the activities of the leaders of the Old Lutheran migration. For descendants of these leaders, there would seem to be no remedy, excepting to read the text in its entirety, because the volumes are not indexed.

Reasons for the Migration. Northern Germany had become overwhelmingly protestant and Lutheran at the time of the Reformation. Nearly all the North German princes were Lutheran or Calvinist (Reformed). Since the two churches exercised important civil responsibilities in Prussia, such as control of marriages, registration of births, and care of the dead, good standing in a congregation had great practical implications for every inhabitant of the country. Generally speaking, the philosophical and doctrinal views of the Calvinists favored the rich and powerful, for Jean Calvin of Geneva had put forth a doctrine whereby those in power were to be seen as God's Elect. Thus it was that, for many of the higher nobles, there tended to be a preference for the Calvinist (Reformed) Church over the Lutheran one, in which wealth and power were not always held in such high repute.

Frederick the Great, one of the wisest of the Prussian rulers, had been careful not to favor either of the two confessions, presumably in the conviction

---

1. Wilhelm Iwan, *Die altlutherische Auswanderung um die Mitte des 19. Jahrhunderts.* Published for the Johann-Hess Institut, Breslau (Ludwigsburg: Eichhorn Verlag Lothar Kallenberg, 1943). A copy of this work will be found in the Library of Congress, Washington, D.C.

2. In his Foreword, Herr Iwan states, however, that he was unable to study materials in the archives at Merseburg and Posen; as a consequence, his data on emigrants from Posen Province is incomplete.

3. This monograph is to serve as background material for a paper on the genealogical implications of migration to be presented at the World Conference on Records in Salt Lake City in August, 1980. A paper on the subject is to be published by the Conference.

that religious strife between Lutherans and Calvinists could only weaken the Prussian State. Members of his family, however, were not so wise, and a descendant, King Friedrich Wilhelm III, forced the two confessions to merge; he simply felt, as a Calvinist, that it was a disgrace that divine services at the Hof- und Garnisonskirche (Court and Garrison Church) in Potsdam, where he worshiped, should vary with each change of Lutheran and Calvinist minister. Furthermore, he found it sad that, as a Calvinist, he could not take Holy Communion with his wife, a Lutheran.

The merger of the two confessions came about by royal proclamation on 27 September 1817 under the title *"Entstehung der preussischen Landeskirche"* (Foundation of the Prussian State Church). The proclamation called for the ministers and congregations of both confessions to overcome their narrow sectarian views and to join together in Holy Communion and in church organization. For educated Prussians, imbued, as they already were, with the rationalism of the period, the proclamation came as a logical and acceptable solution to the divisiveness of the past.

As a practical matter, the proclaimed merger meant that creeds and liturgies, as well as the administration of the churches, had to be revised and reorganized. The first positive attitudes began slowly to change; by 1822 there were evident signs of opposition to the unification. Reformed Church members had little use for Lutheran creedal views; the Lutherans were reluctant to change their hallowed order of service. The ministers of both confessions were unenthusiastic but, as state officials, they were bound to obey the direct commands of their King.

Researchers wishing to inquire further into the doctrinal and administrative difficulties occasioned by the unification of the two confessions will find much written on the matter in Iwan's work and elsewhere. From a genealogical point of view, however, several facts are salient:

¶ Those who opposed the merger strongly enough to leave Prussia were almost entirely of the lower classes, there being only one known member of the lower aristocracy among them (Pastor von Roehr).

¶ Excepting for a very few emigrants from the cities of Magdeburg and Erfurt, almost without exception the emigrants were from rural areas and small towns, with occupations usual in such settings, conservative in their views, frugal, and accustomed to hardships (emigrants from cities and towns = 725; emigrants from rural areas = 5,438).

¶ Generally speaking, as devout Lutherans, they were unwilling to emigrate illegally--despite the fact that, at the time, many less punctilious Germans were finding it possible to skip the country to avoid military or family obligations--and therefore many families incurred great hardship in getting exit permits from the authorities.

¶ As members of organized congregations in Prussia, the emigrants tended to leave the country in groups and to settle together in their new homelands.

¶ Since insistence upon the ancient Lutheran form of worship constituted civil disobedience after the merger of the two confessions, governmental authorities--almost entirely members of the lower noble orders--tended to be most unfriendly, when confronted with applications for emigration permits.

Some officials were more spiteful than others, but, generally, great care was taken to make certain the emigrants took care of all possible obligations before leaving. This meant, for example, that grown children who might be left behind in Prussia, had to be given their inheritances, even though the emigrating parents had not died. One wonders how many would-be emigrants were deterred by this requirement, or how many children had to emigrate with their parents, who under under circumstances might have remained in the homeland.

¶ In the first years of emigration, officials were reluctant to admit that there could exist in Prussia a condition tantamount to religious persecution and, therefore, it is likely that some "Old Lutheran" separatists are recorded as having emigrated for reasons other than their faith. Some emigrants are likely to have been overlooked in this study, since their true reason for emigration is not properly recorded in governmental files. About 86% of the emigrants are thought by Herr Iwan to be identified herein.

¶ Extremely important to genealogical researchers is the fact that governmental files often distort the marital status of emigrants: If one had been married by a Lutheran minister, rather than by a minister of the State Church, civil authorities considered the marriage to be null and void; in a few spiteful cases the authorities labeled the relationship as concubinage. Throughout the list of emigrants which follows, there are many examples wherein the husband and wife are not shown under the same surname, and the children's legitimacy is left open to doubt. Thus, one of the practical effects of dissent from the State Church by the Old Lutherans (and the Mennonites) was that one could not be married legally, and one's children, illegitimate in the eyes of the law, could not join a craft guild or attend a university. In one case reported herein, a young Lutheran recruit was ejected from the Prussian army, simply because he could not produce a valid christening certificate from a State Church minister.

Where the Emigrants Settled. Silesia was the first region in which the idea of emigration emerged. At first, it was thought that southern Russia would be an acceptable haven, since the Czars of Russia had encouraged the settlement of Germans in their territory for several generations. Indeed, as will be seen, a few Lutherans actually did immigrate to the neighborhood of Astrakhan, apparently under the care of Pastor Wehrhan-Kunitz, but any plan for a larger group to move there was destroyed by a Polish revolution during the period.

Later groups were influenced to immigrate to the United States by a glowing letter from blacksmith Karl Berger, from Guttmansdorf, Kreis Reichenbach, Silesia, who wrote from America to his parents in Peilau regarding life near Detroit, Michigan. This letter went the rounds among eager Lutherans and probably did much to influence many of them to follow the footsteps of the Mennonites, Labadists, Dunkards, Salzburgers, and Moravian Brethren (Herrnhuter) to the Western Hemisphere. Settlements in the United States were established at the following places:

New York

Buffalo	Johannisburg	Martinville
Eden	Wallmow	Wollcottsville
Bergholz	Tonawanda	Lockport

New York	Cedarburg	Green Bay
Wollcottsburg	Kirchhain	Texas
Canada	Mayville	Galveston
Humberstone	Lebanon	Houston
	Watertown	Rabb's Creek,
Wisconsin	Madison	Bastrop County
Milwaukee	Manitowoc	Serbin
Freistadt	Oshkosh	

Some emigrants may also have settled in Chicago and Dubuque, Iowa. Ten persons also settled in Ohio and were reckoned as members of the Buffalo congregation.

The places of settlement do not entirely agree with the congregational data fór 1851-1852, because there came about a notable schism among the migrants shortly after arrival in the United States. The parish reports for the Buffalo Synod, as the Old Lutheran separatists were called in the United States, showed the following:

Congregation	Pastor	Teachers	Number of Communicants
New York			
Buffalo	Grabau	3	1,400
Neu Bergholz	v. Roehr	3	1,300
Martinville	Wier	1	597
Wallmow	v. Roehr	1	220
Eden	Lange	–	89
Canada			
Humberstone	–	1	288
Michigan			
Detroit	Winkler	–	ca. 120
Macomb County*	Winkler	–	120
Wisconsin			
Milwaukee	Mueller	–	?
Freystadt	Mueller	1	378
Kirchhain	Kindermann	1	456
Cedarburg	Kindermann	1	78
Watertown	Kindermann	1	84
Newark	Mashop**	–	?

*Later, Roseville. **So spelled.

Data on the congregations in Texas are not given in Herr Iwan's study, excepting the revealing remark that the poorest of the immigrants to Texas had to remain in Galveston and Houston, where they could find work, whereas the more affluent immigrants settled inland at Rabb's Creek, Bastrop County, and at Serbin.

With regard to the settlements in Australia, Herr Iwan gives little specific data, although he states in his Foreword that he had worked among the descendants of these immigrants. Apparently, the history of these settlements has been covered in his book, *Um des Glaubens willen nach Australien* [To Australia for Reasons of Religion](Breslau, 1931), which has not been available in the United States. We do know that the first Old Lutheran settlers to Australia arrived at Port Adelaide aboard the *Solvay* on 16 October 1837. One family (Kleemann) was for a while at Kingscote, Kangaroo Island, but later moved to Tanunda, north of Adelaide. The major colony was at Klemzig, South Australia.

LIST OF EMIGRANTS

Following is the list of emigrants, their relationships, occupations, and places of origin and destinations. Abbreviations used are: b = born (maiden name), c = child, d = daughter, f = family, s = son, w = wife.

1835

From: Silesia, Kreis Liegnitz
To: Russia, neighborhood of Astrakhan, 1835

HOFFMANN, Johanna Elisabeth, 57, widow	Gross Tinz
HOFFMANN, Johann Gottlieb, 20, s	
HOFFMANN, Maria Rosina, 24, d	
BINNER, Johann Gottlieb, 35	Wangten
BINNER, Johanna Eleonore, b KEIL, 31, w	
BINNER, Johann Christian, 8, c	
BINNER, Maria Rosina, 4, c	
BINNER, Maria Rosina, 38, widow	Wangten
BINNER, Maria Rosina, 18, c	
BINNER, Johann Christian, 17, c	
BINNER, Karl Gottlieb, 14, c	
BINNER, Johanna Eleonore, 11, c	
BINNER, Karl Wilhelm, 7, c	
BINNER, Anna Rosina, 1-1/2, c	

From: Silesia, Breslau and immediate neighborhood
To: U.S.A., New York, Buffalo, 1835

ZUENGLER (also ZANGLER), J. G., f	Breslau
LANGNER, F., f?	Breslau
KRIEG, Ernst, cabinetmaker, f?	Breslau
SIEFFERT, J. Ch., cutler, f?	Breslau
HASCHMANN, Wilhelm, lumber dealer, f?	Breslau

1836

From: Silesia, Breslau
To: North America, 1836

PIETSCH, Willhelm August, 35	Breslau
PIETSCH, Rosina, b SCHOENFELD, 20, w	
PIETSCH, Bertha, 6, c	
PIETSCH, Hermann, 5, c	

From: Silesia, Kreis Freistadt
To: Southern Australia

KITTLAU, Luis, 22, restaurateur	Neusalz

1837

From: Pomerania, Kreis Kammin
To: America, 1837

KROENING, --, 26 bookbinder	Kammin
KROENING, Sophia, b BOLLING, w	
KROENING, --, 2, c	
KROENING, --, 8 months, c	
BUROW, --, hired hand & farmer's s	Kammin
ZUEHLSDORF, --, 36, carpenter	Kammin
ZUEHLSDORF, Anna Katharina, b SCHEER, w	
ADAM, Gottlieb, 40, shoemaker	Kammin
ADAM, Charlotte, b ZINGLER, w	
ADAM, --, 4 children, 3-12	
SARNOW, --, shoemaker	Kammin
SARNOW, --, w	
RAPPRAEGER, --, 44, property owner	Kammin
RAPPRAEGER, Maria, b LANGEN, w	
RAPPRAEGER, --, 4 children, 7-16	
GANDT, Luise, 25, unmarried servant girl	Kammin
SCHWARZ, --, shoemaker	Kammin
SCHWARZ, --, w	
FAEHRMANN, --, 49 day laborer	Kammin
FAEHRMANN, Luise, b FAEHRMANN, w	
HANUTH, August, journeyman sadler	Kammin
WILL, --, day laborer	Knurrbusch
KASSNER (or KASTEN), Dorothea, 47, unmarried	Scheffin
GUST, --, hired hand	Platchow
GUST, --, w	
GUST, --, 2 children	

From: Pomerania, Kreis Wollin
To: America, 1837

SCHREIBER, --, shepherd	Schwantus
SCHREIBER, --, 4 children	
LUEDKE, --, blacksmith	near Greifenberg
LUEDKE, --, w	
LUEDKE, --, 2 children	

From: Pomerania, Kreis Naugard
To: America, 1837

BAGANS, --	Hakenwalde
BAGANS, --, w	

From: Silesia, Kreis Goerlitz
To: America, 1837

HARTMANN, Johann Gottlieb, journeyman cabinetmaker, 25	Koenigshain

From: Pomerania, Kreis Kammin
To: South Australia (probably all the persons hereinafter, but destination is not always clearly stated), 1837

KLEEMANN, Friedrich, 38, farmer	Raddack
KLEEMANN, Maria, b. HELM, w	
KLEEMANN, --, 5 children, 3 months-8 years	
PIEPKORN, David, 31, hired hand	Raddack
WESTPHAL, Dorothea, 22, unmarried fiancée of Piepkorn	
GRUENHAGEN, --, former policeman [Schulze]	Polchow
GRUENHAGEN, Auguste, b TRIGLAFF	
GRUENHAGEN, --, 3 sons, 5, 6, 8	
CHRISTIAN, Gottlieb, 28, journeyman tailor	Schnatow
CHRISTIAN, Wilhelmine Friderike, unmarried servant girl, sister of Gottlieb	
CHRISTIAN, Karoline, 21, bride of Gottlieb	
WALLSCHLAEGER, --, 25, herdsman	Schnatow
WALLSCHLAEGER, Maria, b FAEHRMANN, 34, w	
WALLSCHLAEGER, --, 3 children, 3, 5, 7	
SCHAEFFER, --, separated	Kammin
SCHAEFFER, --, underaged child	
ROHDE, Gottfried, hired hand	Kucklow

From: Silesia, Glogau
To: South Australia (destination not clear), 1837

HASEMANN, Franz, shoemaker	Glogau
HASEMANN, Christiane, b BACKSTAEDT, 49, w	
HASEMANN, Mathilde, 26, d	

1838

From: Silesia, Breslau
To: America, 1838

FAUDE, Johann Gottlieb, 45, landscape gardener	Breslau
FAUDE, Rosina, b SCHULZ, 36, w	
KRAUSE, Leberecht Friedrich, 34, pastor	Breslau

From: Silesia, Kreis Glogau
To: America (to Hamburg in 1838 only)

DARTSCH, --, journeyman wheelwright, 39	Denkwitz

From: Silesia, Kreis Liegnitz
To: America (to Hamburg in 1838 only)

RIESE, Johann Gottlieb, inhabitant	Kummernick
RIESE, Elisabeth, b BARTSCH, w	
RIESE, Johanna Elisabeth, 17, d	
RIESE, Johanne Christiane, 16, d	
RIESE, Johann Karl, 13, s	
RIESE, Johanne Eleonore, 11, d	
RIESE, Johann Karl August, 8, s	
RIESE, Anna Rosina, 2, d	

4

From: Silesia, Kreis Oels
To: America (only to Hamburg in 1838)
BIEROSCH, Christian, 45, weaver   Juliusburg
BIEROSCH, Maria Elisabeth, b PFEIFFER, 37, w
BIEROSCH, Ernestine Luise, 7, c
BIEROSCH, Karl Gottlieb, 5 months, c

From: Silesia, Kreis Liegnitz
To: America (only to Hamburg in 1838)
HEGWER, Benjamin Karl, farmer   Kunitz
HEGWER, Maria Rosina Anna, b ILGNER
HEGWER, Christiane Charlotte Heinriete, d
HEGWER, Ernestine Luise, d
HEGWER, Anna Rosina Christiane, d
HEGWER, Maria Rosina Karoline, d
HEGWER, Karl Traugott Bleibtreu, s
HEGWER, Maria Dorothea, d
HEGWER, Gottlieb August Benjamin, s

From: Brandenburg, Kreis Zuellichau
To: Australia, 1838
LANGE, Christian, 43, gardener   Klemzig
LANGE, Anna Dorothea, b KURZWEG, 44, w
LANGE, Marie Elisabeth, 18, c
LANGE, Johann Friedrich, 16, c
LANGE, Johann Christian, 8, c
LANGE, Gottfried, 62, father of Christian
LANGE, Anna Rosina, b RAU, 73, mother of Christian
RAU, Gottfried, 45, tailor   Klemzig
RAU, Christiane, b KURZMANN, 42, w
RAU, Johann Friedrich, 12, s
BOTHE, Johann Gottlob, 33, gardener   Klemzig
BOTHE, Maria Elisabeth, b RAU, 31, w
BOTHE, Luise, 12, d
RAU, Anna Maria, b BITTEROTT, 54, mother-in-law
RAU, Joh[anne] El[isabeth], 21, sister-in-law
FISCHER, Friedrich, 32, landscape gardener   Klemzig
FISCHER, Joh[anne] Eleonore, b BOTHE, 25, w
FISCHER, Friedrich Wilhelm, 4, c
FISCHER, Joh[anne] Karoline, 2, c
PETRASS, Joh[ann] Gottfried, 37, wheelwright   Klemzig
PETRASS, Joh[anne] Luise, b STELLMACHER, 36, w
PETRASS, Johanne Luise, 11, c
PETRASS, Wilhelm, 9, c
PETRASS, Anna, 9, c
PETRASS, August, 2
HOENKE, Christian, tailer   Klemzig
HOENKE, Elisabeth, b SCHULZ, w
HOENKE, Friedrich Ernst, 10, c
HOENKE, Johann August, 6, c
FIEDLER, August, 41, hunter   Klemzig
FIEDLER, Maria, b KOEHLER, widow of PEUSSLER, 38, w
FIEDLER, Johann August, 16, c
FIEDLER, Bertha Mathilde, 15, c
FIEDLER, Johanne Luis, 9, c
FIEDLER, Karl Wilhelm, 4, c
HOENKE, Gottlob, 29, day laborer   Klemzig
HOENKE, Anna Elisabeth, b ZEUNERT, 30, w
SCHULZ, Johann Gottfried, hired hand, 26   Klemzig
SCHULZ, Eleonore, b TEUBER, 24, w
SCHULZ, Johann Friedrich, 1-1/2, s
MIEGEL, Johann Georg, hired hand, 41   Klemzig
MIEGEL, Maria Elisabeth, b ZERNACK, 38, w
MIEGEL, Johanne Eleonore, 13, c
MIEGEL, Johanne Luise, 8, c
JAENSCH, Johann Christian, hired hand, 24   Klemzig
JAENSCH, Eleonore, b RAU, 24, w
JAENSCH, Gottfried, 2, s
RAU, Christian, 33, laborer   Klemzig
RAU, Elisabeth, b SCHROCK, 34, w
HOENKE, Gottfried, 31, gardener   Klemzig
HOENKE, Maria Luise, b BOTHE, 32, w

HOENKE, Johanne Luise, 3, d
HOENKE, Maria Elisabeth, b SCHULZ, 60, m
HOENKE, Anna Elisabeth, 28, unmarried s
BOTHE, Georg, 57, gardener   Klemzig
BOTHE, Eleonore, b RIEPKE, 54, w
BOTHE, Gottfried, 28, s
BOTHE, Anna Maria, 22, d
BOTHE, Christian, day laborer, 62   Klemzig
SCHULZ, Friedrich, 53, gardener   Klemzig
SCHULZ, Anna Elisabeth, b WOIDT, 56, w
SCHULZ, Johanne Eleonore, 20, d
SCHULZ, Anna Dorothea, 18, d
SCHULZ, Johann Samuel, 16, s
SCHULZ, Johanne Luise, 12, d
RAU, Anna Rosina, unmarried daý laborer   Klemzig
RAU, Johann Georg Friedrich, 43, gardener   Klemzig
RAU, Anna Dorothea, b LEDER, 45, w
RAU, Christian, 19, s
RAU, Anna Eleonore, 13, d
RAU, Anna Luise, 11, d
RAU, Friedrich, 6, s
SCHUMANN, Christian, 53, farm laborer   Klemzig
SCHUMANN, Maria Elisabeth, b SCHUBERT, 53, w
SCHUMANN, Johanne Eleonore, 24, d
THIELE, Samuel, 56, cottager   Harthe
THIELE, Rosina, b SCHULZ, 50, w
THIELE, Johann Friedrich, 26, s
THIELE, Johann Wilhelm, 19, s
THIELE, Johann August, 4, s
SCHULZ, Gottfried, 50, journeyman mason and
  cottager   Harthe
SCHULZ, Dorothea, b HAHN, 40, w
SCHULZ, Dorothea, 19, d
SCHULZ, Johann Gotthilf, 13, s
SCHULZ, Johanne Eleonore, 11, d
SCHULZ, Maria Elisabeth, 9, d
SCHULZ, Anna Elisabeth, 1-1/2, d
HOFFMANN, Johann Friedrich, 61, gardener   Harthe
HOFFMANN, Anna Maria, b. KOERBER, 54, w
HOFFMANN, Luise, 21, d
POELCHEN, Christoph, 35, day laborer   Goltzen
POELCHEN, Maria Elisabeth, b POELCHEN, 34, w
POELCHEN, Luise, 13, d
POELCHEN, Johann Gottlieb, 6, s
POELCHEN, Johanne Eleonore, 4, d
POELCHEN, August, 4, s
WEBER, Christian, 42, cottager   Goltzen
  (He left wife and children in Germany be-
  cause they did not belong to his confes-
  sion and he could not convince them other-
  wise.)
ZILM, Christian, 40, day laborer   Goltzen
ZILM, Anna Dorothea, b MATHISKE, w
ZILM, Friedrich Wilhelm, 10, s
ZILM, Johann Friedrich, 7, s
ZILM, Gottlob, 34, brother
ZILM, Anna Dorothea, 28, sister
GROCKE, Gottlieb, 27, day laborer   Goltzen
GROCKE, Dorothea, b SCHULZ, 25, w
GROCKE, Johann Friedrich, 2-3/4, s
GROCKE, Christian, 2 months
WUNDTKE, Johann Gottfried, 32, day laborer   Langmeil
SCHILLING, Christian, 33, cottager   Langmeil
SCHILLING, Johanne Rosina, b BOTHE, 33, w
SCHILLING, Johanne Luise, 9, d
SCHILLING, Maria Elisabeth, 1/4, d
EISEN, Christian, 60, gardener   Langmeil
EISEN, Johann Samuel, 23, s
EISEN, Luise, 20, d
EISEN, Johanne Eleonore, 18, d
SCHILLING, 36, gardener   Langmeil
SCHILLING, Anna Rosina, b LANGE, 34, w

SCHILLING, Maria Elisabeth, 15, d
SCHILLING, Luise, 12, d
SCHILLING, Johann Gottfried, 9, s
SCHILLING, Anna Rosina, 6, d
SCHILLING, Johann Gottlieb, 3, s
SCHILLING, Christian, 1, s
KUCHEL, Johann Georg, 55, night watchman   Langmeil
KUCHEL, Anna Dorothea, b SEIFFERT, 51, w
KUCHEL, Gottfried, 26, s
KUCHEL, Samuel, 23, s
KUCHEL, Johann Friedrich, 19, s
KUCHEL, Gottlieb, 16, s
SEELAENDER, Gottfried, 50, gardener   Langmeil
SEELAENDER, Anna Rosina, b KOENIG, 50, w
SEELAENDER, Anna Dorothea, 25, d
SEELAENDER, Johann Gottfried, 21, s
SEELAENDER, Johanne Luise, 12, d
  (Another son, Johann Gottlob SEELAENDER,
  27, emigrated in 1841.)
BODATSCH, Anna Rosina, b KOCKEJOY, 68, in-
  habitant   Langmeil
KOCKEJOY, Anna Elisabeth, 19, unmarried
  foster daughter
NEUMANN, Gottfried, 42, cottager   Kay
NEUMANN, Anna Maria, b PFEIFFER, 44, w
NEUMANN, Luise, 12, d
NEUMANN, August, 10, s
NEUMANN, Wilhelm, 7, s
NEUMANN, Maria Elisabeth, 3, d
STOIKE, Samuel, 40, day laborer   Kay
STOIKE, Johanne Dorothea, b PAECH, 36, w
STOIKE, Johann Gottlieb, 14, s
STOIKE, Johanne Eleonore, 13, d
STOIKE, Maria Elisabeth, 5, d
STOIKE, Johanne Luise, 2, d
NITSCHKE, Gottfried, 58, cottager   Kay
NITSCHKE, Johanne Dorothea, b WOLFF, 58, w
NITSCHKE, 35, journeyman mason   Kay
NITSCHKE, Maria Elisabeth, b SUESS, 35, w
NITSCHKE, Johann Karl, 10, s
NITSCHKE, Johann Wilhelm, 8, s
NITSCHKE, Johanne Karoline, 6, d
  (Gottfried Nitschke is the son-in-law of
  Johann Friedrich SUESS.)
JAENSCH, Christian, 40, farmer   Kay
JAENSCH, Maria Elisabeth, b KLENKE, 39, w
JAENSCH, Johanne Dorothea, 15, d
JAENSCH, Johann Gottlob, 13, s
JAENSCH, Johann Christian, 9, s
JAENSCH, Johann Friedrich Traugott, 6, s
JAENSCH, Maria Elisabeth, 4-1/2, d
JAENSCH, Johanne Luise, 1-1/2, d
JAENSCH, Maria, 44, unmarried sister of
  Christian Jaensch
SUESS, Johann Friedrich, 67, cottager   Kay
SUESS, Christiane, b THIELE, 67, w
SUESS, Eleonore, 43, d
KLENKE, Christian, 51, day laborer   Kay
KLENKE, Elisabeth, b GIERKE, 49, w
KLENKE, Anna Dorothea, 21, d
THIELE, Christian, 29, shoemaker   Kay
THIELE, Johanne Dorothea, b KLENKE, 32, w
PFEIFFER, Johann Georg, 47, gardener   Kay
PFEIFFER, Anna Rosina, b NEUMANN, 47, w
PFEIFFER, Johann Gottlieb, 19, s
PFEIFFER, Johann Gottfried, 17, s
PFEIFFER, Anna Elisabeth, 12, d
PFEIFFER, Johann Georg, 8, s
PFEIFFER, Anna Luise, 6, d
PFEIFFER, Johann Christian, 3 s
NITSCHKE, Johann Gottlob, 30, wheelwright   Kay
NITSCHKE, Anna Dorothea, b HIRTHE, 34, w

NITSCHKE, Friedrich Wilhelm, 6, s
NITSCHKE, Maria Elisabeth, 3, d
NITSCHKE, Anna Dorothea, 3 weeks, d
PAECH, Johann Georg, 46, farmer   Kay
PAECH, Rosina, b RICHTER, age?, w
PAECH, Johann Christian, 17, s by first marriage
PAECH, Johann Gottlob, 14, s by first marriage
PAECH, Johann Georg, 11, s by first marriage
PAECH, Johanne Luise, 7, d by first marriage
PAECH, Maria Elisabeth, 3-1/2, d by second marriage
PAECH, Johann Friedrich, 1-1/2, s by second marriage
  (A son, Johann Gottfried Paech, of the first mar-
  riage, emigrated in 1841.)
LIEBELT, Johann Christoph, tailor, 33   Nickern
LIEBELT, Anna Dorothea, b WOLF, 30, w
LIEBELT, Johann Friedrich, 7, s
LIEBELT, Johanne Luise, 4, d
LIEBELT, Johann Gottfried, 1, s
RICHSTEIG, Eleonore, 55, widow of day laborer Nickern
SCHIRMER, Johann Christian, 33, gardener   Nickern
SCHIRMER, Anna Dorothea, b KIRSCH, 34, w
SCHIRMER, Gottlob, 4, s
SCHIRMER, Friedrich, 56, father of J. Christian
SCHIRMER, Johann Georg, 16, s of Friedrich
SCHIRMER, Eleonore, 11, d of Friedrich
KIRSCH, Friderike, 56, widowed mother-in-law
LIEBELT, Johann Christian, 40, shepherd   Nickern
LIEBELT, Maria Elisabeth, b KUCHEL, 35, w
LIEBELT, Johann Gottlieb, 14, s
LIEBELT, Christoph, 12, s
LIEBELT, Johanne Eleonore, 5, d
PAECH, Friedrich, 32, cottager & cabinetmaker Nickern
PAECH, Luise, b JACHNING, 30, w
PAECH, Johanne Karoline, 7, d
PAECH, Eleonore, 4, d
PAECH, Luise, 1, d
DOHNT, Gottfired, 43, cottager   Guhren
DOHNT, Anna Dorthea, b NEUMANN, 45, w
DOHNT, Anna Dorothea, 20, d
DOHNT, Johann Gottlieb, 18, s
DOHNT, Johanne Luise, 16, d
DOHNT, Johann Gottfried, 13, s
DOHNT, Johann Christian, 10, s
DOHNT, Johann Georg, 8, s
DOHNT, Maria Elisabeth, 3, d
WITWER, Friedrich Wilhelm, 38, water miller   Guhren
WITWER, Henriette, b GERLACH, 34, w
WITWER, Friedrich Wilhelm, 8, s
WITWER, Johanne Karoline, 2 months, d
SCHIRMER, Gottlob, 28, hired hand to F. W. Witwer
SCHMIDT, Gottlob, 50, day laborer   Skampe
SCHMIDT, Anna Dorothea, b KLUGE, 50, w
SCHMIDT, Anna Dorothea, 20, d
SCHMIDT, Dorothea Elisabeth, 17, d
SCHMIDT, Gottfried, 16, s
SCHMIDT, Johann Gottlob, 12, s
BARTSCH, Samuel, 37, cabinetmaker   Skampe
BARTSCH, Eleonore, b MEISSNER, 38, w
BARTSCH, Johann Gottlieb, 16, s
BARTSCH, Johann Friedrich, 7, s
BARTSCH, Johann Christian, 5, s
BARTSCH, Johann August, 3, s
BARTSCH, Johanne Eleonore, 1-3/4, d
BARTSCH, Johann Samuel, 3 weeks, s
JANETZKY, Johann Georg, 32, cottager & mason Muschten
JANETZKY, Luise, b LUDE, 28, w
JANETZKY, Johann Gotthilf, 3, s
JANETZKY, Johanne Luise, 1-1/4, d
BOEHME, Johann Georg, 41, cottager & journeyman
  carpenter   Muschten
BOEHME, Karoline, b KOENIG, age?, w
BOEHME, Luise, 15, d

BOEHME, Eleonore, 11, d
BOEHME, Ernst, 8, d
BOEHME, Karoline, 6, d
BOEHME, Dorothea, 3, d
BOEHME, Wilhelm, 1, s
RITBRICHT, Gottfried, 44, peasant   Friedrichsfelde
RITBRICHT, Anna Dorothea, b WOITH, age? w
RITBRICHT, Johann Gottlob, 19, s
RITBRICHT, Dorothea Elisabeth, 17, d
HELLWIG, Friedrich, 35, peasant   Friedrichsfelde
HELLWIG, Eleonore, b KOCH, 37, w
HELLWIG, Johann Wilhelm, 7, s
KOCH, Anna Katharina, b PFEIFFER, 69, mother-in-law
KLUGE, Christian, 27, day laborer   Langheinersdorf
KLUGE, Dorothea, b STEIN, 28, w
KLUGE, Johanne Luise, 1/2, d
KNISPEL, Gottfried, 42, gardener   Langheinersdorf
KNISPEL, Anna Rosina, b PFEIFFER, 41, w
KNISPEL, Anna Dorothea, 16, d
KNISPEL, Christian, 14, s
KNISPEL, Johann Gottfried, 10, s
KNISPEL, Johanne Luise, 7, d
KNISPEL, Johanne Eleonore, 2, d
KNISPEL, Hans, 71, father [of Gottfried]
KNISPEL, KNISPEL, Christian, 31, day laborer,
  brother [of Gottfried]
WILKSCH, Johann Georg, 57, day laborer Langheinersdorf
WILKSCH, Anna Dorothea, 10, d
LIEBELT, Johann Gottfried, 40, tailor   Schoenborn
LIEBELT, Anna Elisabeth, b POHLE, 38, w
LIEBELT, Johanne Luise, 14, d
LIEBELT, Anna Dorothea, 4, d
LIEBELT, Johann Gottfried, 2-1/2, s
LIEBELT, Johann Christoph, 59, cottager   Schoenborn
LIEBELT, Anna Elisabeth, b STEINBORN, 64, w
SCHULZ, Anna Elisabeth, b SCHMIDT, 47,
  farmer's widow   Schoenborn
SCHMIDT, Anna Dorothea, 18, d of brother
  [of Schulz]
WEIMANN, Christian, 42, cottager   Schoenborn
WEIMANN, Anna Dorothea, b SCHNEIDER,
  formerly married to JANDKE, 49, w
WEIMANN, Gottlieb, 14, s
WEIMANN, Eleonore, 9, d
JANDKE, Johann Christian, 21, stepson
  of [Christian] Weimann
JANDKE, Samuel, 18, stepson of [Christian]
  Weimann
SCHUBERT, Christian, 51, day laborer   Moestchen
SCHUBERT, Elisabeth, b BARTEL, 48, w
SCHUBERT, Johann Christian, 16, s
BARTEL, Christian, 44, gardener   Moestchen
BARTEL, Maria Elisabeth, b KIRSCHKE, 41, w
BARTEL, Johanne Luise, 21, d
BARTEL, Anna Maria, 16, d
BARTEL, Dorothea Elisabeth, 12, d
BARTEL, Karoline, 6, d
BARTEL, Gottlob, 41, cottager   Moestchen
BARTEL, Elisabeth, b BINDER, 40, w
BARTEL, Johann Wilhelm, 19, s
BARTEL, Maria Elisabeth, 14, d
BARTEL, Johann Gottfried, 8, s
BARTEL, Johann Gottlob, 4, s
BARTEL, Johann Christian, 1/2, s
HOFFMANN, Johann Gottfried, 32, day
  laborer   Crummendorf
HOFFMANN, Eleonore, b RINNERT, 26, w
HOFFMANN, Johann Friedrich, 4, s
HOFFMANN, Johanne Luise, 2, d
BOTHE, Christian, 59, merchant   Crummendorf
BOTHE, Anna Maria, b KOERBER, 54, w
BOTHE, Luise, 21, d

SCHULZ, Johann Christoph, 47, villager   Klippendorf
SCHULZ, Johanne Dorothea, b FRANK, 49, w
SCHULZ, Johann Christian, 28, s
SCHULZ, Karl August, 20, s
SCHULZ, Johanne Luise, 7, d
PFEIFFER, Johann Georg, 59, gardener   Rackau
PFEIFFER, Christiane, b SCHLIEFKE, 56, w
PFEIFFER, Johanne Eleonore, 30, d
PFEIFFER, Johann Christian, 26, s
PFEIFFER, Maria Elisabeth, 18, d
PFEIFFER, Johann Gottlieb, 15, s
PFEIFFER, Johann Wilhelm, 12, s
SCHLIEFKE, Johann Gottlob, 42, tailor   Keltschen
SCHLIEFKE, Johanne Eleonore, b MAHN, 35, w
MAHN, Luise, 27, sister-in-law
ZIMMERMANN, Johann Friedrich, 38, gardener   Ichser
ZIMMERMANN, Anna Elisabeth, b ZIMMERMANN, 39, w
ZIMMERMANN, Johanne Luise, 11, d
ZIMMERMANN, Johanne Eleonore, 8, d
ZIMMERMANN, Maria Elisabeth, 1, d
PHILIPP, Andreas, 47, cottager   Ostritz
PHILIPP, Maria, b KURZMANN, age?, w
PHILIPP, Johann Wilhelm, 21, s
PHILIPP, Anna Rosina, 17, d
PHILIPP, Johanne Luise, 11, d
PHILIPP, Johann Christian, 7, s
HARTMANN, Johann Georg, 46, gardener   Salkau
HARTMANN, Johanne Luise, b PRESCHEL, 34, w
HARTMANN, Johanne Karoline, 10, d
HARTMANN, Johann Gottlob, 6, s
NITSCHKE, Samuel, 48, cottager   Lochow
NITSCHKE, Anna Elisabeth, b GRIEGER, 42, w
NITSCHKE, Johann Gottlieb, 18, s
NITSCHKE, Gottfried, 14, s
NITSCHKE, Johanne Eleonore, 12, d
NITSCHKE, Johann, 6, s
NITSCHKE, Johann Traugott, 2, s
NITSCHKE, Johanne Luise, 2 weeks, d
PAECH, Johann Friedrich, 36, former farmer Rentschen
PAECH, Anna Dorothea, b KRAMM, 33, w
PAECH, Johann Friedrich Wilhelm, 11, s
PAECH, Johann August, 9, s
PAECH, Johanne Dorothea, 5, d
PAECH, Johann Gottlieb, 2, s
PAECH, Johann Friedrich, 8 weeks, s
  (The guardianship authorities [Vormundschafts-
  behoerde] denied emigration permits to the sis-
  ter of Paech and her children, as follows:
  SCHULZ, Dorothea Elisabeth [b PAECH], 42 widow
  SCHULZ, Johanne Eleonore, 12, d
  SCHULZ, Johann Gottnilf, 8, s)
LUBASCH, Gottfried, 49, cottager   Rissen
LUBASCH, Anna Dorothea, b GREISER, 41, w
LUBASCH, Johanne Eleonore, 16, d from first marriage
LUBASCH, Anna Dorothea Luise, 13, d from second mar.
LUBASCH, Karoline, 11, d from second marriage
LUBASCH, Anna Dorothea, 5, from second marriage
LUBASCH, Maria Elisabeth, 2-1/2, from second marriage
LUBASCH, Anna Elisabeth, 18 weeks, from second mar.
  (A daughter, Johanne Luise LUBASCH, made declaration
  that she would not emigrate.)
SCHULZ, Johann Georg, 56, farmer   Graeditz
  (The wife, -- Schulz, b PAECH, and their son,
  Johann Georg SCHULZ, 11, remained in Germany;
  Schulz sold his farm to his wife.)
BEHREND, Gottfried, 35, shoemaker   Schwiebus
BEHREND, Beate, b LICHTENSTEINER, 35, w
BEHREND, Auguste Emilie, 11, d
DONNER, Karl, 39, shoemaker   Schwiebus
DONNER, Karoline, b SCHUETTRICH, 38, w
DONNER, --, 9, s
DONNER, --, 2, d

THOMAS, August, 24, journeyman shoemaker   Zuellichau

From: Brandenburg, Kreis Guben
To: Australia, 1838
WARMBRUNN, Friedrich Traugott, 35, journeyman
  cloth weaver [Tuchmacher]   Stadt Guben
WARMBRUNN, Luise Auguste, b SAGITZ, 31, w
WARMBRUNN, Traugott Hermann, 6-1/2, s (legitimate)
WARMBRUNN, Traugott Christian Emanuel, 2-3/4, s
  (legitimate)
WARMBRUNN, Paul Daniel Johannes, 4 months (legitimate)
WARMBRUNN? Traugott Albrecht August, 9-1/4, illegit-
  imate s of his first wife
WARMBRUNN? Juliana Maria, 4, illegitimate d of his
  second wife
  (Friedrich T. Warmbrunn stated clearly that he
  intended to emigrate with his coreligionists
  from Zuellichau [Kreis] above.)

From: Silesia, Kreis Jauer
To: Australia, 1838
HERMANN, Friederike, b KAESTNER, age? w
  of a painter   Stadt Jauer
HERMANN, Maria Klara Ernestine, 9, d
HERMANN, Karl Julius, 6, s

From: Silesia, Kreis Freistadt
To: Australia, 1838
SCHWARZ, Johann Friedrich, 41, tailor   Seiffersdorff
SCHWARZ? Eva Rosina, b LIEBIG, 37, w
SCHWARZ? Hanna Dorothea, 9, d
SCHWARZ? Johann Gottlieb, 7, s
SCHWARZ? Johanne Christiane, 4, d
SCHWARZ? Dorothea Elisabeth, 2, d
HEINRICH, Johann Gottlieb, 38   Seiffersdorff
HEINRICH, Anna Rosina, b PFEIFFER, 38, w
HEINRICH, Johanne Juliane, 9, d
HEINRICH, Friedrich Wilhelm, 5, s
HEINRICH, Gustav Adolf, 4, s
TSCHAKSCH, Gottlieb, 38, tailor, unmarried   Niebusch
TSCHAKSCH, Anna Rosina, 48, unmarried
TSCHAKSCH, Christian, 21, her son

From: Silesia, Kreis Sagan
To: Australia, 1838
PRIEDEMANN, Samuel, son of a gardener   Reichenau
SPIELBERGER, Anna Rosina b GIERACH (also
  GIERATH), widow   Reichenau
GIERACH (or GIERATH), Christian, 57, farmer Reichenau
GIERACH, Rosina, b RIEGER, 53, w
GIERACH, Georg Friedrich, 23, s
GIERACH, Anna Elisabeth, 21, d
GIERACH, Anna Rosina, 19, d
GIERACH, Christian, 16, s
GIERACH, Maria Elisabeth, 14, d
GIERACH, Johanne Dorothea, 10, d
GIERACH, Samuel, 1, s
SCHULZ, Samuel, 43, cottager   Reichenau
SCHULZ, Anna Rosina, b HOFFMANN, 41, w
SCHULZ, Johanne Eleonore, 15, d
SCHULZ, Anna Elisabeth, 10, d
PFENNIG, Samuel, 38, cottager   Cosel
PFENNIG, Maria Elisabeth, b RIEGER, 38, w
PFENNIG, Christiane, 16, d
PFENNIG, Anna Dorothea, 9, d
PFENNIG, Anna Rosina, 5, d
RIEGER, Christian, 38, farmer's son and
  hired hand   Cosel

RIEGER, Anna Elisabeth, 32, sister
RIEGER, Johann Friedrich, 28, b?

From: Province Posen
To: Australia, 1838
Note: The ship Katharina sailed in 1838 fully loaded
with emigrants from Province Posen. We must state
that the following list is somewhat uncertain, inasmuch as the relevant Posen governmental files granting permission to emigrate are not available. The
list is probably accurate, however, since it is com-
piled from two lists, made separately by the two commissioners for 1838, Councillor [Regierungsrat] Süv-
ern and General Superintendent von Freymark, which
agree on a total of 267 persons. From this number,
41 persons were detained, however, either through
renunciation of intent to emigrate during their inter-
rogation or by denial of exit permit, leaving a total
of 226 actual emigrants. Since we have these two
sources, plus a letter from a fellow passenger and
later Australian reporter, we know that the Katharina
carried about 130 emigrants from Posen to Australia,
leaving a difference of 96 persons unaccounted for.
This discrepancy is made somewhat smaller by Lodewydkx'
list of passengers for the Prinz Georg including an
eight-member KALESKE family from Posen. Likewise, it
is known that some Posener emigrants were aboard the
Australian ship Zebra in 1838, although a list of them
has not been preserved. It is likely, also, that some
Posener emigrants waited to leave until 1841, during
the second largest wave of migration to Australia, but
for which we also lack a list. Furthermore, there appears also to have been considerable loss through
deaths during the trip-- a known total of 55 persons
in 1841, for example. Taking all this into account,
it appears that not too many of the 96 persons unaccounted for remained in Germany, although it may be
that from the following list of 226 persons some might
not have left the country. The list is given in its
entirety, even though uncertain; perhaps, later dis-
coveries in the Posen governmental files will clarify
the matter. Certain of the emigrants, known to have
reached Australia, are identified by an asterisk hereinafter.
BRIESE, Johann Gotthilf, 68, lessee of a
  garden, widower   near Meseritz
ZIMMERMANN, Johann Daniel, 33, day
  laborer, with w and 2 children   near Meseritz
SEMMERAU, --, 36, shoemaker, with
  w and 2 children   near Meseritz
BORRMANN, --, 45, shoemaker, with w
  and 5 children   near Meseritz
SIEVERS, Joachim, 38, shoemaker, with
  w and 2 children   near Meseritz
THOMAS, Johann, 47, clothmaker, with
  w and 4 children   near Meseritz
THOMAS, Samuel, 76, clothmaker, f of
  Johann Thomas, with 2 children   near Meseritz
HANDSCHKE, Johann Gotthilf, 59, hatter,
  with w and d   near Meseritz
FELSCH, Johann Gottlieb, 52, shoemaker,
  with w   near Meseritz
GUENTHER, Johann Ferdinand, 28, mechanic,
  with w and 2 children   near Meseritz
RETTIG, Dorothea, 45, unmarried seam-
  stress   near Meseritz
HOFFMANN, Friederike, 37, unmarried
  seamstress   near Meseritz
HOFFMANN, Rosalie, 29, sister of the
  above, also seamstress   near Meseritz
GENGE, Anna Rosina, widow of a tailor,
  with 5 children   near Meseritz

SCHROEDEL, Therese, 54, housekeeper
  to [Johann Gotthilf] Briese   near Meseritz
MUENCHENBERG, Anna, 45, widow of a
  day laborer, with 3 sons, aged
  22, 18, and 13 years   near Meseritz
MUENCHENBERG, Johanna, 47, widow of a
  day laborer, with 3 sons, aged 20,
  14, and 7 years, and 4 daughters   near Meseritz
WELKE, Gottlieb Ferdinand, apprentice
  mechanic with [Johann Ferdinand]
  GUENTHER   near Meseritz

From: Province Posen, near Bentschen
To: Australia, 1838
See previous note
LINKE, Gottlieb, 34, cabinetmaker   Chlastawe
ROTHE, Christian, 28, horseshoer
  [Kalüpner], with w and 3 children*   Chlastawe
AURICHT, Christian, 32, blacksmith and
  horseshoer [Kalüpner], with w and 2
  children*   Chlastawe
AURICHT, Samuel, 32, horseshoer [Kalüp-
  nerpächter], with w and 3 children;
  brother of Christian Auricht*   Chlastawe
AURICHT, Rosina, 21, maid with Rothe
  family above, sister of Christian
  Auricht   Chlastawe
AURICHT, Anna Elisabeth, 19, sister
  of Christian Auricht   Chlastawe
WILKSCH, Wilhelm, 32, shoemaker, with
  w and 2-year-old s; brother-in-law
  of Christian Auricht   Chlastawe
ADAM, Rosina, 28, maid   Chlastawe
HAHN, Christian, 30, gardener   Chlastawe
MATTNER, Georg, 43, with w and 6 children Chlastawe
KAPPLER, Christian, 35, with w and 4 chil-
  dren, 12 years and under   Chlastawe
REISCH, Christian, 20, journeyman miller Chlastawe
RATSCH, Gottfried, 34, cablemaker, with w
  and 1 c   Chlastawe
GRAETZ, Johann, 44, journeyman mason,
  with w and 4 children, 13 years and under Chlastawe
SCHULZ, Johann Georg, 65, retiree   near Tirschtiegel
BRAUNAK, Karl, 57, clothmaker, with w
  and 5 children; chairman [Vorsteher]
  of his Lutheran congregation   near Tirschtiegel
HAMPEL, Wilhelm, 41, clothmaker and
  chairman [Vorsteher], with w and
  4 children, 9 years and under   near Tirschtiegel
KALESKE, --, 42, merchant, with
  w and 6 children, 20 years and
  under; he is messenger [Boten-
  gänger] of the Lutherans*   near Tirschtiegel
HAMDORF, Christian, age? wheelwright
                                       near Tirschtiegel
HAMDORF, Gotthilf, 32, with w and
  1 child   near Tirschtiegel
BRAUNAK, Friedrich, 47, with w and
  5 children; aged 16 and under;
  brother of Karl Braunak   near Tirschtiegel
HEINEL, --, journeyman mason, & w   near Tirschtiegel
SCHILLER, Gotthilf, 28, tailor,
  unmarried; from Schierziger Hau-
  land   near Tirschtiegel
BRETKE, --, 42, shoemaker, with w
  and 2 children, the older being
  12 years; from Braetz   near Tirschtiegel
WEBER, Gotthif, 26, hired hand,
  unmarried; from Eschenwalde   near Tirschtiegel

From: Province Posen, Kreis Birnbaum
To: Australia, 1838
HAHN, Georg, gardener   Prittisch
KARG, Gottfried, 43, farmer, with w and
  1 s, 8 years old   Prittisch
WAHLSCHUETZ, Johann, 24, master cabinet-
  maker, widower, with c 1-1/2 years
  (it is said that he now wishes to go
  to Poland)   Prittisch
MULLAK, Karl August, 50, day laborer, with
  w and 4 children, of whom the oldest s,
  20 years, is not a Separatist
WEBER, Gottlob, 26, farmer, with w   Prittisch
KINTZEL, Gottlob, 47, farmer, with w and
  5 children, 17 years and under   Prittisch
HEINZE, Friedrich, 43, lead worker, with
  w and 5 children, 14 years and under Prittisch
HOFFMANN, Wilhelm, 44, shoemaker, with
  w and 4 children, 17 years and under Prittisch
HOFFMANN, Beate, 66, widow, mother of
  Wilhelm Hoffmann   Prittisch
ULM, Johann, 45, farmer, with w and 4
  children, 19 years and under (the
  w and stepdaughter say they are not
  Separatists)   Prittisch
WORNEST, 67, landowner [Hauländer Wirt]
  with w and 7 children, of which 2 sons,
  aged 22 and 12 years; the older son is
  not a Separatist   Prittisch
WORNEST, Gottfried, 63, houseowner, with
  w and 1 d, age 23   Prittisch
HEINZE, Christian, 36, farmer, with w
  and 2 children, 11 years and under   Prittisch
SAUER, Christian, 30, houseowner and
  tailor, with w and 3 children, 10
  years and under   Prittisch
SAUER, Gottlieb, 35, houseowner and
  tailor, with w and 1 child, 3 years Prittisch
FRESCHNER, Gottfried, 36, farmer, with
  w and 2 children, 4 years and under Prittisch
SELCHE, Gottlieb, 55, tailor, with w
  and 4 children, 22 years and under   Prittisch
PASCHKE, Martin, 40, tailor, with w
  and 2 children, 6 years and under   Prittisch

From: Province Posen, Kreis Bomst
To: Australia, 1838
Note: As a consequence of the Cabinet orders of March
and April 1837 regarding emigration, a number of addi-
tional would-be emigrants from Kreis Bomst have come
to light. Persons hereinafter whose names are followed
by an asterisk are known to have emigrated (see Permit
files)
KAVEL, Albrecht Christian, 71, tailor*
  with w* and 3 children [names follow];
  Albrecht Christian Kavel was the father
  of the Pastor [Kavel]   Chwalim
KAVEL, Johann Ferdinand, 34, s*
KAVEL, Friedrich Daniel Samuel, age? s*
KAVEL, Maria Charlotte Sabine, age? d*
  (in Australia she married the widowed
  forester -- FIEDLER)
FIEDLER, Julius, s of combmaker [Kamm-
  setzmeister, could also be chimney
  mason] Samuel FIEDLER*   Karge
SCHMIDT, Anna Elisabeth, 36,   Borui
SCHMIDT, Johanne Anna, 2, d
FITZNER, Dorothea, 43, inhabitant,   Borui
FITZNER, Gottlieb, 9, s
FITZNER, --, 17, d
FITZNER, --, 8, d

JAESCHKE, Johann Georg* from Scharker
Hauland   Borui

    Total Emigrants for year 1838:
    to America from Silesia   25
    to Australia from the Mark
      [Brandenburg]   386
    to Australia from Province
      Posen   239
    to Australia from Silesia   40
                       665

        Total   690

1839

From: Pomerania, Kreis Wollin
To: America, 1839
Note: All the Lutheran [Separatists] emigrating dur-
    1838 went to America
HECKENDORF, --, 48, shepherd lessee   Schwantus
HECKENDORF, --, b EHLKE, 41, w
HECKENDORF, Christian Friedrich Wilhelm, 21, s
HECKENDORF, Karl Friedrich August, 20, s
HECKENDORF, David Heinrich Wilhelm, 14, s
HECKENDORF, Johann Gottlieb, 9, s
HECKENDORF, Wilhelm Friedrich, 3, s
HECKENDORF, Franz Ferdinand, 1, s
HECKENDORF, Ernestine Charlotte Wihlemine, 17, d
HECKENDORF, Friderike Luise Maria, 16, d
HECKENDORF, Friderike, Luise Henriette, 12, d
HECKENDORF, Sophie Maria Elisabeth, 7, d
HECKENDORF, Johanna Ernestine, 5, d
FINCK, Friedrich Wilhelm, 29, day laborer   Schwantus
FINCK, Friderike Luise Henriette, b SCHMIDT, 26, w
FINCK, Karl Friedrich Wilhelm, 1, s
HINZ, --, 35, inhabitant   Schwantus
HINZ, --, w
HINZ, Karoline Sophie Friderike, 9, d
HINZ, Ernestine Albertine Wilhelmine, 7, d
HINZ, Wilhelmine Friderike, 4, d
HINZ, Albertine Auguste Maria, 2, d
MILBRATH, Karl Philipp Ludwig, 28, cottager Schwantus
MILBRATH, Karoline Friderike Wilhelmine, b
   HOECKENDORF, 23, w
MILBRATH, Hanna Wilhelmine Friderike, 2 d
SCHMIDT, --, 51, cottager   Schwantus
SCHMIDT, --, b GOETZKE, 54, w
SCHMIDT, Friedrich Wilhelm, 23, s
SCHMIDT, Friderike, 25, d
SCHMIDT, Wilhelmine Sophie Friderike, 17, d
FINCK, Ernst Karl Friedrich, 32, day laborer Wartlow
FINCK, Dorothea Elisabeth, b HOEFT, 35, w
FINCK, Hanna Karoline, 3, d
FINCK, Friderike Wilhelmine Karoline, 2, d
TRAPPE, August Friedrich Samuel, 47, shepherd Wartlow
TRAPPE, Dorothea Sohpia, b KRAUSE, 56, w
KRAUSE, Maria, 22, stepdaughter
KRUEGER, Martin Gottfried, 19 adopted son
ACKERMANN, Erdmann Friedrich, 41, cottager   Warnow
ACKERMANN, --, w
ACKERMANN, August Friedrich Wilhelm, 13, s
ACKERMANN, Johann Wilhelm, 7, s
ACKERMANN, --, d
KRAUSE, Wilhelmine, 25, unmarried laborer   Warnow
KRUEGER, Johann, 37, owner   Fernowsfelde
KRUEGER, --, w
KRUEGER, Dorothea Frid[erike] Albertine, 14, d
KRUEGER, Charlotte Maria Karoline, 11, d
KRUEGER, Johann Wilhelm, 9, s
KRUEGER, --, 1/2 year, d

WILDE, Peter, 66, owner   Fernowsfelde
WILDE, --, w
WILDE, Joachim Wilhelm, 26, s
WILDE, Johann Gottlieb, 24, s
WILDE, Michael Friedrich, 20, s
LEMCKE, Franz Wilhelm, 48, tailor   Kolzow
LEMCKE, Christine Charlotte, b ZUEHLCKE, 43, w
LEMCKE, August Friedrich Wilhelm, 19, s
SCHOESSOW, Martin Friedrich, 47, farmer Kolzow
SCHOESSOW, --, w
SCHOESSOW, Michael Friedrich Wilhelm, 18, s
SCHOESSOW, Johann Karl Friedrich, 12, s
SCHOESSOW, Wilhelmine, 16, d
PARLOW, Karl Friedrich, owner   Coesenthin
BACHMANN, Johann Christian, 41,
   tailor   Vietziger Ablage
BACHMANN, --, 41, w
BACHMANN, Johanna Albertine Sophie, 13, d
BACHMANN, August Friedrich, 3, s
BACHMANN, Ferdinand Christian, 3, s

From: Pomerania, Kreis Greifenberg
To: America, 1839
KNUTH, Johann, with w and 5 children   Schwessow
KNUTH, Gottfried, old owner   Schwessow
KNUTH, Ernest Ludwig Gottfried   Schwessow
PAGENKOPF, Johann Gottlieb, laborer, with
  w and 2 children   Schwessow
ROGGENBUCK, Johann, inhabitant, with w
  and 5 children   Schwessow
HARTWIG, Friedrich, wheelwright, with w
  and 7 children   Schwessow
RIEBE, August, wheelwright, with w and
  1 c   Schwessow
SCHENZEL, Wilhelmine and Johanna Karoline
  Maria, unmarried sisters   Schwessow
FIEBRANZ, Karl Gottlieb, hired hand   Schwessow
ZION, --, former school teacher   Schwessow
LUEDCKE, Friedrich, tailor, and w   Treptow a. Rh.
            [probably Treptow an der Rega]
GRUENHAGEN, Joachim, merchant, with w
  and 2 children   [probably Treptow an der Rega]
FIEBRANZ, Johann Gottlieb, butcher, with
  w and 9 children · [probably Treptow an der Rega]
NATZKE, Johann, labor supervisor, with
  w and 3 children   Triglaff
OTT, Johann Gotthilf, day laborer, with
  w and 5 sons   Triglaff
PRITZLAFF, --, shepherd boy (accompanied
  them without permission)   Triglaff
SCHMIDT, Johann Wilhelm Gotthilf, 54, peas-
  ant   Darsow
SCHMIDT, Karoline Maria Elisabeth, b
  SCHLEDDERMANN, 49, w
SCHMIDT, Karl Albert Theodor, 12, s
SCHMIDT, Hermann Wilhelm Eduard, 10, s
RADTKE, Friedrich Wilhelm, 34, inhabitant Darsow
RADTKE, Charlotte Sophie, b BRUESSKE, w
RADTKE, Johann Friedrich Wilhelm, 6, s
RADTKE, Charlotte ERnestine Friederike, 5, d
RADTKE, Ernst Daniel Wilhelm, 4, s
RADTKE, Wilhelmine Sophie, 1, d
HILGENDORF, Ernst Friedrich, 43, farmer   Dresow
HILGENDORF, Benigna Christiane, b PLACK, 42, w
HILGENDORF, Karl Ludwig Ferdinand, the oldest
  son was in military service but was discharged
HILGENDORF, Christian Friedrich, 19, s
HILGENDORF, Wilhelm Ludwig, 17, s
HILGENDORF, Franz Gottlieb Friedrich, 14, s
HILGENDORF, Ernst Heinrich Friedrich, 11, s
HILGENDORF, August Wilhelm Friedrich, 3, s

HENSEL, Friedrich Wilhelm, peasant, with
w and 5 children   Pribbernow
PRAHL, Friedrich Lorenz, cottager, with
w and 1 c   Horst
DREWS, Johann Joachim, day laborer, with
w and 6 children   Gruchow
WALLSCHLAEGER, Johann Gottlieb, coachman   Dorphagen

From: Pomerania, Kreis Regenwalde
To: America, 1839
RADUE, August, 38, shoemaker   Plathe
RADUE, Ernestine, b KLUG, 34, w
RADUE, Ernestine, 7, d
RADUE, August, 5, s
RADUE, Bertha, 2, d
KLUG, Gottlieb, 22, journeyman shoemaker
(brother of Frau Radue)   Plathe
NEUMANN, Friedrich, 36, master cabinetmaker   Plathe
NEUMANN, Friderike, b GROTH, 37, w
NEUMANN, Bertha, 9, d
NEUMANN, Johann, 7, s
NEUMANN, Karl, 3, s
NEUMANN, Gustav, 1, s
WOLF, Anna Maria Elisabeth, b EHLKE, 56,   Plathe
widow
WOLF, Karl Friedrich Wilhelm, 18, hired hand, s
WOLF, Sophie Luise Friderike, 22, d
WOLF, Sophie Maria Karoline, 20, d
WOLF, Hanna Maria Elisabeth, 13, d
WOLF, Friedrich Philipp, 27, day laborer   Plathe
WOLF, Luise Dorothea, b UEBEL, 27, w
KLUG, Karl Friedrich, 40, farmer   Muddelmow
KLUG, Gottlieb, 63, former owner, father
of Karl Friedrich Klug
KLUG, Sophie, b SCHUHMACHER, 60, mother
of Karl Friedrich Klug
KLUG, Franz, 15, brother, blind
KLUG, Wilhelm Christoph, 58, farmer   Muddelmow
KLUG, Ester Maria, b SCHUHMACHER, 57, w
KLUG, Heinrich Friedrich Wilhelm, 21, s
KLUG, Heinrich Gottlieb August, 18, s
KLUG, August Karl, 16, s
LYNSE, alias HELL, Wilhelm, 22, hired hand,
who emigrated without permission   Muddelmow
KLUG, Johann Friedrich Ferdinand, 37, shep-
herd   Wisbu
KLUG, Wilhelmine, b MANTHEY, 28, w
KLUG, --, 2, c
PETERMANN, Johann Christoph, 44, shepherd   Wisbu
PETERMANN, Karoline Dorothea, b KOELLER, 40, w
PETERMANN, --, six children, 16, 14, 12, 10, 4,
3/4 years
KLUG, Charlotte, b KLUG, 40, widow   Zimmershausen
KLUG, Karl Gottlieb, 28, shepherd boy,
stepson
KLUG, Johann Friedrich Gotthilf, 16, s
STREY, Kaspar Friedrich, 42, tailor   Ruebenhagen
STREY, Karoline, b LUEDKE, 25, w
STREY, --, 1, c
SCHUMACHER, Johann, 42, worker   Ruebenhagen
SCHUMACHER, Henriette, widow of LUEDKE,
b SEEFELD, 52, w
LUEDKE, Friderike, 18, d by first husband
KNUTH, Christian Friedrich, 33, blacksmith   Zowen
KNUTH, Charlotte, b HAMANN, 28, w
KNUTH, --, three children, 3, 2, and 11 weeks

From: Pomerania, Kreis Greifenhagen
To: America, 1839
BRISS, Johann, 32, teacher, Jewish prose-
lyte   Kranzfelde

From: Pomerania, Kreis Naugard
To: America, 1839
BARTELT, Christian Friedrich, owner, with
w and 2 sons   Hakenwalde
HOEPFNER, Johann Karl Friedrich, laborer,
with w and 4 children   Hakenwalde

From: Pomerania, Kreis Kammin
To: America, 1839
BRUSS, Martin Friedrich, 40, journeyman
ship's-carpenter   Kammin
BRUSS, Sophie, b STIEMKE, 37, w
BRUSS, August, 9, s
BRUSS, Martin, 6, s
BRUSS, Johann, 4, s
DREYER, Gottfried, 37, school teacher   Kammin
DREYER, Wilhelmine, b WUSSOW, 28, w
DREYER, August, 2, s
BRUSS, Martin, farmer, with w and 4 children   Kammin
KRUEGER, Johann, laborer, with w and 4 chil-
dren   Kammin
KRUEGER, Friedrich, laborer, with w and 2
children   Kammin
SCHULZ, Friedrich, journeyman mason, with
w and 3 children   Kammin
NEUMANN, --, widow, with 3 children   Kammin
BUESTRIN, Martin, laborer   Kammin
GAEHNZ (or GAHNS), --, with w   Kammin
CHRISTIAN, Charlotte, maid   Kammin
SUCKOW, Karl Heinrich August, 30, master
weaver   Kammin
SUCKOW, Dorothea Karoline, b KLINKHARD, 26, w
SUCKOW, Auguste Maria Emilie, 3, d
HEUER, Michael, farmer, with w and 6
children   Gross-Justin
DIEDRICH, Friderike, maid   Gross-Justin
KOEPSEL, Johann, farmer, with w and
4 grown children   Gross-Justin
GANGER, Johann, shepherd, with w and
4 children   Gross-Justin
STEFFEN, --, cabinetmaker, with w   Gross-Justin
ZIRBEL, Friedrich, tailor   Gross-Justin
GANGER, Johann, tailor, from Klein-
Justin   Gross-Justin
HEUER, Johann, peasant, with w and
6 children   Knurrbusch
HEUER, Joachim   Knurrbusch
WILL, --, widow   Knurrbusch
RAMTHUN, Gottfried, 67, cottager   Knurrbusch
RAMTHUN, Henriette Friderike, b LEMCKE, w
RAMTHUN, Johann Friedrich Wilhelm, 19, s
RAMTHUN, Charlotte Friderike Karoline Wil-
helmine, 14, d
RAMTHUN, August Ernst Ferdinand, 7, s
RAMTHUN, Philippine Albertine Auguste, 4, d
TEWS, Johann, 34, peasant   Benz
TEWS, Friderike Christine, b RIEMER, 30, w
TEWS, August Friedrich, 3, s
TEWS? Karoline Luise, 30, sister
TEWS, --, 76, widow
HEUER, Daniel, 34, day laborer   Benz
HEUER, Dorothea Luise, b TRETIEN (also TRITTIN),
30, w, with 3 children
FLEISCHFRESSER, --, b TRITTIN, w of   Benz
HELM, Michael, 48, policeman   Scharchow
HELM, Katharine, b KRUEGER, 45, w
HELM, Friedrich, 25, s
HELM, Friderike, 24, d
HELM, Henriette, 21, d
HELM, Albertine, 19, d
HELM, Maria, 17, d
HELM, Johann, 11, s

HELM, August, 6, s
HELM, Sophie, 8, d
HELM, David, 45, farmer   Scharchow
HELM, Helena, b FLEISCHFRESSER, 30, w
HELM, Dorothea Wilhelmine, 6, d
HELM, Johann Friedrich, 4, s
KRUEGER, Martin, 42, seaman   Scharchow
KRUEGER, Sophie, b BUROW, 33, w
KRUEGER, Ernst Friedrich, 10, s
KRUEGER, Johann Heinrich, 9, s
KRUEGER, Rosaline, 4, d
BRUSS, Johann Gottlieb, 37, peasant   Scharchow
BRUSS, Charlotte, b MARX, 29, w
BRUSS, August, 5, s
BRUSS, Wilhelm, 3, s
BRUSS, Heinrich, 1, s
MILDEBRATH, Karl, 45, farmer   Reckow
MILDEBRATH, Friderike, b RAPPRAEGER, 47, w
MILDEBRATH, Wilhelmine, 22, d
MILDEBRATH, August, 20, s
MILDEBRATH, Wilhelm, 18, s
MILDEBRATH, Ernestine, 16, d
MILDEBRATH, Johann, 12, s
MILDEBRATH, Johanna, 10, d
MILDEBRATH, Sophie, 8, d
MILDEBRATH, Karoline, 6, d
MILDEBRATH, Wilhelm, 43, cottager   Reckow
MILDEBRATH, Dorothea, b JUST, 45, w
MILDEBRATH, Wilhelmine, 16, d
MILDEBRATH, Johann, 14, s
MILDEBRATH, Ernst, 12, s
WUSSOW, Gottlieb, 40, blacksmith   Reckow
WUSSOW, Wilhelmine, b SCHROEDER, 38, w
WUSSOW, August, 10, s
WUSSOW, Gottlieb, 7, s
WUSSOW, Ferdinand, 5, s
WUSSOW, Karoline, 15, d
WUSSOW, Wilhelmine, 9, d
WUSSOW, Henriette, 1, d
BECKMANN, Johann, 35, hired hand   Reckow
SCHARLOCK, Wilhelm, age? hired hand   Reckow
SUELFLOW, August, age? shepherd boy   Reckow
BARTELT, Fridrich Wilhelm, 36, farmer   Tonnebuhr
BARTELT, Henriette Charlotte, b ULBRICH, w,
  and 3 children?
BARTELT, Johann, 36, day laborer   Tonnebuhr
BARTELT, --, b HORN, 28, w
BARTELT, Karl, 6, s
BARTELT, Wilhelm, 2, s
MILDEBRATH, Ernst Friedrich, cottager   Tonnebuhr
MILDEBRATH, Sophie, b BARTELT, w, with
  4 children
WILKE, Heinrich, former land owner   Tonnebuhr
WILKE, Christiane, b BARTELT, w, with
  4 children
WILKE, Christian, invalid inhabitant   Tonnebuhr
WILKE, Charlotte, b KREI, w, with 3
  children
WILKE, Karl, peasant son (but appar-   Tonnebuhr
  ently not the son of the above)
CHRISTIAN, Christlieb Friedrich, 63, jour-
  neyman carpenter   Schnatow
CHRISTIAN, Maria Elisabeth, b KOEHLER, 63, w
CHRISTIAN, Ernestine Luise, 22, d
CHRISTIAN, Heinrich Friedrich, 32, journey-
  man carpenter, son of the above Christ-
  lieb Friedrich Christian   Schnatow
CHRISTIAN, Sophie Elisabeth, b RIESELBACH,
  35, w
CHRISTIAN, Friederike Karoline, 6, d
CHRISTIAN, Johann, farmer, with w and 5
  children   Schnatow

BUTH, (also BUTT), 43, day laborer   Pemplow
BUTH, Maria Elisabeth, b EHMKE, 45, w
BUTH, Johann Ernst Friedrich, 20, s
BUTH, Ernestine Wilhelmine, 14, d
BUTH, Johanna Friderike, 6, d
WOLDT, Johann Gottlieb, 40, day laborer   Pemplow
WOLDT, Sophie Ernestine Friderike, b JAEGER,
  47, w
WOLDT, Hanna Friderike Heinriette, 17, d
WOLDT, Wilhelmine, 15, d
WOLDT, Johann Christian Gotthilf, 14, s
WOLDT, Friderike Christiane Henriette, 11, d
WOLDT, Johann Wilhelm, 8, s
WOLDT, Franz Wilhelm Friedrich, 3, s
TEWS, Gottlieb, day laborer, with w and
  6 children   Pemplow
GRUEL, Martin, 41, inhabitant and former
  tenant farmer   Gristow
GRUEL, Katharine, b BOHLMANN, age? w
DUMSTREY, Joachim, 47, former farmer   Gristow
DUMSTREY, Engel, b BOHLMANN, 55, w
DUMSTREY, Wilhelm Friedrich Ferdinand, 20, s
DUMSTREY, Friderike Wilhelmine, 16, d
BELLIN, Michael, 41, cottager   Gristow
BELLIN, Dorothea Karoline, b WETZEL, 33, w
KRUEGER, Johann, 55, former landowner   Polchow
KRUEGER, Dorothea, b LANGE, 56, w
KRUEGER, David, 23, s
KRUEGER, Maria Elisabeth, 29, d
KRUEGER, Christiane, 30, d from first marriage
PIEPKORN, Gottfried, 38, cottager   Grabow
PIEPKORN, Engel, b VOIGT, 28, w
PIEPKORN, Maria Friderike, 6, d
PIEPKORN, Gottlieb August, 3-1/2, s
PIEPKORN, Martin Friedrich, 1, s
PIEPKORN, Joachim, tenant farmer, with w
  and 4 children   Grabow
FRENZ, Dorothea, unmarried   Grabow
BAUMGARTEN, Johann, peasant, and 1 child   Grabow
JAHNCKE, Friedrich, 25, tailor   Koenigsmuehl
JAHNCKE, Anna Friderike, b KNOLL, 26, w
JAHNCKE, Johann Gottlieb Friedrich, 1, s
KNOLL, --, widow, with 2 children   Koenigsmuehl
UTECH, Karoline, unmarried   Koenigsmuehl
HAVEMEISTER, Ernst Friedrich, day laborer,
  with w and 6 daughters   Morgow
ZIRBELL, Gottlieb Bogislav, herder, with
  w and 5 children   Morgow
WALLSCHLAEGER, Johann Friedrich, hired hand   Morgow
BEESEMANN, --, blacksmith, with w and 3
  children   Revenow
STOCK, Martin, mill owner, with w and 2
  children   Revenow
KRUEGER, Johann, carpenter   Jassow
STROEVE, Michael, hired hand   Jassow
GUST, Martin, fisherman, with w   Berg Dievenow
GUST, Martin Friedrich, s of Martin Gust
KIST, Engel Benigna, unmarried [apparently
  accompanied the GUST family]
STOCK, Michael, landowner, with w   Kucklow
ILLIES, Karl Wilhelm, private tutor   Stresow
MAASS, Johann Friedrich, daylaborer, with
  w and 2 sons   Bandelow
MAASS, Karl Friedrich, tailor, with w and
  2 sons   Baumgarten
WUSSOW, Karl, 51, master tailor   Weistenthin
WUSSOW, Friderike, b GRUETZMACHER, 52, w
WUSSOW, Johanna, 23, d
WUSSOW, Charlotte, 22, d
WUSSOW, Luise, 19, d
WUSSOW, Auguste, 16, d
WUSSOW, Hermann, 10, s

PIEPKORN, Gottlieb, hired hand   Fritzow
BUESTRIN, David, 48, peasant   Soltin
BUESTRIN, Anna Maria, b GRUENHAGEN, 36, w
BUESTRIN, Wilhelmine, 17, d
BUESTRIN, Friderike, 14, d
BUESTRIN, Heinrich, 8, s
BUESTRIN, Albertine, 5, d
BUESTRIN, Franz Ferdinand, 3, s
LUCK, Joachim, former school teacher, with
   w and 5 children   Buennewitz
BRUEGGEMANN, (Johann, inhabitant   Bussentin
KOEHLER, Joachim, hired hand   Bussentin
KRUEGER, August, shepherd boy   Kahlen
KRUEGER, Friedrich, shepherd boy   Schwirsen

From: Pomerania, Kreis Neu Stettin, Bezirk Coeslin
To: America, 1839
HILDEMANN, Gottlieb, 42, lessee   Gramenzer Busch-
HILDEMANN, Sophie, b KLUCK, 51, w   kathen
HILDEMANN, Wilhelm, 18, s
HILDEMANN, August, 14, s
HILDEMANN, Gottlieb, 12, s
HILDEMANN, Heinrich, 7, s
HILDEMANN, Franz, 4, s
HILDEMANN, Ernestine, 20, d
HILDEMANN, Henriette, 15, d
HILDEMANN, Johanna, 9, d
HILDEMANN, Christiane, 1-1/2, d
KLUG, Wilhelm August, 26, lessee   Gramenzer Busch-
KLUG, Karoline, b WINTER, 27, w   kathen
KLUG, August, 5, s
KLUG, Gottlieb, 3, s
KLUG, Heinrich, 2, s
KLUG, Wilhelm, 3/4, s
WINTER, Michael, 56, invalid inhab-
   itant   Gramenzer Busch-
WINTER, Christiane, b STRAEDE, 45, w   kathen
WINTER, Wilhelmine, 23, d
WINTER, Sophie, 22, d
WINTER, Luise, 20, d
WINTER, Friedrich, 18, s
WINTER, Martin, 16, s
WINTER, Michael, 14, s
WINTER, Johanna, 12, d
   (Frau Karoline Klug, above, is the eighth child)
LEMKE, Johann Heinrich, 41, shepherd   Raffenberg bei
LEMKE, Johanna, b GOEHRKE, w   Gramenz
LEMKE, Christian Daniel, 1, s

     Total for all of Pomerania:
     Kreis Wollin   68
     Kreis Greifenberg   103
     Kreis Regenwalde   54
     Kreis Greifenhagen   1
     Kreis Naugard   10
     Kreis Kammin   305
     Kreis Neu Stettin   29
                Total   570

1839 [continued]

From: Provinz Sachsen [Saxony], *Regierungsbezirk*
       [governmental district] Erfurt
To: America, 1839
DOPF, Georg, 46, master glazier, with w
   and 4 sons, aged 19, 16, 13, and 11
   and a d of 1   Stadt Erfurt
MUELLER, Philipp, 44, dealer in second-
   hand wares, with w and s (age 4) and

a d of 2 years
ZACHER, Martin, 46, gardener, with   Stadt Erfurt
   w and 3 sons, 17, 9, and 3 years
   and a d of 4 years
MUELLER, Johann August Ferdinand, bar-
   ber's assistant   Stadt Erfurt
FICKEL, Friedrich, 27, shoemaker, with
   w, 2 sons 2 and 1/2 year, and 1 d of
   12 years   Stadt Erfurt
SCHMELZER, Christoph, 40, tailor, with
   w, 2 sons, 14 and 12 years, and 2 daughters, 5 and 2 years   Stadt Erfurt
SCHMEDTCHEN, --, 50, shoemaker, with w   Stadt Erfurt
DAMMERT, Gottlob, 33, baker, with w   Stadt Erfurt
SCHROTH, Friedrich, 38, journeyman
   carpenter, with w and 1 s of 5 years   Stadt Erfurt
DISSMAR, Christian, 40, journeyman car-
   penter, with w and 1 d of 21 years   Stadt Erfurt
BARTHEL, Johann Markus, 46, shoemaker,
   with w, 2 sons, 9 and 7 years, and 2
   daughters, 20 and 18 years   Stadt Erfurt
FRICKMANN, Johanna Magdalena, 62, widow
   of a day laborer   Stadt Erfurt
FRICKMANN, Christian Friedrich, 18, s
FRICKMANN, Gottfried, 22, s
HAENSEL, Gottlob, 46, day laborer, with
   w   Stadt Erfurt
JACOBI, Johann, 51, gardener, with w
   and 3 sons, 20, 17; third son is
   Jakob Friedrich JACOBI, 13, s   Stadt Erfurt
SCHAEFER, Christiane, 42, widow of a
   day laborer, with s and d   Stadt Erfurt
STURM, Margarete, 25, maid   Stadt Erfurt
SCHORR, Ernst, 36, comb maker, with w
   and 1 s (1 year) and 6 daughters
   (12, 11, 9, 7, 5, 3 years)   Stadt Erfurt
SCHLOEFFEL, Christoph, 28, weaver, with
   w and 1 s (1 year) and 2 daughters
   (7, 2 years)   Stadt Erfurt
ZACHARIAE, Rosina, maid (accompanied
   the others secretly)   Stadt Erfurt
MEISSNER, Johanna Christiane, 42, laundress, with 1 son (15 years);
   another son, Karl, 21 years, is a soldier in the 3d C[ompany], 31st R[egi-
   ment] and was unable to obtain a permit to emigrate   Stadt Erfurt
WEHSER, Karl, 48, tailor, with w and
   1 s (8 years) and 1 d (5 years)   Stadt Erfurt
KUEHNEMANN, Friedrich, 40, grocer, with
   w, 2 sons (4 and 1 year), and 3 daughters (16, 10, 2 years)
HOERNLEIN, Jakob, 48, weaver, with his
   two oldest children, a daughter of 16
   and a son of 9 years, while his wife
   and son, 3 years, remained behind   Stadt Erfurt
GRABAU, Johann Andreas August, pastor   Stadt Erfurt
GRABAU, --, b BURGGRAF, w, and s (3 years)
PFEIFER, Karoline, maid to the Grabau
   family
SCHOENAU, Johann Christoph, master shoe-
   maker   Nordhausen
SCHOENAU, Johanna Friderike, b FREYBE, w
SCHOENAU, Johann Emanuel, 20, s
SCHOENAU, Heinrich August, 17, s
WENIG, Sebastian, 48   Schmira
WENIG, --, 48, w
WENIG, --, 16, d
WENIG, Oswald, 14, s
BALZER, Luise, stepdaughter
BALZER, Auguste, d, illegitimate
BEYER, --, 27   Schmira

BEYER, --, w
BEYER, Johann Friedrich, 4, s
BEYER, Karl Friedrich, 2, s
HEINEMANN, --, 27, unmarried

From: Provinz Sachsen [Saxony], *Regierungsbezirk*
     [governmental district] Magdeburg
To: America, 1839
BONEBERG, David, 33, factory worker   Stadt Magdeburg
BONEBERG, Wilhelmine, [b?] PASSAU, 32, w
BONEBERG, Wilhelm August, 5, s
BONEBERG, Maria Dorothea, 2-3/4, d
    (Residents of Französiche Kolsawe 7 [street ad-
    dress])
SCHULZE, Peter, 42, grocer   Stadt Magdeburg
SCHULZE, Katharina, b DAMMEYER, 37, w
SCHULZE, Maria, 2, d
SCHULZE, Friedrich, 3/4, s
    (Residents at Wasserkunst 10 [street address])
STREIBER, Andreas, 40, shoemaker   Stadt Magdeburg
STREIBER, Dorothea, b FAHSEL, 38, w
STREIBER, Karoline, 15, d
STREIBER, Eduard, 8, s
STREIBER, Maria, 2, d
    (Residents at Schuhbrücke 11 [street address])
GUENTHER, Karoline, 27, unmarried   Stadt Magdeburg
    (Resident at Kammelsberg 15 [street address])
GRASHOFF, Johann, 33, coachman   Stadt Magdeburg
GRASHOFF, Dorothea, b HESCHEL, 24, w
GRASHOFF, Dorothea, 2, d
GRASHOFF, Karoline, 1, d
    [Address not given.]
BERNHARD, Wilhelmine, age? unmarried, Stadt Magdeburg
    seamstress, resident of Werft 4 [street address]
FISCHER, Karl, 39, shoemaker   Stadt Magdeburg
FISCHER, Elisabeth, b OTTO, age? w
FISCHER, Karl, 9, s
FISCHER, Heinrich, 1/4, s
    (Residents at Pfeiffersberg 11 [street address])
KEMPFE, Dorothea, b RUSCHE, 71,   Stadt Magdeburg
    shoemaker's widow, resident at Stock-
    hausstrasse 27 [street address]
MUELLER, Friedrich, 30, musician and Stadt Magdeburg
    tutor, resident Katharinenstrasse 9
    [street address]
LUECKE, Heinrich Andreas, 40, tailor Stadt Magdeburg
LUECKE, Christiana, b NEIMANN, w
LUECKE, Hermine, 15, d
LUECKE, Luise, 7, d
LUECKE, Albertine, 5, d
    (Residents at Petersstrasse 2 [street address])
LUETZEL, Margarete, 30, unmarried   Stadt Magdeburg
    seamstress
KOERNER, Heinrich, 31, tailor   Stadt Magdeburg
KOERNER, Dorothea, b WEICHHARDT, w
    (Residents at Altes Fischerufer 9 [street address])
MARTIN, Johann, 35, tailor   Stadt Magdeburg
MARTIN, Elisabeth, b GOETZE, 29, w
MARTIN, --, 2-1/2, s
    (Residents at Schopenstrasse 1 [street address])
TAUTE, Martin, 40, factory worker Stadt Magdeburg
TAUTE, Dorothea, b HENNIGES, 43, w
    (Residents at Schopenstrasse 1 [street address])
GRAM, Johann Karl, 29, tailor   Stadt Magdeburg
GRAM, Charlotte, b NEUBAUER, 34, w
GRAM, Karl, 4-1/2, s
GRAM, Friedrich, 1/4, s
von ROHR, Karl Georg Heinrich, 42, Stadt Magdeburg
    retired [Army] captain and antiquarian
von ROHR, Julie, 3, d
KRUEGER, Johann Andreas, 22,journey- Stadt Magdeburg
    man tailor

EBELING, Katharina, unmarried, resi- Stadt Magdeburg
    dent of Schopenstrasse 1 [street address]
GUETTNER, Gottfried, 48, retired cor- Stadt Magdeburg
    poral [*Unteroffizier*] resident of
    Katharinenstrasse 10 [street address]
SCHOENFELD [so-called], Gottfried,   Stadt Magdeburg
    35, tailor
SCHOENFELD, Johanna Martha, b LOTZING, 28, w
SCHOENFELD, Gottfried, 1/2, s
    (Residents of Stockhausstrasse 27 [street ad-
    dress]; [Dorothea] KEMPFE, above, is the
    mother of the so-called? Gottfried SCHOENFELD)

From: Provinz Sachsen [Saxony], Kreis Jerichow
To: America, 1839
SCHULZE, Johann Andreas, 50, tailor   Woltersdorf
SCHULZE, Maria Elisabeth, b FRIEDRICH, 46, w
SCHULZE, Sophie Elisabeth, 21, d
SCHULZE, Johann Peter, 16, s
SCHULZE, Georg Anton, 12, s
SCHULZE, Karl Andreas, 3, s
PROBST, Christian, basketmaker   Gommern
PROBST, Johanna, b HOLLMANN, w
PROBST, --, d

From: Provinz Sachsen [Saxony], Kreis Osterwieck
To: America, 1839
KAUFFUNG, Christoph, baker, with w   Osterwieck
    and 3 children (7, 3, and 1 years)
KAUFFUNG, Karl, shoemaker, with w and Osterwieck
    3 children (5, 3, and 1/2 years)
MAUER, Friedrich, clothmaker, with w   Osterwieck
    and 4 children (10, 7, 4, and 2 years)
BAHNS, Heinrich, laborer, with w   Osterwieck
SCHMALIAN, -- [uncertain whether emi- Osterwieck
    grated]

From: Provinz Sachsen [Saxony], *Grafschaft* [terri-
      tory of a count]
To: America, 1839
BARTHAUER, Karl Ludwig, 58, master tailor Wernigerode
BARTHAUER, Johanne Christiane Elisabeth,
    b NEBE, 61, w
KOEHLER, Heinrich Gottlieb, 37, shoemaker Wernigerode
KOEHLER, Karoline, b RICHTER, 30, w, with
    1 s (5 years) and 3 daughters (9, 7-1/2,
    and 2-1/2 years)
EHRHOFF, Christian, 30, master shoemaker Wernigerode
GRAEBE, Ernst, master cablemaker   Wernigerode
GRAEBE, --, w
GRAEBE, Karl Julius, 17, s (already in Pittsburgh)
GRAEBE, Anna Maria, 15, d
GRAEBE, Gustav Heinrich, 13, s
GRAEBE, Andreas August Franz, 12, s
GRAEBE, Sophie Dorothea Elisabeth, 8, d

From: Provinz Sachsen [Saxony], Kreis Kalbe
To: America, 1839
LANGE, Friedrich, 31, journeyman black- Foerderstedt
    smith, unmarried, illegitimate s of
    the late Henriette EWALD, b LANGE

From: Provinz Sachsen [Saxony], Quedlinburg
To: America, 1839
SIEBERT, *called* BRANDT, Wilhelm Rudolph,
    candidate for Doctor of Theology   Quedlinburg
    (He was certainly an emigrant but the

following eight persons probably also
emigrated, although this is unclear
from the records.)

GRAM, Johann August, journeyman tailor   Magdeburg
GRAM, Johann Wilhelm, journeyman tailor,   Magdeburg
    brother of Johann August GRAM
BONDIECK, Ernst, linen weaver   Wedringen, Kreis
BONDIECK, Elisabeth, b LUEPKEN, w,   Neuhaldensleben
    with 4 children (15, 13, 11, and
    2 years)

With these eight persons the total of 103 emigrants is reached, as set forth in the list of
the *sächsischen Oberpräsidium* [Saxon central
administration]. It is possible, however, that
the following person also emigrated, although
he would have had to make application in Silesia:

BLAESCHKE, Anton Josef, 23, journeyman   Breslau
    mechanic

From: Provinz Sachsen [Saxony], *Regierungsbezirk*
       [governmental district] Merseburg
To: America, 1839
Note: From a total of 103 persons said to have emi-
       grated, only 18 can be identified

HARNISCH, Johann Gottfried, wagoner   Schkoelen, Kreis
HARNISCH, Wilhelmine, b STOLL, w   Weissenfels
HARNISCH, Marie, 3, d
KRIEG, Karl Friedrich, widower,   Schkoelen, Kreis
    journeyman potter   Weissenfels
KRIEG, Johann Gottfried, 3, s
KRUG, Johann Gottlieb, master but-   Schkoelen, Kreis
    cher   Weissenfels
KRUG, Therese, b SCHIRMER, w
KRUG, Marie Therese, 3, d
KRUG, Karl Benjamin, 1-1/2, s
WEHE, --, tax collector, with w and 7   Halle
    small children

From: Provinz Brandenburg, Berlin
To: America, 1839

KUPFERSCHMIDT, Jakob, journeyman tailor,   Berlin
    with w and 8 children
POHLE (*possibly* PROTE), Friedrich, master   Berlin
    baker, with w and 6 children
SCHEIDLER, Johann, journeyman tailor, with w   Berlin
SCHEIDLER, Friedrich, mason, with w and   Berlin
    3 children
WILL, Christoph, bookbinder, with w and   Berlin
    4 children
KOMPAKT, Friedrich, mechanic, with w and   Berlin
    2 children
BUSE, Tobias, shoemaker, with w and 5   Berlin
    children
HESSE, Anna, widow   Berlin
HOLLE, Johann Friedrich, shoemaker, with w   Berlin
    and 6 children
KARL, Johanna, widow   Berlin
LANGE, --, shoemaker, with w and 3 children   Berlin
ALTENSTEIN, --, with w and 1 child   Berlin
WOLF, --, laborer, with w and 3 children   Berlin
UNVERDORBEN, --, former office assistant,   Berlin
    with w
HERING, Anna Maria, widow   Berlin
EXNER, Johann August, journeyman shoemaker   Berlin
STREIBER, Gottfried, journeyman baker   Berlin
TOELGE, --, sugar refiner, and w   Berlin
RICHTER, Johann, coachman, with w and 1 child   Berlin
DETERLING, Johann Christian, laborer   Berlin
KORN, Friedrich, shoemaker, with w and 6   Berlin
    children

SCHEIDLER, Johann Nic., mason, with w   Berlin
PROTE, --, baker (*possibly the same as*   Berlin
    POHLE above)
AMREY, --, tailor   Berlin

From: Brandenburg, Kreis Crossen
To: America, 1839

BEISSER, Johann Gottlieb, gardener   Plau
BEISSER, --, w
BEISSER, Friedrich August, 14, s
BEISSER, Johanna Dorothea, 11, d
    (The two oldest sons, Christoph Valentin, 21,
    and Johann Gottlieb, 17, remained in Germany)

From: Provinz Silesia, Stadt Breslau
To: America, 1839

MEYER, Karl, 50, municipal tax collector   Breslau
MEYER, Dorothea, 41, w
MEYER, Amalie, 11, d
FAUDE, Ernst, 35, landscape gardener   Breslau
HANTSCHKE, Josef, 45, master shoemaker   Breslau
HANTSCHKE, Susanna, b MROSKE, 40, w
HANTSCHKE, Mathilde, 14, d
HANTSCHKE, Maria, 6, d
HANTSCHKE, Robert, 4, s
ZEDLER, Karl, 34, journeyman tailor   Breslau
    (His w remains behind for the time being)
HARTTERT, Gottlob, 40, master tailor   Breslau
HARTTERT, Christiane, b WERNER, 38, w
HARTTERT, Gottlob, 16, s
HARTTERT, Karl Samuel, 6, s
HARTTERT, Wilhelm, 5, s
GUERCKE, Friedrich, 51, houseboy   Breslau
GUERCKE, Johanna, b ZAENSCHER, 41, w
GUERCKE, Pauline, 14, d
GUERCKE, Julius, 7, s
STEIN, Gottlieb, 56, mill-farmer   Breslau
STEIN, Rosina, b SOMMER, 43, w
STEIN, Luise, 23, d
STEIN, Eduard, 21, s
STEIN, Moritz, 16, s
STEIN, Johanna, 8, d
PELZEL, Ignaz, 48, shoemaker   Breslau
PELZEL, Anna Rosina, b KUHNERT, 48, w
PELZEL, Amalie, 13, d
PELZEL, Wilhelm, 7, s

From: Provinz Silesia, Kreis Breslau
To: America, 1839

ROTHER, Christian, 43, blacksmith   Cammelwitz
ROTHER, Anna Rosina, b HOFFMANN, 44, w
ROTHER, Johann Gottlieb, 32, blacksmith   Cammelwitz
ROTHER, Anna Rosina, b WOLF, 22, w
ROTHER, Christiane, 1 year, 3 months, d
ROTHER, Johann Ernst, 20-1/2, cabinetmaker   Cammelwitz
    (probably brother of the above men)
ROTHER, Julius Gustav, 18-1/2, wheelwright   Cammelwitz
    (probably brother of the above men)
MEISSNER, Ernst Gottlieb, 54, teacher   Rothsuerben
MEISSNER, Anna Rosina, b SOFFKE, age?, w
MEISSNER, Heinrich Wilhelm Robert, 25, s
MEISSNER, Ernestine Wilhelmine Salome, 22, d
MEISSNER, Ernst Gottlieb Wilhelm, 18, s
MEISSNER, Christiane Wilhelmine Dorothea, 16, d
MEISSNER, Auguste Wilhelmine Amalie, 10, d
MEISSNER, Friedrich Wilhelm Julius, 7, s
MEISSNER, Anna Rosina Pauline, 5, d
MEISSNER, Wilhelm August Hermann, 2-1/2, s
MEISSNER, Emanuel Gottsworth, 3/4, s
    (Herr Meissner stated that he had been engaged as

second teacher with the emigrating Lutheran
congregation of Pastor Krause.)
SIEGERT, Samuel, teacher   Maria Hoefchen
SIEGERT, Friderike Luise Wilhelmine, b
  BOEHNISCH, w
SIEGERT, Bertah Wilhelmine, 18, d
SIEGERT, Bernhard Theodor, 15, s
SIEGERT, Julie Ernestine, 8, d
SIEGERT, Ernst Friedrich, 6, s
  (Herr Siegert stated that he was the other
  teacher engaged with Pastor Krause's congre-
  gation.)
WERNER, Karl Wilhelm, 42, wheelwright   Pilsnitz
WERNER, Johanna, b KUNICK, 36, w
WERNER, Johann Karl, 14, s

From: Provinz Silesia, Kreis Oels
To: America, 1839
BIEROSCH, Christian, master weaver   Juliusburg
BIEROSCH, Maria Elisabeth, b PFEIFFER, 37, w
BIEROSCH, Ernestine Luise, 7, d
BIEROSCH, Karl Gottlieb, 5 months, s
GRAESER, Christian, 26, weaver   Buckowinke
GRAESER, Anna Rosina, b RADEMACHER, 24, w
GRAESER, Johanne Ernestine Luise, 3 weeks, d
STANGE, Gottlieb, 42, inhabitant   Gross-Graben
STANGE, Helene, b STANGE, 37, w
STANGE, Rosina, 9, d
STANGE, Karl Gottlieb, 7, s
STANGE, Wilhelm, 4, s
STANGE, Johanne Dorothea, 3 weeks, d
MUECHLING, Daniel, 60, inhabitant   Gross-Graben
MUECHLING, Anna Rosina, b QUARG, 50, w
BUENDIG, Helene, 51, shepherd's widow   Kurzwitz
BUENDIG, Maria Elisabeth, 15, d
BUENDIG, Ernst Samuel, 13, s
PUSCHEK, Christoph, 37, inhabitant   Kurzwitz
PUSCHEK, Anna Rosina, b HUEBSCH, 38, w
PUSCHEK, Helen, 13, d
PUSCHEK, Karl, 11, s
PUSCHEK, Anna Rosina, 8, d
PUSCHEK, Wilhelm, 5, s
PUSCHEK, Karl, 2-1/2, s
BUENDIG, Helene, 30, maid; d of the widow   Lacumme
  Helene BUENDIG, above
SCHMIDT, Ernst, 44, houseowner   Lacumme
SCHMIDT, Anna Rosina, b GORSEGNER, 36, w
SCHMIDT, Johanna, 11, d
SCHMIDT, Ernst, 9, s
SCHMIDT, Christian, 6, s
SCHMIDT, Dorothea, 3, d
SCHMIDT, Elisabeth, 1, d
SCHMIDT, Maria Auguste, 3 months, d
SCHMIDT, Anna Rosina, b PFEIFFER, 71, mother
REIMANN, Gottlieb, 35, inhabitant   Lacumme
REIMANN, Anna Rosina, b JAECKEL, 39, w
REIMANN, Karl Gottlieb, 14-1/2, s
TRAUTWEIN, Wilhelm, 38, tanner   Bernstadt
TRAUTWEIN, Johanna, b MATHIAS, 36, w
TRAUTWEIN, Wilhelmine, 12, d
TRAUTWEIN, Wilhelm, 9, s
SCHNEIDER, Dorothea, 21, maid to the Traut-
  wein family
POLCE, Anna, 27, maid to the Trautwein family
MATHIAS, Karl, 31, clothmaker   Bernstadt
MATHIAS, Johanna, b PEUCKER, 27, w
MATHIAS, Wilhelm, 4, s
STORZ, Gottlieb, 39, baker   Bernstadt
STORZ, Johanna, b KUNZE, 38, w
STORZ, Henriette, 7, d
SCHLOSSER, Friedrich Wilhelm, journeyman   Bernstadt
  clothmaker

GOELDNER, Anton, 31-1/2, stall owner   Langenhoff
GOELDNER, Susanna, b SACHSCHALL, 29-1/2, w
GOELDNER, Anna, 4, d
GORSEGNER, Christian, 39, blacksmith   Strehlitz
GORSEGNER, Johanne Christiane, b BRUEGER, 30, w
GORSEGNER, Wilhelm, 9, s
GORSEGNER, Julius, 5, s
GORSEGNER, Christiane, 2, d

From: Provinz Schlesien [Silesia], Kreis Trebnitz
To: America, 1839
ROLLE, Christian, 44, inhabitant   Lutzine
ROLLE, Elisabeth, b ROLLE, 38, w
ROLLE, Elisabeth, 14, d
ROLLE, Maria, b GRUTTKE, 62-1/2, widow and mother
  of Christian Rolle or of Elisabeth Rolle
ROLLE, Helene, 38, inhabitant   Lutzine
HEILMANN, Ernst, 25, shoemaker   Lutzine
KELLER, Daniel, 27, inhabitant   Lutzine
KRICKE, Elisabeth, b SCHOLZ, 43, widow
KRICKE, Johann Ernst, 18, s
KRICKE, Karl Gottlieb, 15, s
BARTSCH, Gottlieb, 34, [profession ?]   Lutzine
BARTSCH, Elisabeth, b LEPACH, 33, w
BARTSCH, Johanna, 8, d
BARTSCH, Karl, 6-1/2, s
BARTSCH, Heinrich, 1, s
RODER, Christian, 41, weaver and private   Lutzine
  gardener
RODER, Elisabeth, b PFEIFFER, w
RODER, Karl Gottlieb, 8, s
PRESSGOTT, Gottlieb, 28-1/2, weaver and   Polnisch
  cottager   Hammer
PRESSGOTT, Anna Rosina, b ROSORKE, 29, w
PRESSGOTT, Gottlieb, 9, s
PRESSGOTT, Friedrich Gustav, 6, s
PRESSGOTT, Moritz Ferdinand, 4, s
HAHM, Christian, 38, inhabitant   Polnisch
HAHM, Rosina, b MATZKE, 31, w   Hammer
HAHM, Christian, 8-1/2, s
HAHM, Gottlieb, 5-3/4, s
HAHM, Karl Wilhelm, 2-1/2, s
GROTTKE, Karl, 47, cottager   Polnisch
GROTTKE, Christiane, b STOBER, 38, w   Hammer
GROTTKE, Karl, 20-1/2, s
WIESNER, Gottlieb, 41, inhabitant   Polnisch
WIESNER, Anna Rosina, b BARTSCH, 41, w   Hammer
WIESNER, Friedrich Wilhelm, 16, s
WIESNER, Luise, 13, d
WIESNER, Juliane, 11, d
WIESNER, Dorothea, 7, d
WIESNER, Gottlieb, 3/4, s
SCHEIGERT, Gottlieb, 43, inhabitant   Polnisch
SCHEIGERT, Johanna, b RICHEL, 38, w   Hammer
  and midwife
SCHEIGERT, Juliane Wilhelmine, 14-1/2, d
SCHEIGERT, Friedrich Erdmann, 11-1/2, s
BARTSCH, Johann, 37, inhabitant   Polnisch
BARTSCH, Susanna, b SCHREIBER, 35, w   Hammer
BARTSCH, Susanna, 11-1/2, d
BARTSCH, Gottlieb, 9, s
BARTSCH, Karl Wilhelm, 7-1/2, s
BARTSCH, Karl, 5, s
BARTSCH, Dorothea, 2, d
JORDAN, Rosina, 30, married; the husband   Polnisch
  is not a Separatist and will not emigrate; Hammer
  there has been no divorce
GORSEGNER, Gottlieb, 36, weaver and cot-   Zantkau
  tager
GORSEGNER, Anna Rosina, b KLOSE, 33, w
KEIL, Wilhelm, 21, Züchnergeselle?   Zantkau

KRAUSE, Gottlieb, 48, mover   Biadauschke
KRAUSE, Anna Rosina, b KUEHN, 47, w
TUCH, Franz Friedrich, 37, wheelwright   Lossen
TUCH, Maria, 36, w
TUCH, Auguste, 5, d
TUCH, Emilie, 4, d
TUCH, Karl, 3, s
TUCH, Gustav, 1, s
WERNER, Friedrich, 60, leader [*Vogt*]   Dockern
WERNER, Johanna Renate, b ENKNER, 56, w
SCHEIGERT, Christoph, 30, farmer   Schawoine

From: Provinz Schlesien [Silesia], Kreis Wartenberg
To: America, 1839
HOMELIUS, Heinrich, 43, citizen and mas-   Polnisch
  ter shoemaker   Wartenberg
HOMELIUS, Maria, b IGEL, 40, w
HOMELIUS, Karl Wilhelm Emanuel, 12, s
HOMELIUS, Gotthard Heinrich Benjamin, 8 s
HOMELIUS, Maria Gottliebe, 4, d
HOMELIUS, Paul Samuel Theophil, 1, s
SCHULTHES, Karl, 37, citizen and master Festenberg
  tailor
SCHULTHES, Martha, b ZIEGLER, 39, w
GRUTTKE, Johann, 69, mover   Festenberg
GRUTTKE, Freimann Gottfried, 40, son of
  the above Johann Gruttke
GRUTTKE, Johanna, b METZNER, 30, w
GRUTTKE, Friedrich Wilhelm, 10, s
GRUTTKE, Wilhelm Heinrich, 5, s
GRUTTKE, Susanne Dorothea, 2, d
GRUTTKE, Freimann Johann, 34, son of   Festenberg
  Johann Gruttke
GRUTTKE, Elisabeth, b ALTMANN, 27, w
GRUTTKE, Johann Gottlieb, 2, s
  (Note: The name Freimann may be a status
  title, rather than a given name, for both
  of the sons above; if so, it means simply
  that they are freemen.)

From: Provinz Schlesien [Silesia], Kreis Gruenberg
To: America, 1839
SCHMIDT, Karl Friedrich, Senior, 55, rag
  collector   Schloin
SCHMIDT, Anna Maria, b JAECKEL, w
SCHMIDT, Johanna Dorothea, 10, d
SCHMIDT, Christian Friedrich, Junior, rag Schloin
  collector (probably son of Karl Fried-
  rich SCHMIDT)
SCHMIDT, Anna Rosina, b SANDER, w
SCHMIDT, Johanna Eleonore, 5, d
SCHMIDT, Johann August, 4 weeks, s
JOCHMANN, Johann Georg, gardener   Schloin
JOCHMANN, Christian, 29, s
JOCHMANN, Anna Elisabeth, 23, d
JOCHMANN, Anna Rosina, 21, d
JOCHMANN, Anna Dorothea, 14, d
HIRTHE, Gottfried, coachman   Schloin
HIRTHE, Maria Elisabeth, b JOCHMANN, w
HIRTHE, Johann August, 16, s
HIRTHE, Johann Friedrich, 10, s
HIRTHE, Johanna Eleonore, 23, d
HIRTHE, Johanna Rosina, 14, d
  (Two older sons, Karl, 21, and Christian, 18,
  who are in service in Berlin, do not wish to
  emigrate.)
FRANKE, Samuel, coachman, with w and   Laettnitz
  6 children (18, 16, 14, 12, and 4)
KLOSE, Heinrich, hired hand   Laettnitz

From: Provinz Schlesien [Silesia], Kreis Glogau
To: America, 1839
DOBSCHAL, Gottfried, day laborer   Glogau
HEINRICH, Theodor Leberecht, invalid day Glogau
  laborer, with w and 5 children
GRUNIG, Anna Rosina, 37, widow of a cab-   Brieg
  inetmaker
GRUNIG, Johanna Elisabeth, 16, d
GRUNIG, Anna Rosina, 15, d
WAEDEL, Karl Friedrich, 41, with w and   Brieg
  4 children
ROTHE, Samuel, 38, gardener, with w and   Brostau
  3 children
ZEIHN, Karl   Polwitz
ZEIHN, Ernst, 24, brother
ZEIHN, Gottfried, brother
BORCHERT, Rudolf Gottfried, master cabinet- Goldberg
  maker, with w and 2 sons
POHL, Anna Maria, widow of a day laborer, Polkwitz
  with 3 children
MUELLER, Wilhelm Emanuel Gottlieb, 28, har- Sprottau
  nessmaker [*Riemergeselle*]

From: Provinz Schlesien [Silesia], Kreis Sagan
To: America, 1839
WALTER, Georg Ferdinand, inhabitant   Reichenau
WALTER, Anna Rosina, b SEUL, w
SEUL, --, foster child

From: Provinz Schlesien [Silesia], Kreis Freistadt
To: America, 1839
SCHWARZ, Johann Georg, 39, tailor   Seifersdorf
SCHWARZ, Dorothea Elisabeth, b HOFFMANN,
  32, w
SCHWARZ, Gottlieb August, 7, s
SCHWARZ, Karl Johann Gotthilf, 5, s
SCHWARZ, --

From: Provinz Schlesien [Silesia], Kreis Rothenburg
To: America, 1839
WAGNER, Gustav Wilhelm, owner of a print- Rothenburg
  shop

  Thus, the total Old Lutheran emigration for the
  year 1839 totals as follows:

Pomerania	570
Saxony	230
Mark Brandenburg	91
Silesia	<u>265</u>
Total	<u>1156</u>

The names of 83 emigrants from the Merseburg region are missing.

1840

Emigration for the year was not large, excepting from
Silesia, as reported by the Silesian Oberpräsident
From: Provinz Schlesien [Silesia], Kreis Trebnitz
To: America, 1840
SCHNEIDER, Christian, 54, farm owner   Zantkau
SCHNEIDER, Anna Rosina, b RODER, 44, w
SCHNEIDER, Ernst, 20, s
SCHNEIDER, Anna Rosina, 18, d
SCHNEIDER, August, 16, s
SCHNEIDER, Karl, 10, s
SCHNEIDER, Johanna, 6, d

KEIL, Silvius, 21, journeyman tailor   Zantkau
KAMMER, Christian Gottlieb, 54, ceramic   Schlottau
  painter
KAMMER, Anna Rosina, b SATTLER, 53, w
KAMMER, August, 16, s
  (The emigration of this family is not certain.)
KANTHER, August, 20, journeyman shoemaker   Luzine
  (The emigration of this person is not certain.)
NITSCHKE, Daniel, 38, miller and inhabitant Schawoine
NITSCHKE, Helene, b STAHR, 36, w
NITSCHKE, Daniel, 6, s
NITSCHKE, Dorothea, 2, d
GARBSCH, Georg, 41, gardener   Klein Ujeschuetz
GARBSCH, Maria Elisabeth, b RIEDEL, 36, w
GARBSCH, Gottlieb, 18-1/2, s
GARBSCH, Georg, 15, s
GARBSCH, Johanna Helene, 12, d
GARBSCH, David, 10, s
GARBSCH, Daniel, 8, s
GARBSCH, Gottfried Hermann, 6, s
GARBSCH, Johann, 4, s
STERNITZKE, Friedrich, 33, houseowner   Klein Uje-
STERNITZKE, Helene, b VIETZ, 28, w   schuetz
STERNITZKE, Karl, 8, s
STERNITZKE, Susanna Helene, 6, d
STERNITZKE, Gottlieb, 3, s
STERNITZKE, Wilhelm August, 1/2, s
HILLERT, Rosina, 62, widow of inhabitant   Klein Uje-
                                     schuetz

From: Provinz Schlesien [Silesia], Kreis Oels
To: America, 1840
SCHMIDT, Karl, 40, livery stable owner   Lacumme
SCHMIDT, Dorothea, b REITZIG, 33, w
SCHMIDT, Christiane, 12, d
SCHMIDT, Johanna, 11, d
SCHMIDT, Ernst, 9, s
SCHMIDT, Dorothea, 8, d
SCHMIDT, Karl, 6, s
SCHMIDT, Elisabeth, 4, d
SCHMIDT, Wilhelm, 3, s
SCHMIDT, Anna Rosina, 2, d
MATHIAS, Gottlieb, 61, businessman   Bernstadt
MATHIAS, Sophia, b METZNER, 61, w
MATHIAS, Julius, 24, s
STERNAHL, Gottlieb, 35, gardener   Nieder Muehlwitz
STERNAHL, Maria, b HAYN, 33, w
STERNAHL, Johann Christian, 10, s
STERNAHL, Ernst August, 8, s
  (The emigration of this family is not certain.)
HEYNE, Gottlieb, 34, farmer and grocer Nieder Muehl-
HEYNE, Anna Rosina, b GUENTHER, 27, w   witz
HEYNE, Karoline, 7, d
HEYNE, Karl August, 6, s
HEYNE, Karl Wilhelm, 4, s
HEYNE, Karl Friedrich, 2, s
  (The emigration of this family is not certain.)
BLASE, Johann, 26, gardener   Galbitz
BLASE, Anna Rosina, b SCHLEIER, 24, w
BLASE, Auguste Pauline Emilie, 2/3, d
  (The emigration of this family is not certain.)
SCHIRDEWAHN, Gottlieb, 33, inhabitant   Galbitz

From: Provinz Schlesien [Silesia], Kreis Sagan
To: America, 1840
KNOBEL, Ernst Wilhelm, journeyman cabinet- Kottwitz
  maker

From: Provinz Schlesien [Silesia], Kreis Sprottau
To: America, 1840
LINCKE, Johann Gottlieb, 29   Kunzendorf

From: Provinz Sachsen [Saxony]
To: America, 1840
MENTE, --, journeyman roofer   Halle

1841

The list of emigrants to Australia is fairly complete
but that for America is very incomplete.
From: Provinz Brandenburg, Kreis Zuellichau
To: Australia, 1841
SCHULZ, Johann Gottlieb, 43, journeyman Zuellichau
  mason
SCHULZ, Johanna Luise, b FECHNER, 48, w
GROSSMANN, Ewald, 32, journeyman mason Zuellichau
GROSSMANN, Luise, b SCHMIDT, 30, w
GROSSMANN, Wilhelmine, 4-3/4, d
GROSSMANN, Johann Karl, 3, s
GROSSMANN, Julius, 3/4, s
THIEDEMANN, Ernst Daniel, 41, tobacco Zuellichau
  worker [Tabaksspinner]
THIEDEMANN, Luise, b BEGEN, 41, w
THIEDEMANN, Gottlieb, 11, s
THIEDEMANN, Daniel, 4, s
THIEDEMANN, Maria, 1, d
  Due to a printing failure, the name of one
  family is missing; there were five children,
  whose names are recorded as follows:
  --, Wilhelm, 14, s
  --, August, 12, s
  --, Karoline, 10, d
  --, Johanna, 6, d
  --, Ernestine, 5, d
GROCKE, Johann Luis, 28, shoemaker   Amt Zuellichau
GROCKE, Anna Elisabeth, b MATZANKE, 30, w
GROCKE, Elisabeth, 1, d
PAECH, Gottfried, 24, coachman   Amt Zuellichau
  (His parents emigrated in 1838.)
STEICKE, Johann Gottfried, 40, prin-   Kay
  cipal servant [Grossknecht]
STEICKE, Anna Rosina, b SCHRECK, 36, w
STEICKE, Johanna Luise, 10, d
STEICKE, Traugott, 6, s
STEICKE, Gottlieb, 3, s
STEICKE, Gottfried, 3/4, s
EGEL, Gottlob, 27, sailor   Kay
EGEL, Johanna Elisabeth, b EDLICH, 28, w
EGEL, Johanna Eleonore, 1, d
ZEINERT, Georg, 30, day laborer   Kay
ZEINERT, Maria, b DRUDTKE, 66, mother
NEUMANN, Christian, 39, cottager   Kay
NEUMANN, Anna Dorothea, b MEYER, w
NEUMANN, Johanna Luise, 9, d
NEUMANN, Johanna Karoline, 8, d
NEUMANN, Johanna Dorothea, 6, d
NEUMANN, Wilhelm, 3, s
NEUMANN, Gottlieb, 3/4, s
PFEIFER, Johann Georg, 25, shepherd boy   Kay
STEICKE, Gottfried, 66, watermiller   Kay
STEICKE, Gottlieb, 27, s
STEICKE, Wilhelm, 24, s
STEICKE, Dorothea, 32, d
STEICKE, Johanna Luise, 28, d
STEICKE, Auguste, 22, s
  [Note: No wife and mother listed.]
SOMMER, Johann Georg, 24, servant boy   Kay
SCHULZ, Christian, 32, gardener   Klemzig
SCHULZ, Karoline, b GRADE, 30, w
SCHULZ, Johanna Eleonore, 26, sister
WENZEL, Christian, 43, cottager   Harthe
WENZEL, Anna Dorothea, b HAMPEL, 38, w
WENZEL, Friedrich Wilhelm, 9, s

18

WENZEL, Luise, 6, d
WENZEL, Johanna Eleonore, 4, d
HENTSCHKE, Christian, 36, houseowner   Kutschlau
  and journeyman mason
HENTSCHKE, Apollonia, b SPARMANN, 36, w
HENTSCHKE, Johann Gottlieb, 10, s
HENTSCHKE, August, 8, s
HENTSCHKE, Wilhelm, 5, s
HENTSCHKE, Johanna Luise, 4 months, d
HENTSCHKE, Martin, 28, gardener   Kutschlau
HENTSCHKE, Anna Christiane, b KRUEGER, 25, w
HENTSCHKE, Anna Dorothea, 4, d
HENTSCHKE, Johanna Luise, 2, d
KRUEGER, Wilhelm, 47, baker   Rackau
KRUEGER, Anna Rosina, b WABERSITZKY, 38, w
KRUEGER, Ernst, 14, s
KRUEGER, Christian, 13, s
KRUEGER, Ernestine, 11, d
KRUEGER, Emilie, 6, d
KRUEGER, Auguste, 6, d
FELSCH, Johann Gottlieb, 54, shoemaker   Klein Dammer
FELSCH, Wilhelmine, b SPERLING, 48, w
FELSCH, Eduard, 18, s
FELSCH, Henriette, 15, d
THIELE, Johann Georg, 45, shoemaker   Crummendorf
THIELE, Anna Rosina, b KLUGE, 42, w
THIELE, Karoline, 17, d
THIELE, Anna Eleonore, 15, d
THIELE, Johanna Luise, 13, d
KUCHEL, Johann Gottfried, 30, ox boy   Lochow
KUCHEL, Johanna Dorothea, b KUCHEL, 30, w
KUCHEL, Johanna Luise, 1-1/4, d
KUCHEL, Johanna Dorothea, 1/4, d
STAUDE, Gottlieb, 36, cottager   Klippendorf
STAUDE, Johann Wilhelm, 9, s
STAUDE, Gottlieb, 6, s
STAUDE, August, 3, s
PREUSS, Johanna Luise, b BITROFF, 58, mother-in-law
GERLACH, Samuel, 35, master clothmaker   Schwiebus
GERLACH, Charlotte Friderike, b HAUPT, 36, w
GERLACH, Albertina, 19, d
GERLACH, August, 17, s
GERLACH, Henriette, 15, d
GERLACH, Julius, 10, s
GERLACH, Juliane, 6, d
GERLACH, Auguste, 3, d
GERLACH, Mathilde, 4 months, d

From: Provinz Brandenburg, Kreis Crossen
To: Australia, 1841
SEELAENDER, Johann Gottlieb, 32, car-   Blumberg
  penter (from the Rollmuehle near the
  Kreis town of Blumberg)
SEELAENDER, Karoline, b HAMSELL, 27, w
SEELAENDER, Friedrich August, 2, s
  (Father of Johann Gottlieb Seelaender emi-
  grated to Australia in 1838.)
KLIMKE, Johann Gottlieb, gardener
KLIMKE, Anna Rosina, b RIEMER, w
KLIMKE, Johann Gottlieb, 5, s
KLIMKE, Karoline, 3, d
KLIMKE, Wilhelmine, 1, d

From: Provinz Schlesien [Silesia], Kreis Gruenberg
To: Australia, 1841
NITSCHKE, Georg Friedrich, houseowner   Januy
  and shoemaker
NITSCHKE, Anna Elisabeth, b FELLENBERG, 33, w
NITSCHKE, Gottlieb, 9, s
NITSCHKE, Johanna Rosina, 8, d

NITSCHKE, Anna Rosina, 7, d
NITSCHKE, Johanna Helene, 5, d
NITSCHKE, Johanna Ernestine, 1-1/2 (twin), d
NITSCHKE, Johanna Luise, 1-1/2 (twin), d
NITSCHKE, Helen, 22, sister
BAER, Georg Friedrich, coachman   Januy
BAER, Anna Elisabeth, b MERSCH, w
BAER, Christian, s
BAER, Heinrich, s
BAER, Ernestine, d
BAER, Pauline, d
HOHENBERG, Johann Georg, 52, farmer   Sawade
HOHENBERG, Anna Rosina, b IRMLER, 47, w
HOHENBERG, Anna Rosina, 21, d
HOHENBERG, Johanna Dorothea, 10, d
HOHENBERG, Gottlob, 7, s
HOHENBERG, August, 2, s
LEHMANN, Gottfried, 42, grocer   Sawade
LEHMANN, Anna Elisabeth, b IRMLER, 36, w
LEHMANN, Christiane Pauline, 12, d
LEHMANN, Johanna Elisabeth, 10, d
LEHMANN, Christiane Ernestine, 8, d
LEHMANN, Johanna Auguste, 6, d
LEHMANN, Heinrich, 4, s (twin)
LEHMANN, Friedrich Reinhold, 4, s (twin)
LEHMANN, Johann Gottfried, 2, s
LEHMANN, Johanne Auguste, 3 months, d
KOWALD, Anna Rosina, 58, inhabitant   Sawade
KOWALD, Anna Elisabeth, widow of FELLENBERG, 26,
  daughter
KOWALD, Friedrich, 25, s
KOWALD, Anna Dorothea, 18, d
KOWALD, Luise, 12, d
SCHULZ, Georg August, 30, journeyman butcher Sawade
SCHULZ, Eleonore, b KLEBER, 32, w
MATTNER, Christian, 40, gardener   Sawade
MATTNER, Elisabeth, b MATZANKE, 42, w
KLICHE, Gottfried, 41, houseowner   Sawade
KLICHE, Anna Elisabeth, b PIETSCHKE, 32, w
KLICHE, Johanna Dorothea, 7, d
KLICHE, Auguste, 5, d
KLICHE, Ernestine, 1, d
KRAUSE, Gottfried, 33, houseowner   Sawade
KRAUSE, Anna Elisabeth, b BARREIN, 25, w
KRAUSE, Ernestine, 3, d
KRAUSE, Auguste, 1, d
HOEPPNER, Daniel, 32, journeyman mason   Sawade
HOEPPNER, Luise Dorothea, b NETTENBERG, 28, w
HOEPPNER, Johann Friedrich August, 5, s
HOEPPNER, Johann Friedrich, 3, s
HOEPPNER, Karl Gottlob, 1, s
NICOLAI, Johann Christof, 53, coachman   Prittag
NICOLAI, Elisabeth, b FROEHLICH, 51, w
NICOLAI, Gottfried, 27, s
NICOLAI, Johann Christof, 24, s
NICOLAI, Eva Maria, 21, d
SEIDEL, Christian, 54, gardener   Prittag
SEIDEL, Eva Rosina, b KAERGEL, w
SEIDEL, Gottlieb, 18, s
SEIDEL, Christian, 13, s
SEIDEL, Helene, 16, d
WOLF, Anna Dorothea, 23, foster daughter
NITSCHKE, Gottfried, 38, houseowner   Prittag
NITSCHKE, Eva Elisabeth, b ARLT, 38, w
NITSCHKE, Gottlieb, 13, s
NITSCHKE, Eva Elisabeth, 7, d
NITSCHKE, Karl Friedrich, 5, s
NITSCHKE, Friedrich Wilhelm, 3, s
NITSCHKE, Gottfried, 1, s
HENTSCHKE, Christian, 16, stepson
HENTSCHKE, Johann Gottlieb, 13, stepson
HOEPPNER, Johann Georg, 60, gardener   Prittag

HOEPPNER, Rosina, b FROEHLICH, 48, w
HOEPPNER, Christian, 22, s
HOEPPNER, Anna Rosina, 13, d
HELBIG, Maria Elisabeth, 22, hired girl [employed
  by the Hoeppner family]
KLAR, Gottfried Emanuel, 29, mill owner   Deutsch-
KLAR, Luise, b PREUSS, 29, illegal w   Kessel
KLAR, Pauline, 2, d
PREUSS, Gottlob, 61, inhabitant   Deutsch-Kessel

From: Provinz Schlesien [Silesia], Kreis Liegnitz
To: Australia, 1841
HOFFMANN, Samuel, 47, granary owner   Alt Beckern
LUX, Johanna Christiane, 26, housekeeper   Bienowitz
HOFFMANN, Johanna Christiane Henriette, 14 his d
HOFFMANN, Karl Rudolf, 10, his s

From: Provinz Posen
To: Australia, 1841
Note: Only a few names can be identified
FRITZSCHE, Gotthard Daniel, 44, pastor   Turowo
NEHRLICH, Dorchen, his fiancée
NEHRLICH, Hannchen, widow, mother-in-law from Hamburg
WALLAST, Peter, 42, shoemaker   Alttomsyl
WALLAST? Desde, 48, w
WALLAST, Juliane, 19, d
  [It is not clear whether Frau Desde is married
  to Peter Wallast or whether DESDE is a surname.]
HENSEL, --   Pinne
ROEHR, --, shoemaker   Tirschtigel
BORRMANN, --   Tirschtigel
MUELLER, Ferdinand   )   Birnbaum
MUELLER, Johann Friedrich)- brothers
MUELLER, August   )

From: Pomerania
To: America, 1841
Note: None of the Pomeranian emigrants accompanying
  Pastor Krause can be identified. A few of the
  emigrants from Silesia, who emigrated with him, are
  listed hereinafter.

From: Provinz Schlesien [Silesia], Kreis Liegnitz
To: America, 1841
LEOPOLD, Karl Friedrich, inhabitant   Parchwitz
LEOPOLD, Johanna Karoline, b PRELLER, w
LEOPOLD, Karl Friedrich August, s
LEOPOLD, Wilhelm Julius, s
LEOPOLD, Johann Friedrich August, s
LEOPOLD, Johanne Luise Karoline, d
LEOPOLD, Johanne Christiane, d
SCHOEN, Benjamin, 38, mill owner   Pfaffendorf
SCHOEN, Rosina, b ILGNER, 29, w
SCHOEN, Christiane, 11, d
SCHOEN, Hermann Wilhelm, 8, s
SCHOEN, Ernst Heinrich Julius, 5, s
SCHOEN, Emilie, 2, d
SCHOEN, Maria Elisabeth Dorothea, 1-1/4, d

From: Provinz Schlesien [Silesia], Kreis Lueben
To: America, 1841
GROSSER, Albert, master cabinetmaker   Buchwaeldchen
GROSSER, Rosina, b WOGISCH, w
GROSSER, Emilie, 15, d
GROSSER, Eduard, 13, s
GROSSER, Hermann, 8, s
GROSSER, Traugott, 6, s
GROSSER, Maria, 4, d

From: Mark [Brandenburg], Kreis Sternberg
To: America, 1841
REDLICH, Friedrich, 39, master shoemaker   Zielenzig
REDLICH, Charlotte, b FIEDLER, 36, w
REDLICH, Wilhelm, 12, s
REDLICH, Wilhelmine, 10, d
REDLICH, Eduard, 7, s
SCHMIDT, Karl Friedrich, 64, master butcher Zielenzig
REICHHENG, --, 50, divorced sister
  [This is not entirely clear; the divorced
  brother-in-law was a master cablemaker.]

1842

Note: Although the statistical tables which accompany
this work show a total of 45 emigrants for the year,
all of which were said to have been identifiable, the
list gives the names of only two, a brother and sister
STOCK, who emigrated to America from Kreis Kammin and
were followed in 1843 by a brother, Christian Wilhelm
STOCK.

1843

All recorded emigration for the year was to America.
From: Provinz Brandenburg, Kreis Prenzlau
To: America, 1843
STRASBURG, Gottlieb, 60, cottager and weaver Wallmow
STRASBURG, --, b HINZ, 60, w
STRASBURG, Charlotte, 34, d
STRASBURG, Friedrich, 26, s
THIEMKE, Maria, b HINZ, 64, widow   Wallmow
KUHZ, Dorothea, b SCHULZ, 70, day laborer   Wallmow
KIECKHOEFEL, Dorothea Elisabeth, 27, un-   Wallmow
  married hired girl
HASELEY, Friedrich, 31, farmer's s   Wallmow
HASELEY, Wilhelm, 26, farmer's s   Wallmow
HASELEY, --, widow   Wallmow
  (Her husband had given the money for the two
  sons, above, to emigrate; two other brothers,
  David HASELEY and August HASELEY were also
  given permission to emigrate despite their
  military connection. [It is not clear whether
  these two sons actually emigrated with their
  mother and other brothers.])
KRUEGER, Friedrich, 24, hired hand   Wallmow
WENDT, Friedrich Wilhelm, 27, farmer's s   Wallmow
  (May have been prohibited from emigrating
  at Havelberg.)
WIELAND, Gottfried, 40, day laborer   Wallmow
WIELAND, Luise, b KRUMREICH, 46, w
WIELAND, Wilhelm, 21, s
WIELAND, Luise Christine Wilhelmine, 19, d
WIELAND, Christine Friderike, 16, d
WIELAND, Johann Gottfried, 13, s
WIELAND, Karl August, 11, s
WIELAND, Christiane Elisabeth, 9, d
WIELAND, Christiane Luise, 6, d
HASE, Daniel, 39, worker   Wallmow
HASE, Marie, b SCHULZ, w
HASE, Christian Friedrich, 10, s
HASE, Friedrich, Wilhelm, 5, s
HASE, Christine, 2, d
LINDKE, Martin, 43, worker   Wallmow
LINDKE, Christiane, b BARTEL, 43, w
LINDKE, Martin Friedrich Wilhelm, 15, s
LINDKE, Christine Luise, 14, d
LINDKE, Ernestine Wilhelmine, 12, d
LINDKE, Dorothea Luise, 10, d
LINDKE, Johanna Friderike, 8, d
LINDKE, Maria Elisabeth, 2, d

BLUMREICH, Johann Friedrich, 35, weaver — Wallmow
BLUMREICH, Christine, b WOLFF, 31, w
BLUMREICH, Friderike Wilhelmine, 7, d
BLUMREICH, Friedrich Wilhelm, 1, s
STRASBURG, Gottfried, 36, weaver and cottager — Wallmow
STRASBURG, Christine, b REGLING, 23, w
STRASBURG, Wilhelmine Friderike, 6, d (twin)
STRASBURG, Johanna Elisabeth, 6, d (twin)
STRASBURG, Friedrich Wilhelm, 4, s
STRASBURG, August Wilhelm, 2, s
STRASBURG, Johann Gottfried Wilhelm, 4 months, s
BERGHOLZ, Friedrich, 24, hired hand — Wallmow
GRAPENTHIN, Friderike, 26, w
BERGHOLZ? [or GRAPENTHIN], Friedrich Wilhelm, 1-3/4,s
STEFFEN, Johann, 50, herder — Wallmow
STEFFEN, Christine, b AHLBECK, 45, w
STEFFEN, Friedrich Wilhelm, 15, s
STEFFEN, Christian Friedrich, 13, s
STEFFEN, Christina Dorothea Elisabeth, 7, d
STEFFEN, Dorothea Elisabeth, 5, d
STEFFEN, Wilhelm, 2, s
WALK, Christof, 28, farmer — Wallmow
WALK, Wilhelmine Friderike, b WENDT, 25, w
WALK, Christian Friedrich, 1, s
MATZDORFF, Friedrich, 45, shepherd — Wallmow
MATZDORFF, Christine Dorothea, b FAEHRMANN, 44, w
MATZDORFF, Regine, 17, d
MATZDORFF, Dorothea Friderike Wilhelmine, 11, d
MATZDORFF, Johanna Elisabeth, 7, d
MATZDORFF, Ernestine Friederike Luise, 4, d
MATZDORFF, Friederike Karoline, 2, d
FAEHRMANN, --, 69, widow, mother-in-law
BUROW, Michael, 38, hired hand — Wallmow
BUROW, Elisabeth, b GOMBERT, 36, w
BUROW, Friedrich Wilhelm, 9, s
BUROW, Dorothea Elisabeth Friderike, 17, d
BUROW, Wilhelmine Christine, 13, d
BUROW, Wilhelm Ferdinand, 6, s
BUROW, Maria Dorothea Elisabeth, 3, d
BUROW, Christian Friedrich, 4 months, s
  [Note: The age of Friedrich Wilhelm Burow is
  suspect, since he is not listed in sibling se-
  quence.]
BUROW, Christian, 39, tailor — Wallmow
BUROW, Christine, b RAHN, 39, w
BUROW, Johanna Wilhelmine Friderike, 9, d
BUROW, Friderike Justine, 7, d
BUROW, Immanuel Friedrich, 5, s
BUROW, Sophie Elisabeth, 2, d
BALLERT, Johann, cottager and shoemaker — Wallmow
JAHN, Dorothea, 32, w
DAMEROW, Gottfried, cottager and day laborer — Wallmow
  (He is legally separated from his wife.)
MUELLER, Christian, 60, cottager and worker — Wallmow
MUELLER, Luise, b BUROW, 50, w
MUELLER, David, 22, s
MUELLER, Christian, 18, s
MUELLER, Friedrich Daniel Michael, 17, s
MUELLER, Friedrich, 14, s
MUELLER, Albertine Wilhelmine, 23, d
CASSUBE, Johann, 50, worker — Wallmow
CASSUBE, Christine, b BALLERT, 48, w
CASSUBE, Friedrich Wilhelm, 18, s
CASSUBE, Johann, 17, s
CASSUBE, Karoline Friderike, 16, d
CASSUBE, Wilhelm Gottfried, 13, s
CASSUBE, Christian Friedrich, 9, s
CASSUBE, Wilhelmine, 4, d
BECKMANN, --, teacher and church deacon — Wallmow
BECKMANN, Johanna, b KANUTH, 30, w
BECKMANN, Christof Magnus, 1, s
STOLZMANN, Gottfried, 17, s of one of the — Wallmow
  persons detained in the Havelberg affair

BUROW, Christof, 17 — Wallmow
  (Perhaps the son of the above Burow.)
SALINGRE, Johann, farmer — Bergholz
  (Legally separated from his wife.)
KLEE, Frierich, 32, weaver — Bergholz
KLEE, Maria Charlotte, b KRULL, 31, w
MEYER, --, 34, laborer — Bergholz
MEYER, --, 28, w
SCHUESSLER, Maria, 62, widowed day laborer — Bergholz
SCHUESSLER, Luise, 28, d
SUCROW, Christian, 31, farmer's s — Bergholz
RUBBERT, Johann, 26, hired hand — Bergholz
DUCWITZ, Maria, 27, unmarried hired girl — Bergholz
STOWASSER, August, 34, teacher and deacon — Bergholz
STOWASSER, Wilhelmine Henriette, b KRUEGER, 21, w
FERKEN, Friedrich, 43, weaver — Bergholz
FERKEN, Dorothea, b BRUENING, 41, w
FERKEN, Karl Wilhelm, 14, s
FERKEN, Christine Friderike, 8, d
FERKEN, Johann Friedrich, 5, s
BREDOW, Joachim, 42, day laborer — Bergholz
BREDOW, Luise, b NEUMANN, 30, w
BREDOW, Johann Friedrich, 17, s
BREDOW, Christian Friedrich, 11, s
BREDOW, Christine Luise, 12, d
BREDOW, Friedrich Wilhelm, 7, s
BREDOW, Friderike Christine, 4, d
BREDOW, Karoline Wilhelmine, 2, d
PROEFROCK, Johann, 30, day laborer — Bergholz
PROEFROCK, Christine, b VOELKER, 27, w
PROEFROCK, Friderike Christine, 5, d
PROEFROCK, Christine Luise, 1, d
HOLLAND, Christian, 24, tailor — Bergholz
HOLLAND, Maria Dorothea, b KRAUSE, 28, w
HOLLAND, Auguste Karoline, 1, d
WILLIAM, Johann, 31, farmer — Bergholz
WILLIAM, Marie, b ANDRÉ, 31, w
WILLIAM, Johann, 8, s
WILLIAM, Abraham, 28, farmer — Bergholz
WILLIAM, Judith Laramé, 28, w
WILLIAM, Friderike Wilhelmine, 7, d
WILLIAM, Auguste Albertine, 6, d
WILLIAM, Marie, 3, d
WILLIAM, August Wilhelm, 1-1/2, s
FERKEN, Michael, 47, laborer — Bergholz
FERKEN, Karoline, b WITTKOPP, 43, w
FERKEN, Karoline Luise, 18, d
FERKEN, Christian Friedrich, 16, s
FERKEN, Wilhelmine Luise, 10, d
WOLFF, Christian, 32, merchant — Bergholz
WOLFF, Wilhelmine Christine, b SCHULZ, 26, w
WOLFF, Marie Auguste Wilhelmine, 3, d
WOLFF, Albertine Friderike, 2, d
LOGÉ, Peter, 32, cottager — Bergholz
LOGÉ, Christine Luise, b WOLFF, 29, w
LOGÉ, August Ferdinand, 2, s
LOGÉ, Wilhelmine Christine, 1, d
ENGEL, Gottfried, 25, laborer — Bergholz
ENGEL, Marie Sophie, b GRUETZNER, 31, w
ENGEL, Christine Wilhelmine, 6, d
ENGEL, Wilhelm, 4, s
ENGEL, Luise Christine, 2, d
RECKE, Karoline, 24-1/2, unmarried — Bergholz
GENET, 24, unmarried — Bergholz
GROBENGIESSER, --, 29, wheelwright — Bruessow
GROBENGIESSER, Maria Dorothea, b WITTKOPF, 27, w
CAMANN, Friedrich, 35, maker of house slip- — Bruessow
  pers
CAMANN, Luise, b GROBENGIESSER, 27, w
CAMANN, Friedrich August, 3, s
CAMANN, August Wilhelm, 2, s
CAMANN, Wilhelm Julius, 1/2, s

STIEG, Karl Ludwig, 52, shoemaker   Bruessow
STIEG, Christine Luise, b ZEHMS, 41, w
STIEG, Luise Karoline Friderike Wilhelmine, 18, d
STIEG, Karl August, 16, s
STIEG, Luise Albertine, 10, d
STIEG, Wilhelm Ludwig, 7, s
STIEG, Ferdinand Hermann, 4, s
ROSSOW, Johann Friedrich, 44, shoemaker   Bruessow
ROSSOW, Friderike Elisabeth, b FIELITZ, 47, w
ROSSOW, Karl Wilhelm, 16, s
ROSSOW, Johann Friedrich Wilhelm, 14, s
ROSSOW, Karoline Wilhelmine Henriette, 12, d
ROSSOW, Johann August, 8, s
GROBENGIESSER, Johann Justus, 56, wheel-   Bruessow
  wright
GROBENGIESSER, Karoline, b RIBIKE, 67, w
GROBENGIESSER, Justine Friderike, 26, d
GROBENGIESSER, Johanne Charlotte Friderike, 24, d
GROBENGIESSER, Wilhelm Heinrich, 20, s
HANDKE, Johann Christian, 41, shoemaker   Bruessow
HANDKE, Charlotte Luise, b BETTAC, 31, w
HANDKE, Heinrich Wilhelm, 15, s
HANDKE, Johann Gottlieb Leberecht, 4, s
TRIPPENSEE, --, tailor from Broelka near   Bruessow
DUBOI, --, 42, day laborer   Fahrenwalde
DUBOI, Dorothea, b SCHULTZ, 38, w
GENET, Abraham, 25, hired hand   Fahrenwalde
KLEE, Karl Friedrich Wilhelm, 34, weaver Fahrenwalde
KLEE, Friderike, b RETTMANN, 34, w
KLEE, Wilhelmine Friderike, 7, d
KLEE, August, 3, s
KLEE, Marie Friderike Karoline, 1, d
KRULL, Christian, 37, farmer   Fahrenwalde
KRULL, Marie, b BECCUE, 37, w
KRULL, Marie Justine, 9, d
KRULL, Karoline Luise, 7, d
KRULL, Friedrich Wilhelm, 5, s
KRULL, Albertine, 1-1/2, d
BRAUER, Luise, 24, servant girl   Fahrenwalde
ZABEL, Christian Friedrich, 35, shepherd Fahrenwalde
ZABEL, Dorothea Luise, b MUELLER, 28, w
ZABEL, Wilhelmine Friderike Luise, 6, d
ZABEL, Wilhelm Friedrich August, 4, s
ZABEL, Friderike, 1-1/2, d
KRULL, Johann David, 26, journeyman car- Fahrenwalde
  penter
KRULL, Christine Luise, b DUCWITZ, 27, w
KRULL, Friderike Wilhelmine, 6, d
KRULL, Justine Luise, 3, d
KRULL, Johann, 1-1/2, s
BATZLAFF, Friedrich, 17   Fahrenwalde
SCHWEBS, --, 58, cabinetmaker   Falkenwalde
SCHWEBS? Wilhelmine, b RIECKS, 27, w?
WEGNER, Wilhelm, 26, weaver   Falkenwalde
SCHUELER, Dorothea, 25, w
WEGNER, Luise, 31, unmarried   Falkenwalde
SCHUELER, Gottfried, 58, cottager and Falkenwalde
  tailor
SCHUELER, Marie, 48, w
SCHUELER, Christine Wilhelmine, 18, d of first mar-
  riage of the father
SCHUELER, Gottfried, 15, s of first marriage of the
  father
SCHUELER, Johanna Marie Auguste, 6, d of second mar-
  riage
SCHUELER, Heinrich Wilhelm, 4, s of second marriage
WEGNER, Marie, b HOEPFNER, 43, widow Falkenwalde
  and seamstress
WEGNER, Ernst Gottlieb, 15, s
WEGNER, Marie Dorothea Wilhelmine, 8, d
WEGNER, Johann Christian, 5, s
WEGNER, Gottfried, 43, weaver   Falkenwalde

WEGNER, Christine, b WEGNER, 43, w
WEGNER, August Christof Gottlieb, 17, s
WEGNER, Friedrich Johann, 9, s
WEGNER, Marie Christine, 7, d
WEGNER, Johanna Marie Elisabeth, 5, d
  [The notation states that there were five chil-
  dren but only four are listed by name.]
URTEL, Johann Christoph, 45, weaver   Grimme
URTEL, Christine, b SCHULZ, 45, w
URTEL, Johann Wilhelm, 16, s
URTEL, Friedrich, 14, s
URTEL, Karl August, 13, s
URTEL, Ferdinant Wilhelm, 9, s
URTEL, Gottlieb Heinrich, 8, s
URTEL, Christine Friderike, 11, d
SCHULZ, Karl Friedrich, 40, shoemaker   Grimme
TINKELTHEI, Dorothea Luise, 38, w
SCHULZ? Charlotte Friderike, 18, d
SCHULZ? Charlotte Marie Wilhelmine, 16, d
SCHULZ? Wilhelm Friedrich, 10, s
SCHULZ? Dorothea Luise, 8, d
SCHULZ? Wilhelmine Albertine, 4, d
SCHULZ? Augustine, 1-1/2, d
MUELLER, Johann, 39, laborer   Grimme
MUELLER, Christine, b GIESE, 42, w
MUELLER, Friderike, 11, d
MUELLER, Johann, 7, s
MUELLER, Friedrich Wilhelm, 4, s
MUELLER, August, 1, s
BOENING, Wilhelm, 42, farmer's s   Menkin
BOENING, Christian, 26, brother of Wilhelm
BOENING, Luise, 27, sister of Wilhelm
HEUER, Georg, 50, day laborer   Menkin
BOENING, Sophie, 60, w
HEUER? Christine Luise, 24, d
HEUER? Friderike, 16, d
HEUER? Georg Friedrich, 15, s
BISCHOF, Friedrich, 42, day laborer   Menkin
MUELLER, Dorothea Luise, 45, w
BISCHOF? Dorothea Luise, 16, d
BISCHOF? Christine Friderike Luise, 11, d
BISCHOF? Christian Friedrich, 5, s
BISCHOF? Wilhelmine Friderike Sophie, 3, d
BOENING, --, b MARKHOFF, 54, farmer's widow Menkin
KUEHN, Mich[ael], 70, former land owner Schwaneberg
SCHROEDER, Friedrich, 31, weaver and cot- Schwaneberg
  tager
SCHROEDER, Charlotte, b SCHROEDER, w
SCHROEDER, August, s
GLOEGE, Johann, 46, weaver   Schwaneberg
GLOEGE, Christine, b SCHULTZ, 44, w
GLOEGE, Friedrich Wilhelm, 19, s
GLOEGE, Christine Luise, 17, d
GLOEGE, Friedrich Wilhelm, 14, s
GLOEGE, Friderike, 13, d
GLOEGE, Karl Friedrich, 9, s
GLOEGE, Johann Daniel, 2, s
KRULL, Friedrich, 46, official [Statt-   Caselow
  halter]
DESJARDIN, Elisabeth, 50, w
KRULL? Marie Karoline, 20, d
KRULL? Friderike Luise, 17, d
KRULL? Christ[ine?] Wilhelm[ine], 14, d?
KRULL? Friderike Charlotte, 11, d
KRULL? Charlotte Albertine, 8, d
CONRAD, Christian, 46, day laborer   Caselow
MEHLS, Eleonore, 50, w
CONRAD? Wilhelmine, 9, d
KOEHN, Christof, 44, weaver   Wollin
PIPKORN, Marie, 50, w
KOEHN? Mich[ael] Friedrich, 19, s
KOEHN? Wilhelm, 17, s

KOEHN? Ernestine, 15, d
KOEHN? August Gottlieb, 12, s
KOEHN? Johanna Luise, 10, d
KOEHN? Christine Luise, 7, d
GAENZMER, Justine Luise, stepdaughter
SIEBERT, Marie, b BILLIAN, 55, widow   Zerenthin
SIEBERT. Marie. 28, d
SIEBERT, Friedrich, 26, laborer   Zerenthin
SCHMOCK, Gottfried, 30, journeyman cloth   Prenzlau
   maker
RIECK, Amilie, 27, w
SCHMIDT, Georg, 30, master cabinetmaker   Prenzlau
   (His w emigrated in 1844 following him.)
BARTH, --, son of a weaver   Prenzlau
HILDEBRANDT, Dorothea Luise, b STAATS,
   59, widow of a day laborer   Tornow
MERTENS, Justine, b WIELAND, 52, widow of   Tornow
   a farmer
SPANN, Wilhelmine, b WEGNER, 33, divorced   Gruenow
   day laborer
BARTEL, Dorothea, 30, maid   Rollberg
DESJARDIN, Abraham, 27, peasant's s   Woddow
BLANK, Daniel, 20   Wetzenow

From: Provinz Brandenburg, Kreis Ober-Barnim and
       Lebus
To: America, 1843
SCHWEFEL, Ernst Wilhelm, inhabitant   Neu Kietz
SCHWEFEL, Sophie, b CRAMER, w
SCHWEFEL, Ernst Wilhelm, 10, s
SCHWEFEL, Johann Wilhelm, 7, s
SCHWEFEL, Karoline Wilhelmine, 5, d
SCHWEFEL, Auguste, 1, d
   (The KOCH sisters, daughters of the w by her
   first marriage, remained in Germany.)
SCHULZE, Friedrich August, inhabitant   Neu Kietz
BERGMANN, Dorothea Sophie, w
SCHULZE? Friedrich August, 10, s
SCHULZE? Friedrich Wilhelm, 8, s
SCHULZE? Marie Sophie Dorothea, 6, d
SCHULZE? Karl Ludwig, 4, s
SCHULZE? Johann August, 1, s
   (A foster d, -- ALBERTS, was accommodated in
   Germany but then emigrated in 1848 rejoining the
   family.)
SALMSMUELLER, Karl Ludwig, 33, tailor   Sietzing
SALMSMUELLER, Luise, b HOEHNE, 37, w
SALMSMUELLER, Auguste, 1, d
DRECHSLER, Karl Ludwig, 46, master black-   Sietzing
   smith
DRECHSLER, Charlotte Sophie, b SCHERFLING, 43, w
DRECHSLER, Emilie Friderike Wilhelmine, 20, d
DRECHSLER, Charlotte Juliane, 19, d
DRECHSLER, Karl Ludwig Adolf, 16, s
DRECHSLER, Florentine Bertha Emilie, 12, d
DRECHSLER, Karl Ludwig Julius, 10, s
DRECHSLER, Albertine Amalie, 8, d
DRECHSLER, Florentine Charlotte Therese, 3, d
MOLDENHAUER, Johann Rudolf, 54, property   Sietzing
   owner
HOEHNE, Anna Sophie, 45, w
MOLDENHAUER? Martin Gottfried, 24, s
MOLDENHAUER? Dorothea Luise, 21, d
MOLDENHAUER? Sophie Wilhelmine, 20, d
MOLDENHAUER? Wilhelmine Karoline, 19, d
MOLDENHAUER? Johann Heinrich, 12, s (twin)
MOLDENHAUER? Sophie Friderike, 12, d (twin)
MOLDENHAUER? Friedrich Wilhelm, 9, s
MOLDENHAUER? Wilhelm August, 2, s
MOLDENHAUER? Friderike, age? d
HOEHNE, Johann Gottlieb, 30   Sietzing
HOEHNE, Elisabeth, b MIELENZ, 24, w

WOLTMANN, Christian, weaver   Sietzing
WOLTMANN, Maria Elisabeth, b MOLDENHAUER, w
WOLTMANN, Marie Elisabeth, 2, d
WOLTMANN, Wilhelm, weaver   Wuschewire
KRUBSACK, Charlotte Sophie, fiancée
PANKOW, Erdmann, tailor   Alt Levin,
MOLDENHAUER, Sophie, w   Kreis Lebus
   (She is the d of Katharina M[oldenhauer] who
   follows them [to America] in 1844.)
HOEHNE, Johann Friedrich   Beauregard
MAIRE, Henriette, w
ZANDER, Johann Gottfried, day laborer   Beauregard
ZANDER, --, b BUSCHKE, w
KUTZER, Johann Wilhelm, day laborer   Beauregard
BRUNKOW, Anna Luise, w
KUTZER? Friderike Emilie Auguste, 5, d
   (According to a family book of the Kiehn-
   werder Lutheran Congregation, he
   emigrated but returned to Germany in 1846. [The note
   says nothing about the return of the w and
   d.])
KRUEGER, David, day laborer   Alt Letschin,
SCHROEDER, Dorothea, w   Kreis Lebus
KRUEGER? Heinrich Daniel, 15, s
KRUEGER? Friedrich, s
KRUEGER? Maria, s
MOLDENHAUER, Johann, weaver   Gross-Barnim
MOLDENHAUER, Adelheid Auguste Emilie, b VOIGT, w
MOLDENHAUER, Johanna Emilie, 3, d
MOLDENHAUER, Johann Wilhelm, 1, s
   (Johann MOLDENHAUER is the s of Joh[ann]
   Rud[olph] M[OLDENHAUER].)
STEINBORN, Friedrich Wilhelm, cottager   Trebbin
   and master weaver
STEINBORN, Anna Christiane, b MOLDENHAUER, w
STEINBORN, Wilhelmine Friderike, d
STEINBORN, --, c
DUEHRING, Gottfried, mason   Neu Medewitz
DUEHRING, Katharina, b HOEHNE, w
DUEHRING, Friedrich Julius, 8, s
DUEHRING, Karl Friedrich, 6, s
DUEHRING, Friedrich Wilhelm, 5, s
DUEHRING, Marie Friderike, 3, d
DUEHRING, Friedrich August, 1, s
SETZKORN, Gottfried Wilhelm, master   Alt Wriezen
   tailor
SETZKORN, Karoline, b RICHTER, w
SETZKORN, Karl Friedrich Wilhelm, 19, s
FRIESE, Wilhelm, garment maker   Rehfeld
FRANKE, Maria, w
FRIESE? Wilhelm, s
FRIESE? Friedrich, s
FRIESE? Karl Ferdinand, s
FRANKE, Martin, 35, peasant   Sophienthal

From: Provinz Brandenburg, Kreis Angermuende
To: America, 1843
FREY, Johann, 44, citizen and master   Neu Angermuende
   weaver
FREY, Sophie, b BACH, 48, w
FREY, Juliane, 17, d
FREY, Emilie, 16, d
FREY, Johann, 14, s
FREY, Auguste, 12, d
FREY, Albert, 11, s
FREY, Ferdinand, 9, s
FREY, Julius, 8, s
GROSSKOPF, Friedrich, 42, citizen   Neu Angermuende
   and master cabinetmaker
GROSSKOPF, Sophie, b WALTER, 41, w
GROSSKOPF, Friedrich, 14, s
GROSSKOPF, Amalie, 9, d

GROSSKOPF, Gotthold, 4, s
MIEHLE, Ferdinand, 42, citizen and   Neu Angermuende
   master weaver
TIECK, Sophie, 48, w
ERKE, Christian, 52 citizen farmer   Neu Angermuende
   [Ackerbürger]
HUEBNER, Maria, 46, w
ERKE? Emilie Marie, 16, d
ERKE? Wilhelm Friedrich, 14, s
ERKE? August, 12, s
ERKE? Wilhelmine, 6, d
ERKE? Julius, 3, s
ERKE? Auguste, 1, d
CHABOT, Dorothea Sophie, b KOEPPEN,   Neu Angermuende
   71, widow of a hatter
FREY, Johann August, 35, citizen   Neu Angermuende
   and weaver
FREY, Wilhelmine, b EISENFUEHR, 33, w
FREY, Johann August, 6, s
FREY, Gustav Albert, 1, s
JUNGE, Karoline, b HINZ, widow of   Neu Angermuende
   a seaman shipper
JUNGE, Karoline Eleonore, 18, d
JUNGE, Karl Leopold, 16, s
JUNGE, Wilhelm Arnold, 14, s
JUNGE, Henriette Dorothea Wilhelmine, 12, d
JUNGE, Gottfried Heinrich, 10, s
JUNGE, Gottlieb Friedrich, 8, s
JUNGE, Johann August, 2, s
HENNIG, Johann, farmer   Welsow
WALTER, Charlotte, w
HENNIG? Ephraim, 19, s
HENNIG? Johann Friedrich, 17, s
SCHMIDT, Augustine Wilhelmine Karoline, stepdaughter
MEISSNER, Christian, master weaver   Bruchhagen
MEISSNER, Luise, b KUMM, w
MEISSNER, Justine, 14, d
MILIUS, Christian, inhabitant   Guestow
WEGNER, Dorothea, w
MILIUS? Maria, d
MILIUS? Christine Luise, d
MILIUS? Christian, s
MILIUS? Gottlieb, s
MILIUS? Michael, s
MILIUS? August Otto, s
BEITZ, Christian, cabinetmaker   Greifenberg
BEITZ, --, w
BEITZ, Auguste Wilhelmine, 10, d
BEITZ, Hermann August, 8, s
BEITZ, Friderike Wilhelmine, 6, d
BEITZ, Karl Friedrich, 4, s
BEITZ, Maria Luise, 1, d
HUCK, --, weaver   Greifenberg
SACK, Karl, cabinetmaker   Liepe
SIDOW, Karoline, w
SACK? Karl, 1, s
   (The sister of Karl Sack, the unmarried Wil-
   helmine Sack and their parents remained in
   Germany.)
REHWALD, Christian Friedrich, tailor   Guentherberg
TESCH, Dorothea Luise, w
REHWALD? Justine Luise, 13, d
REHWALD? Johanna Wilhelmine Luise, 11, d
REHWALD? Karl Friedrich Sigesmund, 9, s
REHWALD? Christian Friedrich Erdmann, 4, s
REHWALD? Johann Gottfried Erdmann, 1, s
REHWALD, Karl Friedrich, laborer   Guentherberg
WILCKE, Karoline Wilhelmine, w
REHWALD? Karoline Wilhelmine, 4, d
REHWALD, Michael Friedrich, tailor   Guentherberg
BECKER, Luise, w
REHWALD? Johann Gottfried Erdmann, 17, s

HERRMANN, Martin Friedrich, freeman   Guentherberg
WEYER, Christine, w
HERRMANN? Karoline Wilhelmine, 16, d
HERRMANN? Luise Wilhelmine, 12, d
KRUEGER, Johann Gottlieb, shoemaker   Luetzlow
KORF, Christine, w
KRUEGER? Ferdinand Wilhelm Rudolf, 1, s
GENZ, Wilhelmine, foster d
KORFF, Wilhelmine, unmarried   )
KORFF, Maria Dorothea, unmarried   ) sisters
   [Note differences in spelling of surname KORF
   and KORFF in original.]

From: Provinz Brandenburg, Berlin
To: America, 1843
Note: Despite consultation of the city files, only
     one family from Berlin can be identified.
LUDWIG [or LUDEWIG], --, princely chamber   Berlin
   servant [prinzliche Kammerdiener]
LUDWIG, --, w
LUDWIG, --, d
LUDWIG, --, d

From: Provinz Pommern [Pomerania], Kreis Kammin
To: America, 1843
LUECKE, Karl Wilhelm, 36, day laborer   Kammin
MOLDENHAUER, Katharina Dorothea, 43, w
MOLDENHAUER, Karoline Friderike, 14, d of Ka-
   tharina Dorothea MOLDENHAUER
LUECKE? Henriette Wilhelmine, 10, d
LUECKE? Karl Friedrich Wilhelm, 8, s
LUECKE? Johanna Luise, 3, d
KINDERMANN, Gustav Adolf, 38, candidate   Kammin
   [for an academic degree]
HOERNIGK, Maria Charlotte Wilhelmine, 29, w
KINDERMANN? Martin Adolf Michael, 1-3/4, s
SCHALLOCK, Dorothea Sophie, 36, maid
WANGERIN, Franz Konrad, 32, journeyman butcher Kammin
KNOLL, Leopold, 29, hired hand   Kammin
RUSCH, Erdmann Daniel Friedrich, 38, day   Baumgarten
   laborer
PATRATZ, Friderike Luise, 40, w
RUSCH? Gottlieb Ernst Friedrich, 7, s
RUSCH? Wilhelmine Sophie Dorothea, 4, d
RUSCH? Christian Friedrich, 67, father
   [of Erdmann D. F. Rusch? it is not en-
   tirely clear from the context of the
   entry.]
RUSCH? Juliane Friderike, b PATRATZ, mother
   [of Erdmann D. F. Rusch?]
OTTO, Christian Friedrich, wheelwright   Baumgarten
BOETTCHER, Karoline Sophie Henriette, 33, w
OTTO? Albertine Wilhelmine Henriette, 2, d
OTTO? Karl Friedrich Eduard, 1 month, s
POMPE, Ernst Friedrich, 36   )   Baumgarten
POMPE, Michael Friedrich, 43) brothers
VOIGT, Johann David, 49, shepherd   Kutlow
DETTMANN, Anna Maria, 42, w
VOIGT? Johanna Friderike Marie Luise, 9, d
VOIGT? Marie Ernestine Wilhelmine Luise Tugendreich,
   8, d
   [TUGENDREICH could also be a surname.]
KLIESE, Friedrich Eduard, 30, tailor   Hermannsthal
BERNDT, Ulrike Juliane, 28, w
KLIESE? August Friedrich, 4, s
KLIESE? Bertha Friderike, 2, d
KLIESE? Ludwig Eduard, 1, s
KLIESE, Christian Eduard, gardener, father [of
   Friedrich Eduard Kliese]
HOFEMEISTER, Joachim Friedrich Wilhelm, 30,   Tribsow
   master tailor

SCHRAMM, Johanna Friderike, 36, w
HOFEMEISTER? Ernst Ludwig, 3, s
DOBBERPHUL, Christian Friedrich, 28, day   Tribsow
  laborer
BUTH, Ernestine Wilhelmine, 20, w
DOBBERPHUL? Franz Friedrich Wilhelm, 1, s
HOFEMEISTER, Martin Friedrich, 54, cottager   Tribsow
SUELFLOW, Katharina Elisabeth, 52, w
HOFEMEISTER? Johann Gottlieb, 27, s
HOFEMEISTER? Christian Friedrich, 25-1/2, s
HOFEMEISTER? Martin Wilhelm, 23, s
HOFEMEISTER? Ernest, 18, s
SUELFLOW, Johann, 31, farmer   Tribsow
GROTH, Sophie Friderike, 29, w
SUELFLOW? Johann Friedrich Wilhelm, 7, s
SUELFLOW? Bertha Wilhelmine Friderike, 3, d
SUELFLOW, Benigna, b NEUMANN, 66, mother [of
  Johann SUELFLOW]
GRUEL, Michael, 53, cottager   Tribsow
SUELFLOW, Maria Luise, 49, w
GRUEL? Ernestine Maria Friderike, 18, d
GRUEL? Friderike Helene, 16, d
OHM, Wilhelmine, 25, stepdaughter
GROTH, Friedrich, 28, farmer   Tribsow
DOBBERPHUL, Dorothea Friderike, 24, w
GROTH? Ernestine Wilhelmine Friderike, 4, d
GROTH? Franz Friedrich August, 1, s
SCHMELING, Johann Christoph Friedrich, 39,   Tribsow
  day laborer
WILKE, Karoline Friderike, 36, w
SCHMELING? Charlotte Karoline Friderike, 16, d
SCHMELING? Dorothea Ernestine, 14, d
SCHMELING? Karoline Sophie Friderike, 9, d
SCHMELING? Ernestine Dorothea Sophie, 7, d
SCHMELING? Joachim Friedrich Wilhelm, 4, s
SCHMELING? Ferdinand, 1, s
WOLDT, Christoph Friedrich, 41, inhabitant Pribbernow
KIECKHOEFER, Johanna Henriette Ernestine, 27, w
WOLDT, Johann Eduard Julius Ferdinand, 1, s
WOLDT, Dorothea Sophie, 62, mother [of Chris-
  toph Friedrich WOLDT]
WOLDT, Johann Friedrich, 30, farmer   Pribbernow
GRAMEKE, Wilhelmine Friderike, 23, w
WOLDT? Herm[ann] Friedrich August, 10 months, s
KRUEGER, Johann Martin Georg Ewald, 59,   Pribbernow
  [farm?] lessee
BAEHN, Maria Christiane, 55, w
KRUEGER? Karoline Friderike Dorothea, 14, d
KRUEGER? Karl Friedrich Wilhelm, 11, s
  (The wife's son by a former marriage,
  Johann Karl Friedrich BAEHN, was adopted
  by her sister and remained in Germany.)
RETZLAFF, Karl Gottlieb, 32, property owner Cretlow
KIECKHOEFER, Maria Wilhelmine Friderike, 32, w
RETZLAFF? Emilie Wilhelmine Albertine, 11, d
RETZLAFF? Bertha Wilhelmine Elvina Josefine, 10, d
MUELLER, Karl Friedrich, 64, property owner Cretlow
KLAMP, Johanna Sophie, 70, w
MUELLER? Karl Friedrich, 30, s
WOLDT, Christine Luise, 38, daughter-in-law
EGGERT, Johann David, 44, property owner   Cretlow
KLAMP, Christine Luise, 43, w
EGGERT? Karl Friedrich, 12, s
EGGERT? Johann Friedrich, 9, s
EGGERT? Wilhelm Friedrich, 6, s
EGGERT? Hanna Wilhelmine, 2, d
EGGERT, Karl Friedrich, 39, property owner   Cretlow
KRAUSE, Hanna Luise Wilhelmine, 33, w
EGGERT? Karl Friedrich, 7, s
EGGERT? Bertha Marie Elisabeth, 3, d
EGGERT? Martin Gotthilf, 1, s
PRACHNOW, Ernst Ludwig Ferdinand, weaver   Cretlow
BARCKOW, Ernestine Friderike Luise, 21, w

BURMEISTER, Johann Gottfried, 34, inhabitant Cretlow
BARCKOW, Karoline Luise, 33, w
BURMEISTER? Albertine Friderike Wilhelmine, 9, d
BURMEISTER? Wilhelm Friedrich Ferdinand, 1, s
HACKBARTH, Mich[el] Friedrich, 40, lessee of
  cows [Kuhpächter]   Banderow
WINTER, Eva Luise, 40, w
HACKBARTH? Ernst August Heinrich, 9, s
HACKBARTH? Bertha Charlotte Luise, 7, d
HACKBARTH? Karl Friedrich Wilhelm, 5, s
HACKBARTH? Ferdinand Heinrich August, 2, s
HOFEMEISTER, Johann Ludwig, 32, blacksmith Banderow
TEWS, Johanna Wilhelmine, 27, w
HOFEMEISTER? Karl Friedrich Julius, 1, s
MITZLAFF, Martin Friedrich, 45, farmer   Morgow
WOLDT, Sophie Luise Friderike, 32, w
MITZLAFF? Johann Friedrich Ferdinand, 10, s
MITZLAFF? Karl Friedrich Wilhelm, 7, s
MITZLAFF? Wilhelmine Henriette Albertine, 5, d
MITZLAFF? Hermann Friedrich Wilhelm, 2, s
WINTER, Johann Christian Friedrich, 48, day Morgow
  laborer
WOLTER, Maria Elisabeth, 39, w
WINTER? Friderike Ernestine Wilhelmine, 18, d
WINTER? Karl Friedrich August, 15, s
WINTER? Ernestine Wilhelmine Henriette, 9, d
WINTER? Ernst Friedrich Wilhelm, 7, s
WINTER? Wilhelm Friedrich, 4, s
UTTECH, Martin Friedrich, 41, day laborer   Morgow
HOFEMEISTER, Maria Karoline Benigna, 39, w
UTTECH? Johann Christian Friedrich, 10, s
UTTECH? Augustine Wilhelmine Ernestine, 7, d
UTTECH? Ernst Wilhelm Friedrich, 4, s
UTTECH, Kaspar Friedrich, 46, day laborer   Morgow
MITZLAFF, Friderike Luise, 51, w
UTTECH? Karl Friedrich Anton, 20, s
UTTECH? Karoline Friderike Marie, 15, d
UTTECH? Johanna Sophie, 15, d
UTTECH? August, 12, s
UTTECH? Friderike, 8, d
UTTECH? Herm[ann] Friedrich Wilhelm, 5, s
KRUEGER, Karl Friedrich, 24, hired hand   Batzlaff
BRENDEMUEHL, Johann Gottfried, 38, farmer   Nitznow
SCHUSTER, Anna Maria, 41, w
BRENDEMUEHL? August Friedrich, 16, s
BRENDEMUEHL? Gotthilf Wilhelm Ferdinand, 12, s
BRENDEMUEHL? Karl Friedrich Ferdinand, 12, s
BRENDEMUEHL? Johann Ferdinand Wilhelm, 8, s
BRENDEMUEHL? Wilhelmine Karoline Friderike, 6, d
BRENDEMUEHL? Franz Friedrich August, 4, s
BRENDEMUEHL? Hanna Karoline Friderike, 2, d
HELM, Johann Friedrich, 44, hired hand   Buessentin
KRUEGER, Martin, 45, farmer   Jassow
SCHULZ, Juliane Friderike, 40, w
KRUEGER? Karl, 10, s
KRUEGER? Gottlieb, 8, s
KRUEGER? Wilhelmine, 4, d
KRUEGER? Bertha Sophie Friderike, 1/4, d
HACKBARTH, Karoline Wilhelmine Friderike, 25, unmar-
  ried [no explanation of her relationship to the
  family she accompanied]
KRUEGER, Ferdinand Joachim, 23, hired hand   Jassow
HINZ, Johann Friedrich, 40, journeman car-   Reckow
  penter
BRUEGGEMANN, Ernestine Luise, 36, w
HINZ? Ernestine, 12, d
HINZ? Johanna, 9, d
HINZ? Luise, 7, d
HINZ? Auguste, 4, d
HINZ? Friedrich, 2, s
HOEFS, Karl Heinrich, 64, school teacher   Reckow
BUCHHOLZ, Sophie, 64, w
HOEFS? Sophie Friderike, 26, d

HOEFS? Karoline Albertine Wilhelmine, 24, d
WEGNER, Friedrich, 25, future son-in-law
JANKE, Karl Wilhelm Ferdinand, 30, blacksmith   Reckow
WILLE, Dorothea Ernestine, 30, w
JANKE? Albertine Luise Friderike, 4, d
JANKE? Emilie Wilhelmine, 2, d
JANKE, --, 72, father
JANKE, --, 59, mother
JANKE, Anna Luise Christine Regine Karoline,   Reckow
    32, unmarried
NELL, Ernst Gottfried, 42, inhabitant   Denthin
BRUSS, Martin Gottlieb, 36, peasant   Denthin
NOFKE, Charlotte Eleonore, 36, w
BRUSS? Wilhelmine, 8, d
BRUSS? Karoline, 5, d
MUELLER, Johann Friedrich, 50, peasant   Grambow
DOBBERPHUL, Luise, 53, w
DOBBERPHUL, Juliane Wilhelmine, 24, foster daughter
SCHULZ, Peter Gottlieb, 48, tailor   Grambow
GENZ, Sophie Christine Friderike, 42, w
SCHULZ? Sophie Friderike, 13, d
SCHULZ? Karl Wilhelm, 11, s
SCHULZ? Karoline Wilhelmine, 9, d
SCHULZ? August, 7, s
SCHULZ? Karl Friedrich Ferdinand, 5, s
SCHULZ? Ernestine Karoline, 2, d
SCHULZ? --, 2 months, unchristened s
DOBBERPHUL, Christian, 58, farmer   Grambow
KLUG, Karoline Friderike, 45, w
DOBBERPHUL? Karl Friedrich, 27, s
STOCK, Christian Wilhelm, 31, hired hand   Grambow
    (He is the fiancé of [Anna Luise C. R. K.]
    JANKE from Reckow and is a brother of --
    STOCK who emigrated [with a sister] in
    1842.)
SCHULTZ, Karl Heinrich, 44, tailor   Grambow
KUPHAL, Karl Joachim Friedrich, 33, cow-   Luisenhof
    herd
SCHNUCKEL, Anna Sophie Friderike, 37, w
KUPHAL? Karl Friedrich Wilhelm, 11, s
KUPHAL? Ernestine Wilhelmine, 8, d
KUPHAL? Johann Friedrich, 6, s
LAST, Johann Erdmann, 52, day laborer   Luisenhof
PANKOW, Anna Sophie, 50, w
LAST? Johanna Justine Charlotte, 15, d
LAST? Johann Friedrich August, 13, s
LAST? Johann Friedrich Wilhelm, 11, s
LAST? Marie Friderike Wilhelmine, 6, d
STIEMKE, Karl August, 25, inhabitant   Luisenhof
STIEMKE, Karl Friedrich Wilhelm, 59, jour-
    neyman blacksmith, from Coeselitz
SCHALLOCK, Heinrich Friedrich Wilhelm, 38,   Kopplin
    day laborer
MEISTER, Friderike Luise, 33, w
SCHALLOCK? Wilhelmine Charlotte Sophie, 11, d
SCHALLOCK? Johan Heinrich Friedrich, 8, s
SCHALLOCK? Karl Christ[ian] Friedrich Ludwig, 5, s
SCHALLOCK? Johann Friedrich Wilhelm, 2, s
WERNER, Heinrich Wilhelm, 49, tailor   Medewitz
WUERDIG, Regina Charlotte Karoline, 30, w
WERNER? Heinrich Gottfried Erdmann, 4, s
WERNER? Wilhelmine Marie Auguste, 2, d
WERNER? Marie Luise Dorothea, 3/4, d
DIETZ, Joachim Heinrich, 45, inhabitant   Medewitz
RUSCH, Anna Karoline, 45, w
DIETZ? Johanna Sophie Charlotte Wilhelmine, 19, d
DIETZ? August Ludwig, 15, s
DIETZ? Karoline Albertine, 12, d
DIETZ? Marie Wilhelmine, 10, d
DIETZ? Luise Charlotte Sophie, 4, d
JAEGER, Wilhelm Bogislav, 52, miller   Revenow
HELM, Friderike, 40, w

JAEGER? Karl Wilhelm August, 28, s
JAEGER? Karl Heinrich, 20, s
JAEGER? Johann Wilhelm, 14, s
JAEGER? Johann Franz Karl, 5, s
JAEGER? Anna Maria Friderike Wilhelmine, 29, d
JAEGER? Abigail Sophie, 17, d
JAEGER? Johanna Wilhelmine, 12, d
JAEGER? Luise Auguste, 10, d
JAEGER? Friderike Auguste, 7, d
EICHHORST, Gottlieb Wilhelm, 31, cabinet Klein Justin
    maker
MARTEN, Sophie Charlotte, 27, w
EICHHORST? Friedrich Wilhelm, 6, s
EICHHORST? Friedrich August, 3, s
EICHHORST? Ferdinand August Wilhelm, 1, s
BARKOW, Karl Friedrich Wilhelm, 30, farmer   Dargsow
VOELZ, Benigna Dorothea Sophie, 30, w
RAMTHUN, Sophie Luise, 61, mother
BARKOW? Friderike, 27, sister
BARKOW? Wilhelmine, 24, sister
KAAP, Martin, 44, day laborer   Knurrbusch
TANK, Johanna Dorothea Luise, w
KAAP? Wilhelm Ferdinand, 12, s
KAAP? Wilhelmina Dorothea Friderike, 9, d
KAAP? Friedrich Wilhelm, 7, s
KRUEGER, Martin Friedrich, 55, lessor of   Knurrbusch
    cows
KRUEGER, Dorothea Maria, b BUROW, w
BUBLITZ, Johann, 43, farmer   Klemmen
KLOHN, Friderike Luise, 41, w
BUBLITZ? Karl Friedrich Ernst, 19, s
KANNENBERG, Karl Friedrich, 46, cowherd   Kloetzin
KANNENBERG, Karl Friedrich Eduard, 19, s
KANNENBERG, August Friedrich Wilhelm, 17, s
KANNENBERG, Friedrich Wilhelm Hermann, 15, s
KANNENBERG, Karoline Wilhelmine Henriette, 13, d
KANNENBERG, Hermann Friedrich Ludwig, 10, s
KANNENBERG, Johann Karl Friedrich, 7, s
KANNENBERG, Gottfried Karl Wilhelm, 4, s
    [No wife and mother listed.]
GROTH, Joachim Friedrich, 39, property   Neu Tessin
    owner
CHINOW, Dorothea Sophie Karoline, 38, w
GROTH? Wilhelm Friedrich, 7, s
GROTH? Wilhelmine Karoline Charlotte, 5, d
GROTH? Karl August, 1-1/2, s
HEUER, Christian David, 42, day laborer   Brendemuehl
BEHNKE, Johann Christlieb, 40, day   Brendemuehl
    laborer
LANGE, Sophie Luise, 46, w
BEHNKE, Eduard Ferdinand, 10, s
BEHNKE, Bertah Emilie, 8, d
BEHNKE, Julius Bernhard, 5, s
BEHNKE, Theodor Ludiwg, 2, s
SCHREIBER, Christian, 52, day laborer   Wittstock
DREYER, Friderike Sophie, 47, w
SCHREIBER? Sophie Karoline Wilhelmine, 21, d
SCHREIBER? Ferdinand Friedrich Wilhelm, 14, s
SCHREIBER? Luise Friderike Ernestine, 8, d
HACKBARTH, Johann Friedrich, 54, former   Coeselitz
    property owner
HACKBARTH, Dorothea Luise Karoline, 28, d
KOEPKE, Gottfried, 37, inhabitant   Stewen
LANGE, Josefine Wilhelmine Albertine, 28, w
KOEPKE? Karoline Wilhelmine, 2, d
MUELLER, Johann Kaspar Friedrich, 25, hired   Granzow
    hand
VOELZ, Michael, 61, inhabitant   Hagen
VOELZ, Dorothea Luise Friderike, 21, d
VOELZ, Hanna Karoline, 19, d
VOELZ, Johanna Friderike Auguste, 12, d
    [No wife and mother listed.]

HEIDTKE, Karl Wilhelm, 38, farmer   Tonnebuhr
KRUEGER, Dorothea Maria Charlotte, 29, w
HEIDTKE? Emilie Karoline Wilhelmine Therese, 11, d
HEIDTKE? Math[ilde?] Therese, 9, d
HEIDTKE? Bertha Luise, 6, d
HEIDTKE? Luise Wilhelmine, 5, d
HEIDTKE? Anna Maria, 1, d
KRUEGER, Sophie Christine, 65, widow and mother [presumably of Dorothea Maria Charlotte KRUEGER]
HEIDTKE, Johann Friedrich Ludwig, 27, hired hand, brother [of Karl Wilhelm HEIDTKE]
HEIDTKE, Martin Friedrich, 23, farmer   Tonnebuhr
HEIDTKE, Martin Friedrich [senior], 65, father
GERKE, Maria Elisabeth, 66, mother
HEIDTKE, Johann, 73, uncle, former property owner
BARTELT, Erdmann Friedrich, 45, hired hand [accompanying HEIDTKE family members]
LIESNER, Ludwig Friedrich Ferdinand, 32,   Moratz
son of farm lessor
LIESNER, Eduard August Wilhelm, 30-1/2, brother
LIESNER, Friderike Luise, b KOCH, 63, widow and mother
LIESNER, Bertha Emilie Friderike, 24, sister
LIESNER, Wilhelmine Auguste Henriette, 22-1/2, sister

From: Pommern [Pomerania], Kreis Randow
To: America, 1843
Note: Total emigration from this Kreis in 1843 was 183 persons, of which only the following persons can be identified by name:
SCHULZ, Johann Friedrich, laborer   Stornow
FAHRENWALD, --, widow   Ploewen
(It is stated that she emigrated before her children, inasmuch as her three children were stopped in Havelberg, but were later allowed to emigrate; see the "Havelberger" *infra*.)
MOLL, Karl, inhabitant   Ploewen
(He returned to Germany in 1845 and, with his family, returned to America in 1846.)

From: Pommern [Pomerania], Kreis Naugard
To: America, 1843
BRAASCH, Karl Friedrich, 58, peasant   Neu Massow
CRAHN, Charlotte Maria, 66, w
BRAASCH? Wilhelm Friedrich Ferdinand, 29, s
BRAASCH? Karl Ludwig Hermann, 25, s
BRAASCH? Friedrich Wilhelm Julius, 22, s
BRAASCH? Gottlieb Rudolf, 20, s
BRAASCH, Karl, 8, grandchild
BRAASCH, Friedrich, 5, grandchild
(The two grandchildren are sons of Johann Braasch, laborer, in Stettin.)
UTTECH, Johann David, 42, master cabinet-   Fanger
maker
BRAEUNNING, Ernestine Karoline, 28, w
UTTECH? Karl Friedrich, 15, s by first marriage
UTTECH? Wilhelmine Friderike, 11, d by first marriage
UTTECH? Karoline Ernestine, 5 by second marriage
UTTECH? Friederike Johanne, 3, d by second marriage
UTTECH? Johann Friedrich Hermann, 9 months, s by second marriage
KRUEGER, Joachim, 52, property owner   Fanger
SCHUETT, Karoline, 42, w
KRUEGER? --? oldest d [Luise Auguste Friderike]
KRUEGER? Wilhelmine Karoline Friderike, 18, d
KRUEGER? Friderike Dorothea Charlotte, 16, d
KRUEGER? Karl Wilhelm, 12, d
KRUEGER? Karoline Friderike Ernestine, 9, d
KRUEGER? Johann Friedrich, 6, s
KRUEGER? Karl Friedrich August, 3, s of oldest d
(It is stated that the oldest d, Luise Auguste

Friderike, would be married shortly to the father of her child; he is the hired hand -- RABENHORST and presumably her name [and that of her child?] will be changed to RABENHORST.)
BLIESNER, Johann Gustav, 42, property owner   Fanger
HOEFS, Gottliebe, 52, w
RABENHORST, Johann Gottlieb, 18, stepson
JAEGER, Martin Friedrich, 56, shepherd   Maskow
BEHLING, Dorothea Luise, 54, w
JAEGER? Friderike Luise 19, d
JAEGER? Wilhelm Friedrich, 17, s
SELL, Friedrich Christian, 22, hired hand [accompanying JAEGER family]
GOETSCH, Johann Friedrich Ernst, 31   Maskow
JAEGER, Karoline Sophie, 23, w
GOETSCH? Ernestine Karoline Friderike, 3, d
GOETSCH? Johann Friedrich Wilhelm, 9 months, s
GOETSCH, Ernst Heinrich, 66, former property owner, father [of Johann Friedrich Ernst GOETSCH]
GOETSCH, Christliebe, b NASS, 60, w and mother [of Johann Friedrich Ernst GOETSCH]
SCHULZ, Wilhelm, 44, master tailor   Trechel
SCHULZ, Johanne Sophie Karoline, 35, w
SCHULZ, Karl Friedrich, 14, s
SCHULZ, Ernestine Wilhelmine, 9, d
[This is one of the few times that the compiler has not given the maiden surname of the wife.]
TIMMEL, Johann, 42, cottager   Friedrichsberg
STUEWE, Friderike, 40, w
TIMMEL? August Friedrich Gotthilf, 9, s
TIMMEL? Augustine Luise Friderike, 6, d
TIMMEL? Johann Friedrich Ludwig, 3, s
HOEPFNER, Michael Friedrich, 50, peasant   Ottendorf
RADTKE, Karoline Elisabeth, 44, w
HOEPFNER? Johanne Karoline, 19, d
HOEPFNER? Auguste Emilie, 18, d
HOEPFNER? Wilhelmine, 16, d
HOEPFNER? August Friedrich, 12, s
HOEPFNER? Albertine Luise, 8, d
KORTH, Johann Martin, 58, peasant   Braschendorf
BRAUN, Maria Luise, 51, w
KORTH? Michael Friedrich Ferdinand, 19, s
KORTH? Sophie Wilhelmine Ernestine, 14, d
KORTH? Regine Friderike, 10, d
KORTH? Karl Friedrich Rudolf, 6, s
MARLOW, Martin Friedrich, 58, holder of   Klein
a mortgage [*Pfandbesitzer*]   Leistikow
SCHUETT, Friderike, 48, w
SCHUETT, Friedrich Wilhelm, 28, journeyman miller, stepson
MARLOW, Karl August Ferdinand, 20, s
MARLOW, Eduard Heinrich, 11, s
MARLOW, Wilhelmine, 9, d
(The last three children are stated to have been his own children; one son is in military service and remains in Germany.)
HOFFMEISTER, Johann David, 37, inhabitant   Hakenwalde
and butcher
RADTKE, Anna Regina, 52, w
KANT, Christine, 31, stepdaughter from the wife's first marriage
KANT, Justine Karoline Wilhelmine Johanne, 20, stepdaughter from the wife's first marriage
KANT, Karl Wilhelm Gottfried, 14, stepson from the wife's first marriage
HOFFMEISTER, Hanna, 11, d
HOFFMEISTER, August Rudolf, 8, s
HOFFMEISTER, David, 6, s
(A son [of the wife by her first marriage], Johann Friedrich Wilhelm KANT, 22, remained in Germany.)
BRAASCH, Johann Friedrich Vollrath, 36,   Hakenwalde
inhabitan and former business inspector [*Wirtschaftsinspektor*]

MENGERT, Johanne Karoline, 28, w
BRAASCH? Karoline Friderike Henriette, 3 months, d
LEMCKE, Joachim Christlieb, 58, day   Hakenwalde
   laborer
WILDE, Christiane Elisabeth, 55, w
LEMCKE? Karoline Gottliebe Wilhelmine, 24, d
LEMCKE? Karoline Sophie Wilhelmine, 18, d
LEMCKE? Wilhelmine Friderike Karoline, 16, d
   (A daughter, Sophie Friderike, married to
   the laborer -- KRONENFELD in Moratz, re-
   mains in Germany.)
ZUEHLKE, Johann Daniel, 39, journeyman   Gollnow
   carpenter
OTTERSTEIN, Anna Regina, 35, w
ZUEHLKE? Johann Friedrich, 13, s
ZUEHLKE? August Friedrich, 12, s
ZUEHLKE? Johanne Karoline Friderike Wilhelmine, 10, d
ZUEHLKE? Wilhelmine Charlotte Regina, 8, d
ZUEHLKE? Anna Regina Wilhelmine Ernestine, 6, d
ZUEHLKE? Karl Daniel, 3, s
ZUEHLKE? Albertine Auguste Emilie, 3 months, d
VOLLBRECHT, Karl Friedrich Ludwig, 36,   Ibenhorst
   former hereditary lessee [Erbpächter]
WIETSTOCK, Maria Elisabeth, 34, w
VOLLBRECHT? Maria Luise Emilie, 11, d
VOLLBRECHT? Albertine Wilhelmine Friderike, 9, d
VOLLBRECHT? Ernestine Friderike Karoline, 7, d
VOLLBRECHT? Hanna Christine Bertha, 5, d
SCHLEY, Johann, 47, inhabitant   Ibenhorst
MACHUL, Dorothea Charlotte, 41, w
SCHLEY? Emilie Albertine, 18, d
SCHLEY? Johann Gottlieb, 12, s
SCHLEY? Wilhelm Friedrich, 9, s
SCHLEY? Karl David, 7, s
SCHLEY? Heinrich Christlieb, 5, s
SCHLEY? Friedrich Michael, 2, s
GERBITZ, Gottlieb, 56, farmer   Graevenhagen
GOETSCH, Sophie, 39, w
GERBITZ? Wilhelmine Sophie Christine, 20, d
GERBITZ? Karl Friedrich Wilhelm, 17, s
GERBITZ? Gottlieb, 12, s
GERBITZ? Marie Charlotte Ernestine, 9, d
GERBITZ? Ernestine Johanne Marie, 7, d
KORTH, Karl Julius, hired hand [to the
   GERBITZ family], son of farmer -- KORTH
   in Graevenhagen

From: Pommern [Pomerania], Kreis Greifenhagen
To: America, 1843
WURL, Christ[ian] Friedrich Erdmund, 31, Nipperwiese
   barge builder
WURL, Maria Elisabeth, b WURL, 30, w
WURL, Erdmann Friedrich, 7, s
WURL, Wilhelm Friedrich, 5, s
WURL, August Heinrich, 3, s
WURL, Ernst Leberecht, 1, s
WURL, Christian, 84, barge builder,   Nipperwiese
   father of Christian Friedrich Erdmund WURL
WURL, Anna Christiane, b KOPP, 70, mother [of same]
SATTELBERG, Gottfried, 55, fisherman   Nipperwiese
WURL, Dorothea Maria, 45, w
SATTELBERG? Dorothea Sophie, 25, d
SATTELBERG? Gottfried, 23, s
KRAUSE, Henriette, 23, w of Gottfried Sattelberg [jun.]
SATTELBERG? Karl August, 18, s of Gottfried [senior]
SATTELBERG? Erdmann Friedrich, 9, s of Gottfried [sen.]
KNORR, Emilie, 9, foster daughter of Gottfried [sen.];
   daughter of machinist -- KNORR, brother-in-law of
   SATTELBERG, from Koenigsberg NM [?], who has given
   his consent [for daughter's emigration to America]
SATTELBERG, Christian, 50, laborer   Nipperwiese

FALKENHAEUER, Sophie, 41, w
SATTELBERG? Dorothea Sophie, 21, d
SATTELBERG? Christian Friedrich, 19, s
SATTELBERG? Dorothea Marie, 7, d
FETTGENHAEUER, b BEELING, 70, mother-in-law
   [Note: No explanation is given regarding
   the discrepancy between surnames FALKENHAEUER
   and FETTGENHAEUER.]
SAHR, Karl Friedrich, 29, laborer   Nipperwiese
WURL, Friderike, 29, w
SAHR? Wilhelm Friedrich, 2, s
THIELE, Gottfried Heinrich, 32, laborer   Nipperwiese
KARGE, Dorothea Sophie, 25, w
THIELE? Dorothea Marie, b HAACK, 58, mother
   (the husband has given consent to her emi-
   gration to America)
SAHR, Martin Friedrich, 32, laborer   Nipperwiese
LUECK, Luise, 24, w
SAHR? August Friedrich, 2, s
SAHR? Charlotte, b LUEPKE, 58, mother
WURL, Karl Gottlieb, 33; he is entirely   Nipperwiese
   blind; his relatives, Erdmund WURL and
   Friderike SAHR b WURL, wish to support
   him; his father, fisherman Friedrich
   WURL who is still alive, gives his con-
   sent for his son to emigrate to America
HILGER, Gottfried, 37, laborer   Nipperwiese
GRUNOW, Dorothea Karoline, 39, w
HILGER? Dorothea Sophie, 5, d
PROCHNOW, Karl Friedrich, 44, shoemaker   Nipperwiese
SONNTAG, Wilhelmine, 58, w
PROCHNOW? Karl Friedrich, 17, s
BLANK, Karl Friedrich, 32, shoemaker   Nipperwiese
BRAEUNLICH, Charlotte Wilhelmine, 28, w
BLANK? August Wilhelm Karl, 4, s
BLANK? Sophie Bertha, 2, d
BLANK? Eduard Karl, 4 months, s
PROCHNOW, Wilhelm, 35, cabinetmaker   Nipperwiese
DICKHOFF, Anna, 40, w
PROCHNOW? Henriette, 12, d
PROCHNOW? Wilhelm, 11, s
PROCHNOW? Karl August, 9, s
PROCHNOW? Wilhelmine, 6, d
KOPP, Christian, 44, laborer   Nipperwiese
VORPAHL, Dorothea, 47, w
KOPP? Dorothea, 19, d
KOPP? Gottfried, 18, s
KOPP? Wilhelmine, 15, d
KOPP? Martin, 13, s
KOPP? Wilhelm, 8, s
KOPP? Luise, 6, d
KOPP? Friderike, 4, d
SCHMIDT, Gottfried, 48, laborer   Nipperwiese
KOHN, Anna Sophie, 45, w
SCHMIDT? Wilhelmine, 16, d
SCHMIDT? Dorothea Sophie, 18, d
FUELLNER, Friedrich, 34, fish dealer   Nipperwiese
OERTWIG, Dorothea Sophie, 26, w
FUELLNER? Henriette, 8, d
WURL, Wilhelm Ludwig, 28, hired hand   Nipperwiese
SYDOW, Karl August, 54, tailor   Nipperwiese
SATTELBERG, Rebekka, 47, w
SYDOW? Friedrich August, 21, s, journeyman tailor
SYDOW? Karl Ferdinand, 12, s
SYDOW? Auguste Amalie, 19, d
SYDOW? Emilie Charlotte, 17, d
SYDOW? Friderike Karoline, 15, d
SYDOW? Ottilie Marie, 9, d
SYDOW? Rebekka, 5, d
SCHWARZHOLZ, Gottfried, 46, cattle dealer Nipperwiese
THIELE, Dorothea, 58, w
SCHWARZHOLZ? Dorothea Marie, 25, d

28

SCHWARZHOLZ? Anna Christine, 21, d
SCHWARZHOLZ? Karoline Wilhelmine, 18, d
SPUR, Christian Friedrich, 65, laborer   Jaegersfelde
SCHULZ, Gottfried, 53, peasant   Wilhelmshoehe
SCHROEDER, Dorothea Sophie, 54, w
SCHULZ? Gottffried, 24, s
SCHULZ? Daniel, 23, s
ZELLIN, Johann Friedrich, 31, journey-   Wilhelmshoehe
    man mason
SCHULZ, Regine, 27, w
ZELLIN? Karl August, 1, s
BLUEMKE, David, 65, peasant   Bayershoehe
GOVIEL, Sophie, 44, w
FEHRMANN, Friedrich, 33, former   Schulzendorf
    small farmer
ACHTMANN, Friderike, 30, w
FEHRMANN? Karl Friedrich, 9, s
FEHRMANN? Karoline Wilhelmine, 8, d
KUBE, Michael, 56, laborer   Wildenbruch
GRUENBERG, Henriette, 50, w
KUBE? Henriette, 19, d
KUBE? Karoline Friderike, 8, d
HOEPFNER, August Friedrich, 49, invalid   Fiddichow
ZOBEL, Sophie, 48, w
HOEPFNER? Henriette Friderike, 23, d
HOEPFNER? Friedrich Wilhelm, 16, s
HOEPFNER? Karoline Friderike, 14, d
HOEPFNER? Karoline Albertine, 13, d
HOEPFNER? Johanna, 12, d
HOEPFNER? Wilhelmine, 8, d
HOEPFNER? Karl Friedrich, 7, s
    (A son, Friedrich Wilhelm, 22, had to remain
    behind [in Germany] because of active mili-
    tary duty. [No explanation of why two sons
    have the same name.]
PAGE, Daniel, 35, wheelwright   Fiddichow
PAGE, Dorothea Maria, b ARNDT, widow of
    HOEPFNER, 45, w
PAGE, Wilhelmine, 2, d
HOEPFNER, Johanna Friderike Henriette, 19, d of
    the wife by her first marriage
HOEPFNER, Karl August Friedrich, 16, s of the
    wife by her first marriage
GRAF, Johann Friedrich, 43, merchant   Fiddichow
GRAF, Johanne Dorothea, b MUELLER, formerly
    married to LOEPERIK, 38, w
GRAF, Hermann Friedrich, 19, s [probably by
    the husband's first marriage]
GRAF, Friedrich Eduard, 16, s [ditto]
GRAF, Friedrich Alexander, 14, s [ditto]
LOEPERIK, Wilhelmine Luise, 13, d of the wife
    by her first marriage
LOEPERIK, Karl August, 10, s [ditto]
LOEPERIK, August Hermann, s [ditto]

From: Pommern [Pomerania], Kreis Greifenberg
To: America, 1843
KOLLATH, Johann David, 37, former   Gansken Pribbernow
    small farmer
FRIEDE, Christiane Wilhelmine Friderike, 35, w
KOLLATH? Hanna Karoline Friderike, 11, d
KOLLATH? Johann Ferdinand Hermann, 8, s
KOLLATH? Karl Albert Julius, 5, s
KOLLATH? Hermann Friedrich, 2, s
GAEDTKE, Johann Joachim, 53,   Gansken Pribbernow
    former farmer
FRIEDE, Marie Eleonore, w, widowed
GAEDTKE? Henriette Marie Veronika, 22, d
FRIEDE, Christian Friedrich Wilhelm, 40, s of
    the wife by her first marriage
    (Two stepchildren [presumably children of the

wife by her first marriage] were left behind
in Germany and probably were married.)
BROITZMANN, Joachim, 46, former   Gansken Pribbernow
    small farmer
NICOLAUS, Anselm Friedrich, 41,   Gansken Pribbernow
    property owner
KOHLS, Dorothea Christine, 59, w
NICOLAUS, Hanna Sophie Wilhelmine, 11, d by
    husband's first marriage
BLOCK, Peter, 44, tailor   Holm
SAUER, Katharine Sophie, 46, w
BLOCK? Karoline Wilhelmine, 18, d
KRESSIN, Johann, 36, small farmer   Holm
NEUMOETH, Maria Charlotte Friderike, w
KRESSIN? Wilhelm August Friedrich, 6, s
KRESSIN? Johann Ferdinand Ludwig, 4, s
KRESSIN, Dorothea, b VOLKMANN, 68, widow   Holm
    of a small farmer
MOLDENHAUER, August, 25, inhabitant   Holm
LAABS, Katharine, 34, w
BROITZMANN, Johann Wilhelm, cottager   Holm
VOLKMANN, Anna, 38, w
BROITZMANN? Maria, 11, d
BROITZMANN? Dorothea Friderike, 9, d
BROITZMANN? Karoline Wilhelmine, 7, d
BORCHARD, --, 33, unmarried   Holm
KRESSIN, Gottfried, 32, small farmer   Holm
KRESSIN, Ferdinand, 2, s
KRESSIN, Maria, 1, d
LASKE, Marie Dorothea, 35, unmarried   Holm
LASKE? Karoline Marie Therese, 8, d
KRUEGER, Wilhelmine, 26, unmarried   Holm
ARNDT, Hans, 58, farmer   Darsow
ARNDT, Engel, b LISKOW, 59, w
ARNDT, Hans [junior], 31, s
HOPPE, Charlotte Sophie, 26, w [of s]
ARNDT? Karoline Justine Friderike, 5, d
ARNDT? Wilhelmine Charlotte Dorothea, 3, d
ARNDT? Friderike Sophie Maria, 1, d
WILL, Philipp, 34, policeman and farmer   Darsow
TEWS, Karoline Charlotte Friderike, 27, w
WILL? Therese Dorothea Sophie, 6, d
WILL? Albertine Charlotte Marie, 5, d
RATTKE, Johann Gottlieb, 25, hired hand [to
    WILL family]
BUBLITZ, Christian Friedrich, 61, farmer   Prust
BUBLITZ, Ferdinande Albertine Charlotte, b WENDT,
    42, third wife
BUBLITZ, Hanna Friderike Karoline, 23, d by
    first w
BUBLITZ, Heinrich Ferdinand Gotthilf, 18, s by
    second wife, Charlotte BUBLITZ, b BUCHOLZ
BUBLITZ, Karoline Wilhelmine Henriette, 16, d
    by second wife, Charlotte BUBLITZ, b BUCHOLZ
BUBLITZ, August Friedrich, 13, s by second w
BUBLITZ, Therese Maria Karoline, 3, d by second w
GENZ, Johann Gottlieb Wilhelm, 33, laborer   Zitzmar
SCHEER, Henriette Wilhelm, 29, w
HOGE, August Gottlieb, 29, deacon and   Wittenfelde
    teacher's assistant
RIEBE, Celestine, w
HOGE? Johann Karl Friedrich, 4, s
HOGE? Auguste Sophie Emilie, 2, d
BENTERT, Engel, b RAMTHUN, 73, widow of a   Arnsberg
    small farmer
BENTERT, Peter, 43, s
BENTERT, Engel, 36, unmarried, owner of a   Arnsberg
    small farm
BENTERT, Franz Hermann, 3, s
KOEPSEL, Christian, 45, farmer   Arnsberg
MATTER, Anna Sophie, 39, w
KOEPSEL? Karoline Albertine, 17, d

KOEPSEL? Emilie Ernestine Rosette, 16, d
KOEPSEL? Johann Hermann, 15, s
KOEPSEL? Wilhelm Gottfried, 12, s
KOEPSEL? Friderike Wilhelmine, 11, d
KOEPSEL? Hanna Maria Elisabeth, 9, d
KOEPSEL? Johann Franz, 8, s
KOEPSEL? Sophie Therese, 6, d
    (It may be that not all these children were
    by the wife above listed, as it states that
    the children were "raised by" this mother;
    on the other hand, it may be that the phrase
    means that other children were left behind
    in Germany.)
PETER, Joachim, 57, shoemaker   Treptow
WINKELMANN, Anna Luise, 51, w
WINKELMANN, Marie Luise, 26, stepdaughter
PETER? Hermann Friedrich, 8, s
RUNGE, Joachim, 72, inhabitant   Mittelhagen
BERLOHM, Dorothea, 56, w
RUNGE? Karoline, 24, d
RUNGE? Friedrich Wilhelm, 15, s
LOOK, Karl Bogislaw, 34, farmer   Dresow
KOEPSEL, Sophie Charlotte, 43, w
LOOK? Hanne Marie Friderike, 9, d
LOOK? Ernst Friedrich Wilhelm, 7, s
KOEPSEL? Wilhelmine Sophie Luise, 22, wife's
    illegitimate d
KOEPSEL? Ernestine Karoline Wilhelmine, 15, wife's
    illegitimate d
BAHN, Karl, 64, inhabitant   Neides
STEINGRAEBER, Anna Luise, 51, w
BAHN? Wilhelm, 27, s
BAHN? Karl Johann Eduard, 23, s
BAHN? Karl Friedrich Heinrich, 17, s
BAHN? Auguste Maria Johanne, 14, d
BAHN? Julius Friedrich Christian, 11, s

From: Pommern [Pomerania], Kreis Regenwalde
To: America, 1843
ZIEMER, Johann Gottlieb, 37, farmer   Natelfitz
RAASCH, Johanne Luise Wilhelmine, 33, w
ZIEMER? Karl Heinrich Friedrich, 10, s
ZIEMER? Gotthilf Friedrich Erdmann, 7, s
ZIEMER? August Hermann Eduard, 2, s
FROEMMING, David, 46, small farmer   Natelfitz
PAGEL, Johanne Friedrich [!] Wilhelmine, 33, w
    Four children from [his?] first marriage:
FROEMMING? Hanna Karoline Luise, 23, d
FROEMMING? Hanna Friderike Wilhelmine, 18, d
FROEMMING? Hanna Luise Friderike, 15, d
FROEMMING? Sophie Karoline Charlotte, 13, d
    Three children from [his?] second marriage
FROEMMING? Johanne Albertine, 10, d
FROEMMING? Bertha Auguste Emilie, 7, d
FROEMMING? Charlotte Emilie Ernestine, 4, d
RAASCH, Johann Friedrich, 38, cottager   Natelfitz
    and tailor
ZARLING, Charlotte Christiane Luise, 44, w
RAASCH? Christ[ian] Friedrich Erdmann, 12, s
RAASCH? Johann Christian Friedrich, 9, s
RAASCH? Karoline Maria Friderike, 6, d
RAASCH? Henriette Charlotte Justine, 3, d
KRUEGER, --, 42, cottager and wheelwright Natelfitz
ZACHOW, Dorothea Christine, 47, w
KRUEGER? Johann Friedrich Wilhelm, 16, s
KRUEGER? Friedrich Gottlieb, 14, s
KRUEGER? Johanne Sophie Luise, 12, d
KRUEGER? August Friedrich Wilhelm, 8, s
KRUEGER? Martin Friedrich Wilhelm, 6, s
GROTH, Karl Friedrich Gotthilf, 40,   Natelfitz
    wheelwright

GRUENDEMANN, Ernestine Friderike, 44, w
GROTH? Johann Heinrich Karl, 17, s
GROTH? Emilie Friderike Henriette, 14, s
GROTH? Ottilie Auguste Karoline, 12, d
GROTH? Karl Julius Ferdinand, 10, s
GROTH? Berthan Wilhelmine Friderike, 7, d
GROTH? Johanne Karoline Friderike, 4, d
LUEBKE, Friedrich, 33, shepherd   Natelfitz
LAUTERBACH, Karoline Friderike Henriette, 39, w
LUEBKE? Julius Karl Theodor, 8, s
LUEBKE? Hermann Friedrich Wilhelm, 6, s
LUEBKE? Johann Ferdinand Wilhelm, 3, s
TIETZ, Friedrich, 23, hired hand   Natelfitz
HORN, Johann Gottlieb, 55, inhabitant   Plathe
KOEPSEL, Dor[othea] Luise, 51, w
HORN? Johann Friedrich, 27, s
HORN? Johann Gottlieb, 25, s
HORN? Karoline Friderike Wilhelmine, 22, d
HORN? Henriette Dorothea Sophie, 16, d
LAUCH, Johann Christian Gottlieb, 43, hired Plathe
    hand
FELBAUM, David, 34, day laborer   Zowen
SPIERING, Charlotte, 28, w
FELBAUM? Johann Friedrich August, 3, s
SPIERING, Gottlieb, 45, tailor   Zowen
SELL, Johann, 43, inhabitant   Neu Gabbuhn
SCHMELING, Wilhelmine, 33, w
SELL? Johann Hermann, 10, s
SELL? Karoline Wilhelmine Auguste, 6, d
LETTOW, Karl Bogislav, 44, master tailor Ornshagen
KRAUSE, Dorothea Maria, 36, w
LETTOW? August Karl Friedrich, 13, s
LETTOW? Johann Gottlieb Friedrich, 10, s
LETTOW? Ludwig Friedrich Wilhelm, 8, s
LETTOW? Johanna Wilhelmine Friderike, 4, d
LETTOW? Wilhelm, 2, s
LETTOW? --, 26 days old, unchristened
ZIMDARS, Joachim David, 46, farmer   Wisbow
REIMER, Dorothea Luise, 36, w
REIMER, Dorothea Luise, 15, d [of the w]
ZIMDARS, Hanna Wilhelmine, 18, d
ZIMDARS, Karl Friedrich Franz, 14, s
ZIMDARS, Julius Friedrich Hermann, 9, s
ZIMDARS, August Wilhelm Hermann, 7, s
ZIMDARS? August Karl Wilhelm, 2, s
    [Excepting for the last son, the list is quite
    specific about surnames]
JUEDES, Wilhelm Bogislav, 44, laborer   Wisbow
ZACHOW, Marie Luise, 46, w
JUEDES? Ernestine Wilhelmine Friderike, 13, d
JUEDES? Friderike Dorothea Luise, 11, d
JUEDES? Johann Friedrich Wilhelm, 9, s
JUEDES? Christof Friedrich August, 7, s
JUEDES? Auguste Wilhelmine Henriette, 4, d
JUEDES? Heinrich Friedrich Wilhelm, 2, s

From: Pommern [Pomerania], Kreis Usedom-Wollin
To: America, 1843
WERGIEN, Ludwig, 42, farmer   Warnow
BERNDT, 40, Engel Dorothea, w
BERNDT, Joachim, former owner and father [of w]
WERGIEN? Karl Friedrich Wilhelm, 15, s
WERGIEN? Johanna Friderike, 12, d
WERGIEN? Johanne Regina, 9, d
WERGIEN? Luise Friderike, 6, d
WERGIEN? Christine Karoline, 3, d
WERGIEN? Ludwig, 1, s
WERGIEN, Johann, 52, wheelwright   Warnow
WERGIEN, --, b BROCKHUSEN, 29, w
WERGIEN, Johann Friedrich Wilhelm, 9, s
WERGIEN, Albertine Wilhelmine, 5, d

MAGNITZ, Johann Ludwig, 29, cottager — Warnow
WILL, Gottfried, 58, shepherd — Warnow
LEMKE, Maria, 50, w
WILL? Wilhelmine Luise, 26, d
WILL? Martin Friedrich, 23, s
WILL? Hanna Luise, 21, d
WILL? Franz Friedrich, 18, s
WILL? Karl Christian, 15, s
WILL? Johanna Marie, 11, d
WILL? Auguste Friderike, 7, d
BOENING, Daniel Friedrich, 34, cottager — Warnow
BOENING, --, b KNEISKE, 28, w
BOENING, Henriette Julie, 4, d
BOENING, Karl Friedrich Wilhelm, 3, s
BOENING, Marie Elisabeth, 1, d
REIMANN, Johann Friedrich, 30, cottager — Warnow
WILL, Luise, 28, w
REIMANN? Karoline Marie Auguste, 2, d
PAHLOW, Johann, 41, cottager — Warnow
MAGNITZ, Anna, 42, w
PAHLOW? Ernst Wilhelm, 15, s
PAHLOW? Johann Karl, 9, s
PAHLOW? Friedrich Ludwig, 6, s
PAHLOW? Auguste Wilhelmine, 1, d
GNEWUCH, Christian, 38, cottager — Warnow
BUCHHOLZ, Wilhelmine, 32, w
GNEWUCH? Johanne Luise, 7, d
KUCKAHN, Christian, 42, inhabitant — Rehberg
SCHULZ, Johanne, 32, w
KUCKAHN? Johann Friedrich Wilhelm, 16, s
KUCKAHN? Ferdinand Wilhelm, 14, s
KUCKAHN? Friderike Auguste, 12, d
KUCKAHN? Wilhelm Friedrich August, 10, s
KUCKAHN? Johanna Friderike Dorothea, 8, d
KUCKAHN? Johanna Friderike, 2, d
KUCKAHN, Karl, 38, inhabitant — Rehberg
HASS, Sophie, 41, w
KUCKAHN? Friderike Luise, 12, d
KUCKAHN? Franziska Dorothea, 10, d
KUCKAHN? Rosalie Bernhardine, 5, d
KUCKAHN? Bernhardine Johanne, 1, d
  (A stepson, Robert HASS, remained in Germany.)
EGGERT, Christian Friedrich, 42, inhabitant — Rehberg
EHMKE, Dorothea, 35, w
EGGERT? Wilhelmine Friderike, 11, d
EGGERT? Christof Friedrich, 7, s
EGGERT? Auguste Albertine, 5, d
EGGERT? Dorothea Marie, 3, d
EGGERT? Johann Karl, 1, s
PYRITZ, Martin, 46, peasant — Fernowsfelde
SARNOW, Anna, 41, w
PYRITZ? Friderike Charlotte, 17, d
PYRITZ? Luise Karoline, 41, d
PYRITZ? Martin Friedrich, 12, s
PYRITZ? Gustav Karl, 9, s
PYRITZ? Karoline Ernestine, 6, d
PYRITZ? Auguste Luise, 2, d
  (The oldest daughter, Albertine PYRITZ?, 18,
  remained in Germany.)
BUDAHN, Michael, 41, cottager — Codram
FROMHOLZ, Marie, 34, w
BUDAHN? Friderike, 18, d
BUDAHN? Marie, 9, d
VOSS, Johann Friedrich, 35, lessee [of — Schwantus
  farm?]
VOSS, Martha Dorothea Wilhelmine, 26, w
VOSS, Hermann Gustav Wilhelm, 3, s
VOSS, Hanna Karoline Wilhelmine, 2, d
MILBRATH, --, 61, widowed mother-in-law
KLUTH, Karl Albert Bruno, 26, master fur- — Wollin
  rier
VOELZ, Elvine Luise, 22, w

KLUTH, Marie Klara Math[ilde], 27, sister
BUNDROCK, Daniel, 37, maker of wooden — Wollin
  houseshoes
WOLLER, Charlotte Friderike, 39, w
BUNDROCK? Gottlieb, 16, s, apprentice tailor

From: Pommern [Pomerania], Kreis Saatzig
To: America, 1843
CHRISTIAN, Martin Friedrich, 50, cot- — Alt Damerow
  tager
NASS, Dorothea Sophie, w
CHRISTIAN? Gottlieb, 20, s
CHRISTIAN? Friedrich, 19, s
CHRISTIAN? Charlotte, 16, d
CHRISTIAN? August, 14, s
CHRISTIAN? Luise, 9, d
CHRISTIAN? Wilhelm, 8, s
CHRISTIAN? Karl, 7, s
CHRISTIAN? Augustine, 5, d
CHRISTIAN? Maria Elisabeth, 3, d
CHRISTIAN? Hermann, 2, s

From: Pommern [Pomerania], Regierungsbezirk [govern-
  mental district] Coeslin, Fuerstentumer Kreis
  [township of the Duchy]
To: America, 1843
MANTHEY, Karl Christlieb, gardener — Semerow
GROSSKLAUS, Sophie, unmarried — Drenow
  ("With her supporting sponsor [Brotherr-
  schaft]" who is unnamed [possibly MANTHEY])

From: Pommern [Pomerania], Kreis Prenzlau
To: America, 1843
Note: The following persons were stopped at Havelberg because their papers were not in order; they
  were allowed to continue to America in 1843, how-
  ever. These persons are in addition to those from
  Kreis Prenzlau who have been listed infra. Six per-
  sons in the following list appear not to have been
  allowed to emigrate in October 1843 but presumably
  followed in 1844; they are marked with an asterisk.
WALK, Christian Friedrich*, 26, laborer — Wallmow
  and s of a farmer
WALK, Wilhelmine, b WENDT*, 25, w
WALK, Gottfried*, 23, brother
WALK, Johann, 21, brother
WALK, Friedrich, 19, brother
WALK? --, mother, widow of a farmer
WENDT, Christian*, 23, farmer's son — Wallmow
WENDT, Elisabeth, 16, sister
WENDT, Wilhelm, 10, brother
WENDT? --, mother, widow
  (A brother, Friedrich Wilhelm WENDT, 27, was
  not stopped at Havelberg and possibly the
  mother was allowed to continue her trip also;
  see the Wallmow list infra.)
KRUEGER, --, b WALK, 54, widow of a weaver — Wallmow
KRUEGER, Dorothea Elisabeth, 21, d
KRUEGER, Karl August, 16, s
WOLFF, Friedrich Wilhelm, 16 — Wallmow
WOLFF, Charlotte Wilhelmine, 14
WOLFF, August, 9
  (These three are the children of the widower
  WOLFF, now married to KRUEGER HASELEY. He is
  said to have left by train in advance of these
  children, probably with his wife who is not
  listed among the Havelberg detainees. She does
  not appear in the first list of Wallmow emigrants,
  however, and is mentioned here.)

HEUER, , Johann Friedrich, 22, mourneyman   Wallmow
    weaver
HEUER, --, b STRASBURG, 55, mother & widow
HEUER, Friderike, 19, sister
HEUER, Christian Friedrich, 16, brother
WOLFF, Christian Friedrich, 57, master   Wallmow
    weaver
WOLFF, Sophie, b SCHULTZ, w
SCHULTZ, Christine, 18, foster daughter
STRASBURG, Christine, b KUHN, 35, widow of   Wallmow
    a weaver
STRASBURG, Friedrich, 9, s
MOLL, Christine, b HENSCHEL, 46, widow of   Wallmow
    a weaver
MOLL, Christian Friedrich, 19, s
MOLL, August Wilhelm, 13, s
MOLL, Christiane Elisabeth, 10, d
MOLL, Friedrich Wilhelm, 8, s
RIEBOW, Luise, 27, unmarried   Wallmow
RIEBOW, Georg, 7, s
RIEBOW, Alwine, 5, d
RIEBOW, Wilhelmine, 2, d
WIELAND, Dorothea Christine, b WIESE*, 31,   Wallmow
    married hired hand [!]
DAMEROW, Dorothea*, 24, unmarried   Schwaneberg
DAMEROW, Christine, 19, unmarried
    (These two young women were sisters.)
STOLZMANN, Wilhelm, 42, laborer   Fahrenwalde
HANNEMANN, Charlotte, 50, w, blind
HANNEMANN, Christine, 19, d
    (A son, Gottfried STOLZMANN, is listed
    under Wallmow in the list of persons who
    were not detained; see infra.)
REICH, Charlotte, b WITTKOPF, 52, widow   Bergholz
REICH, Friderike, 19, d
REICH, Charlotte, 15, d, deaf and dumb
REICH, Marie, 11, d
FAHRENWALD, Dorothea, 21, unmarried   Ploewen,
FAHRENWALD, Ulrike, 13   Kreis Randow
FAHRENWALD? Henriette, age not given
    (No further information given regarding
    the Fahrenwald girls, probably sisters.)

From: Pommern [Pomerania], Kreis Kammin
To: Russia, 1843
KUEHL, Martin, 29, weaver   Kammin
WITTE, Amalie Charlotte Dorothea Ulrike, 35, his
    housekeeper
WITTE? Ulrike Elisabeth, b SANSKY, 64, mother
    of the housekeeper

From: Provinz Sachsen [Saxony]
To: America, 1843
STREIBER, A., 44, master shoemaker   Magdeburg
STREIBER, --, w
STREIBER, Karoline, 20, d
STREIBER, Eduard, 13, s
STREIBER, Marie, 7, d
STREIBER, Auguste, 5 months, d
BUCHMANN, Heinrich, journeyman tailor   Magdeburg
SOMMERBURG, Bernhard Franz Jakob, 45   Magdeburg
KORTHAUS, Johanne Katharina, w
SOMMERBURG? Christian Bernhard Franz, s
SOMMERBURG? Eduard Karl Christof, s
SOMMERBURG? Jakob Gustaf Christof, 15, s
SOMMERBURG? Sophie Emilie, 14, d
    (Residents at Neustaedter Strasse 3 [street ad-
    dress]; ages of the older children not given.)
BEISSER, Johann Gottlieb, gardener   Magdeburg
BEISSER? Johanne Dorothea Engel, w

BEISSER, Friedrich August, 17, s
BEISSER, Johanne Dorothea, 14, d
KOENIG, Johann Leberecht Wilhelm   Magdeburg
    (He has three years more duty in the Reserve.)

From: Provinz Sachsen [Saxony], Regierungsbezirk
        Merseburg, Kreis Weissenfels
To: America, 1843
WAGNER, Friedrich, inhabitant   Rosendorf
WAGNER, --, b SCHULZ, w, with 6 children
MEISSNER, --, inhabitant   Uichteritz
MEISSNER, --, w, with 4 children
    (These two families are thought to have been
    Old Lutherans.)

From: Provinz Schlesien [Silesia], Kreis Liegnitz
To: America, 1843
REINSCH, Johann Gottlieb, journeyman tailor Berndorf
OBST, Johann Gottlieb, 42, inhabitant, un-   Wangten
    married
TOBSCHALL, Karl, 30, master wheelwright   Neudorf

From: Hamburg [free city]
To: America, 1843
GRUBE, Hermann, fruit dealer   Hamburg
    (He went to Wisconsin, where he married the
    sister of -- PANKOW.)
DOHRMANN, --, "the largest part of the   Hamburg
    children")
SCHACHT, --, entire family   Hamburg

    To summarize the emigration of 1843:
        From Brandenburg   498
        From Pomerania   832
        The Havelberg detainees   42
        From Saxony   33
        From Silesia   3
        From Hamburg   7
               Total   1,415
    There were 1,599 emigrants, of which the
    above 1,415 are identifiable by name.

1844

From: Brandenburg, Regierungsbezirk Potsdam, Kreis
        Prenzlau
To: America, 1844
Note: Persons identified hereinafter with an aster-
       isks were among the Havelberg detainees of
       1843 who were able to continue their voyages
       only in 1844.
WIELAND, Friedrich*, 24, laborer   Wallmow
WIESE, Dorothea Christine*, 30, w
WIELAND? Johanna Elisabeth*, 1/2 year, d
WALK, Christian, 26, son of a farmer   Wallmow
WENDT, Wilhelmine Friderike, w
WALK? Christian*, 3 months, s
    [It seems strange that only this baby is
    marked by an asterisk as a detainee; it
    seems likely that the entire family re-
    mained behind in 1843.]
WALK, Gottfried, 24, son of a farmer   Wallmow
WENDT, Christian, 24, son of a farmer   Wallmow
DAMEROW, Dorothea, 26, d of a cottager   Schwaneberg
WOLFF, Christian, 58, day laborer   Wallmow
SCHULZ, Sophie, 60, w
    (It is stated that their grown children have
    already emigrated.)

SCHROEDER, Friedrich, cottager and   Schwaneberg
    tailor
SCHROEDER, Wilhelmine, b SCHROEDER, 41, w
SCHROEDER, August, 9, s
SCHROEDER, Ferdinand Wilhelm, 1, s
LANGE, Christian, 40, cottager and   Schwaneberg
    laborer
WOLLENBERG, Christine, 35, w
LANGE? Wilhelm, 11, s
LANGE? August, 8, s
LANGE? Wilhelmine, 6, d
LANGE? Christian, 2, s
SCHROEDER, Michael Friedrich, 37, cot-   Schwaneberg
    tager, unmarried
WOLLENBERG, Christian Friedrich, 27,   Schwaneberg
    day laborer
HAASE, Marie, 31, w
WOLLENBERG? Wilhelm, 3, s
WOLLENBERG? Christian, 1, s
SCHMIDT, Ottilie, b BUCHHOLZ, 29, sep-   Prenzlau
    arated w of a cabinetmaker
POSSIN, Karl Friedrich, her s by first marriage
    (The wife follows her husband who emigrated
    in 1843.)
MAILLEFERT, Samuel, 46, cloth maker   Prenzlau
GNIFFROI, Christine Wilhelmine, 48, w
MAILLEFERT? Karl, 19, s
MAILLEFERT? Wilhelmine, 12, d
BARTH, Nicolaus, 47, weaver   Prenzlau
FRIESE, Wilhelmine, 48, w
BARTH? Gustav Nicolaus, 7, s
BECK, Johann Karl, 43, master weaver   Strasburg
ALBRECHT, Ida Helen Albertine, 42, w
BECK? Johann Christian Friedrich, 14, s
ALBRECHT, Friedrich, 37, master weaver   Strasburg
OTTO, Dorothea Christiane, 37, w
ALBRECHT? Wilhelmine, 11, d
ALBRECHT? Albertine, 7, d
ALBRECHT? Auguste, 6, d
ALBRECHT? Ferdinand, 3, s
RIEBE, Johann Christof, 43, wheelwright   Strasburg
KRUEGER, Charlotte Wilhelmine Karoline, 26, w
RIEBE? Karoline, 2, d
KULOW, Johann Christian Friedrich, 30,   Strasburg
    shoemaker
TRUEHL, Sophie, 42, w
KULOW? Johann, 3, s
SCHUENEMANN, Wilhelm, 10, stepson
SCHUENEMANN, Friedrich, 6, stepson
ANDRÉ, Philipp, 70, former property owner   Bergholz
BILLIEAU, Elisabeth, 64, w
    (Their children emigrated in 1843.)
LOGÉ, Peter, 33, property owner   Bergholz
WOLFF, Luise, 30, w
LOGÉ? August Ferdinand, 3, s
LOGÉ? Christine Wilhelmine, 1, d
WOLFF, --, 61, widowed mother-in-law
DEVANTIER, Johann, 21, hired hand   Bergholz
SALINGRE, Judith, b HOURTIENNE, 40, w of   Bergholz
    a farmer
    (Her husband emigrated in 1843 and she
    will rejoin him.)
STRASBURG, Michael, 31, day laborer   Bagemiel
SIEBERT, Dorothea Marie, 32, w
STRASBURG? Christine Wilhelmine, 2, d
MUELLER, Michael, 36, weaver and property   Menkin
    owner
BOEHMIG, Dorothea, 33, w
MUELLER? Friedrich, 8, s
MUELLER? Friederike, 6, d
MUELLER? Wilhelm, 5, s
MUELLER? Christian, 2, s

BAHLOW, Wilhelm Friedrich, 33, master   Nieden
    miller
GAUDE, Dorothea Sophie, 32, w
BAHLOW? Wilhelmine Ernestine, 4, d
BAHLOW? Auguste Albertine, 2, d
HAACK, Michael Friedrich, 41, laborer   Wismar
MARTIN, Karoline, 31, w
HAACK? Wilhelm Friedrich, 7, s
HAACK? Michael Friedrich, 5, s
HAACK? Karl Friedrich, 1, s
SCHWEBS, Daniel, 52, cabinetmaker   Falkenwalde
RIECK, Wilhelmine, 27, w
FELDHAHN, Friedrich, 33, laborer   Grimme
SCHULTZ, Maria Christine, 27, w
FELDHAHN? Friderike Luise, 5, d
FELDHAHN? Friedrich Wilhelm, 2, s
FELDHAHN? August Friedrich, 1, s
ZELT, Sophie, b SCHULTZ, 50, mother-in-law,
    separated from her husband
MEYER, Karl, 30, hired hand   Gruenow

From: Brandenburg, Kreis Angermuende
To: America, 1844
GLASENAPP, Martin, citizen   Schwedt
GLASENAPP, --, w
GLASENAPP, Auguste, 18, d
GLASENAPP, Martin Friedrich, 10, s
HOFFMEISTER, Christian Friedrich, 30,   Gramzow
    cabinetmaker
    (He is the eldest son of a widowed mother.
    He has seven brothers and sisters, of which
    the eldest sister and the two youngest sis-
    ters will emigrate with him, leaving the
    mother and two unmarried sisters behind.)
    [If so, one brother or sister is not accounted
    for.]
WILCKE, Ludwig, journeyman miller   Frauenhagen
ROSSOW, Gottfried, 28, tailor   Meichow
ROSSOW, Marie, b HOFFMEISTER, 29, w
ROSSOW, --, 5, c
ROSSOW, --, 1, c

From: Brandenburg, [Kreis] Ober-Barnim
To: America, 1844
HENTSCHEL, Gottlieb, 45, shoemaker   Wuschewire
KOPPELIN, Marie Dorothea, 36, w
HENTSCHEL? Marie Charlotte Luise, 8, d
HENTSCHEL? Marie Luise Em[ilie?], 4, d
HENTSCHEL? Luise Auguste, 2, d

From: Brandenburg, Regierungsbezirk Frankfurt [Oder],
    Kreis Koenigsberg
To: America, 1844
HENSCHEL, Friderike, 47, widow   Lietzegoericke
HENSCHEL, Henriette, 17, d
HENSCHEL, Wilhelmine, 13, d
HENSCHEL, Albertine, 11, d
WAGENER, Friedrich, 27, freeman   Lietzegoericke
HOECKENDORF, Elisabeth, 27, w
WAGENER? Luise, 1, d
    [The title *Freimann*, literally freeman,
    could be a title of nobility, as in *Frei-*
    herr, but it is doubted that this is the
    case herein, because the surname is not
    preceded by the noble particle *von*.]
HOECKENDORFF, Friedrich, 42, freeman   Lietzegoericke
HOECKENDORF, Michael, 80, father
HOECKENDORF, Sophie, b STRECKER, 70, mother
    [See preceding note regarding title of freeman.]

DAHMS, Martin, 41, freeman   Lietzegoericke
KUHRT, Sophie, 27, w
DAHMS? Sophie, 5, d
DAHMS? Friderike Luise, 3, d
DAHMS? Albertine Wilhelmine, 9 months, d
   [See preceding note regarding title of freeman.]
ROEHRIKE, Gottlieb, 29, cottager's son Lietzegoericke
HARTMANN, Friedrich, 40, freeman   Lietzegoericke
RAASCH, Dorothea Elisabeth, 35, w
HARTMANN? Elisabeth, 11, d
HARTMANN? Marie Wilhelmine, 9, d
HARTMANN? Johann Christian Friedrich, 7, s
HARTMANN? Martin Ernst, 5, s
HARTMANN? Wilhelm Friedrich, 3, s
HARTMANN? Johann Ludwig, 1, s
GRIMM, Johann Friedrich, 49, laborer   Lietzegoericke
WAGENER, Wilhelmine Sophie, 53, w
GRIMM? Gottlob, 18, s
GRIMM? Christian Ludwig, 17, s
GRIMM? Marie Luise, 15, d
GRIMM? Friedrich Wilhelm, 11, s
FETZENHAUER, Friedrich, 70, laborer   Gross-Wubiser
OTTERSTEIN, Johann, 50, day laborer   Gross-Wubiser
VETKENHEIL, Anna Dorothea, 50, w
OTTERSTEIN? Auguste, 25, d
RAASCH, Martin, 28, freeman   Gross-Wubiser
MESICKE, Friderike Wilhelmine, 23, w
RAASCH? August Wilhelm, 1, s
   [See preceding note regarding title of freeman.]

From: Brandenburg, Kreis Lebus
To: America, 1844
MOLDENHAUER, Katharina, b BOCHO   Letschin
   (She follows her daughter, Sophie, wife of
   the tailor -- PANKOW, who emigrated in 1843.
   The father, small farmer Heinrich MOLDENHAUER,
   is either dead or remains in Germany.)
SCHOENIKE, Karl   Letschin
VOGT, Karl August, 16, cottager's son   Letschin
BOCHOW, Friedrich, hired hand   Alt-Levin
EXNER, August, shoemaker   Alt-Levin
HINZE, Wilhelmine, w
EXNER? Johann Valerius Gustav, 2, s
EXNER? --, unnamed c
POSSIN, Peter, 27, shoemaker   Langsow
POSSIN, Maria Elisabeth, b GLAUKE, 25, w
GLAUKE, Anna Sophie, b HAENISEN, w of small Langsow
   farmer Gottfried GLAUKE
GLAUKE, Johann Friedrich, 15, s of small   Langsow
   farmer Gottfried GLAUKE
FREIERT, Johann Friedrich, 44, machinist   Langsow
GEISLER, Karl Gottlob, 52, cottager and   Ortwig
   flannel weaver [Parchentweber]

From: Provinz Pommern [Pomerania], Kreis Greifenhagen
To: America, 1844
SCHROEDER, Karl Friedrich, 39, citizen   Fiddichow
   and property owner
SCHROEDER, Friderike, b WOLTER, w
SCHROEDER, Johanna Friderike, 15, d
SCHROEDER, Ernst Friedrich, 13, s
SCHROEDER, Martin Daniel, 9, s
SCHROEDER, Georg Gottfried, 7, s
SCHROEDER, Marie Christiane Auguste, 4, d
SCHROEDER, Sophie, 1, d
SCHROEDER, Hanna, b STAHR, 60, mother [of Karl F.]
LUEPKE, Martin, 41, laborer   Nipperwiese
LUEPKE, Dorothea Luise, b OERTWIG, 31, w
LUEPKE, Dorothea Wilhelmine, 8, d
LUEPKE, Dorothea Luise, 5, d

LUEPKE, Karl Friedrich, 2, s
LUEPKE, --, 1 month, c
KOHN, Erdmann Friedrich, 27, day laborer Nipperwiese
Wilke, Sophie Dorothea, 29, w
KOHN? Henriette, 4, d
KOHN? Friderike Wilhelmine, 2, d
BUEDLER, Daniel, 27, cottager   Nipperwiese
GELLERT, Friderike, 25, w
BUEDLER, Wilhelmine, 2, d
BUEDLER, Auguste, 6 months, d
KOPP, Michael Friedrich, 33, tailor   Roderbeck
PAPKE, Friderike, 30, w
KOPP? Luise, 2, d
KOPP? --, 1 month, c
SCHOEN, Karl Friedrich, 34, cottager   Roderbeck
KRAETKE, Charlotte Luise, 36, w
SCHOEN? Wilhelmine Henriette, 10, d
SCHOEN? Auguste, 8, d
SCHOEN? Karl Friedrich August, 2, s
PUCKELWALDT, Christian Friedrich, 51,   Bayershoehe
   small farmer
KLUCK, Karoline, 38, w
PUCKELWALDT? Emilie, 9, d
PUCKELWALDT? Karl, 4, s
LABS, Karl Friedrich, 42, small farmer Bayershoehe
WINTER, Dorothea Sophie, 42, w
LABS? Ernestine Wilhelmine, 4, d
LABS? Karl Friedrich Ferdinand, 1, s
PAPKE, Karl August, 26, hired hand   Uchtdorf
NELL, Wilhelm, 47, day laborer   Wildenbruch
NELL, Friderike Wilhelmine, 19, d

From: Provinz Pommern [Pomerania], Kreis Greifenberg
To: America, 1844
LISKOW, Johann, 24, farmer's son   Zimdarse

From: Schlesien [Silesia], Kreis Freistadt
To: Australia, 1844
HEPPNER, Heinrich, 51, carpenter Town of Freistadt
DECKOW, Johanna, 56, widow [joining persons
   who have already emigrated]
HOFFMANN, Ernst August, 33, hoop? smith   Town of
   [Zirkelschmied]   Freistadt
HOFFMANN, --, w
HOFFMANN, Luis, 5, s
HOFFMANN, Johann Georg, 45, tailor   Town of
HOFFMANN, --, w   Freistadt
HOFFMANN, Karl, 18, s
HOFFMANN, Gottlieb, 14, s
HOFFMANN, Friedrich, 11, s
HOFFMANN, Johannes, 1, s
HOFFMANN, --, 17, d
HOFFMANN, --, 9, d
HOFFMANN, --, 3, d
PFEIFFER, Johann Friedrich, 28, in- Langhermsdorf
   habitant
PFEIFFER, --, w
PFEIFFER, Karl Friedrich Ernst, 13, s
PFEIFFER, Johann Friedrich Wilhelm, 9, s
PFEIFFER, Johann Friedrich, 2, s
PFEIFFER, Johanna Juliane, 11, d
PFEIFFER, Marie Elisabeth, 6, d
LAUTERBACH, Gottfried, coachman   Langhermsdorf
LAUTERBACH, Eva Rosina, b LAUTERBACH, w
LAUTERBACH, Johann Karl Friedrich, s
LAUTERBACH, Eva Rosina, d
LAUTERBACH, Anna Maria, d
   (Family joins persons already emigrated.)
PFEIFFER, Samuel, 72, inhabitant   Langhermsdorf
PFEIFFER, Johanna Eleonore, 28, d

34

FELLENBERG, Gottfried, 53, houseowner   Ober-Siegers-
FELLENBERG, Dorothea Elisabeth, w   dorf
FELLENBERG, Dorothea Elisabeth, 22, d
FELLENBERG, Karl Gottlob, 18, s
FELLENBERG, Maria Dorothea, 16, d
IRRGANG, Johanna Rosina, b KRAUSE, 34,   Ober-Siegers-
  widow, inhabitant   dorf
IRRGANG, Wilhelm August, 5, s
IRRGANG, Johanna Christiane, 4, d
HEPPNER, Gottfried, 56   Ober-Siegers-
HEPPNER, Karl, 24, s   dorf
HEPPNER, Hermann, 16, s
HEPPNER, August, 11, s
  (The Heppners to rejoin family members who
  have already emigrated.)
FECHNER, Christian, 53, houseowner   Niebusch
APELT, Anna Elisabeth, w
FECHNER? Johann Friedrich Ernst, 24, s
FECHNER? Karl Friedrich, 18, s
BUCHWALD, Johann Sigismund, farmer   Niebusch
BUCHWALD, Johanna Dorothea, d, unmarried
  (The Buchwalds to rejoin family members who
  have already emigrated.)
SCHULZ, Johann Karl Erdmuth, 24, son of   Steinborn
  a gardener
GROSSMANN, Johanna Elisabeth, w
SCHULZ, Johann Georg, 61, gardener   Steinborn
SCHULZ, Johanna Helena, b Jentsch, w
WALTER, Johann Karl, 21, inhabitant   Hartmannsdorf
SCHULZ, Gottfried, gardener   Weichau
  (Schulz to rejoin family members who
  have already emigrated.)
ULBRICHT, Johann Friedrich, 40   Brunzelwaldau
ULBRICHT, --, w, with two daughters
LIEBIG, Johann Friedrich, 46, house-   Seiffersdorf
  owner
JENTSCH, Dorothea Elisabeth, w
LIEBIG? Johann Gottlob, 19, s
LIEBIG? Dorothea Elisabeth, 12, d
SPORN, Johann Friedrich, 38, coachman   Seiffersdorf
JENTSCH, Maria Elisabeth, w
SPORN? Johanna Helena, 24, d
SPORN? Johann Friedrich, 19, s
KRAUSE, Johann Karl, 26, son of a   Seiffersdorf
  gardener

From: Schlesien [Silesia], Kreis Gruenberg
To: Australia, 1844
FIEDLER, Karl August, 25   Town of Gruenberg
  (Fiedler to rejoin family members who
  have already emigrated.)
KAHLE, Karl Gottlieb, 42   Town of Gruenberg
KAHLE, --, w
KAHLE, Karl, 19, s
KAHLE, Johann, 11, s
  (The Kahle family to rejoin members who
  have already emigrated.)
MACKENZIE, Ernst Wilhelm, 24, jour- Town of Gruenberg
  neyman nailsmith
ALTMANN, Johann Josef, 48, journey-   Schloin
  man mason
REIMANN, Anna Maria, w
ALTMANN? Johann Karl August, 20, s
ALTMANN? Johann Josef, 18, s
ALTMANN? Johanne Eleonore, 16, d
ALTMANN? Justina, 8, d
ALTMANN? Anna Rosina, 4 (twin), d
ALTMANN? Ernst, 4 (twin), s
ALTMANN? --, 1, d
KLOSE, Samuel, 42, coachman   Schloin
KRAUSE, Marie Elisabeth, w

KLOSE? Anna Rosina, 14, d
KLOSE? Anna Eleonore, 8, d
KLOSE? Gottlieb, 5, s
SEIDEL, Christian Friedrich, 46, share-   Schloin
  cropper
SCHULZ, Anna Elisabeth, w
SEIDEL? Maria Elisabeth, 22, d
SEIDEL? Anna Rosina, 19, d
SEIDEL? Johann Karl, 17, s
SEIDEL? Anna Eleonore, 14, d
SEIDEL? Anna Rosina, 10, d (twin)
SEIDEL? Christian, 10, s (twin)
SEIDEL? --, 4, c
SEIDEL? --, 1, c
KAETHNER, Johann Gottlieb, 43, schoolteacher Schloin
KAETHNER, --, w
KAETHNER, Johannes, 9, s
KAETHNER, --, 15, d
KAETHNER, --, 12, d
KAETHNER, --, 8, d
KAETHNER, --, 5, d
  (Kaethner wanted to emigrate in 1841 with Pastor
  -- Fritzsche, but fellow emigrants of 1841 wrote
  in their travel reports that Kaethner became
  frightened and turned back when he saw the large
  ship [on which they were to sail].)

From: Schlesien [Silesia], Kreis Sagan
To: Australia, 1844
ULBRICHT, Anna Rosina, 22, unmarried   Reichenau
RAETHEL, Johann Gottlob, 33, son of a
  coachman, stepbrother of Anna Rosina
  Ulbricht
PRIEDEMANN, Johann Christian, 27, inhab-   Reichenau
  itant
PRIEDEMANN, Anna Elisabeth, b HOFFMANN, w
PRIEDEMANN, Johann Georg, 72, father
GRAETZ, Anna Elisabeth, 42, widow   Reichenau
GRAETZ, Johann August, 16, s
  (Mrs. Graetz and her son were to rejoin
  family members who have previously emi-
  grated.)
NIPPE, Johann Georg, son of a farmer   Cosel
  (To rejoin family members who have al-
  ready emigrated.)
POHL, Gottlieb August, 16   Klein-Dobritsch
  (To rejoin family members who have al-
  ready emigrated.)

From: Brandenburg, Kreis Sorau
To: Australia, 1844
WALTER, Heinrich, 29, citizen and   Christianstadt
  linen weaver
SCHRAPEL, Anna Ernestine, 33, w
WALTER? Simeon Nathanael, 9 months, s
WALTER, Johanna Christiane, b WALTER, 60, mother
SCHNEIDER, Johann Christof, 27, cloth   Christianstadt
  weaver
WALTER, Ernestine Philippine, 26, w
SCHNEIDER? Johann Gottlieb, 1, s
IRRGANG, Johann Gottlieb, 43, day   Christianstadt
  laborer
SCHMIDT, Johanna Dorothea, 33, w
IRRGANG? Johanna Auguste, 13, d
IRRGANG? Emma Pauline, 6, d
STILLER, Johann Samuel, 40, day laborer   Nismenau
SCHRAPEL, Johanna Karoline, 27, w
STILLER? Johann Gottlieb 5, s
STILLER? Johann Christian, 3, s

SCHRAPEL, Johann Gottlieb, 50, former   Friedersdorf
   housepainter, now farmer
SCHEFLER, Maria Dorothea, 49, w
SCHRAPEL? Johann Gottlieb, 19, s
SCHRAPEL? Johann Friedrich, 17, s
SCHRAPEL? Johann Traugott, 14, s
SCHRAPEL? Johanna, 12, d
SCHRAPEL? Marie Dorothea, 9, d
LINDNER, Johann Gottlieb, 39, blacksmith   Guschau
SCHUETZE, Dorothea Elisabeth, 42, w
LINDNER? Johann Christian, 10, s
LINDNER? Karl Traugott, 8, s
LINDNER? Johann Gottlieb, 5, s
LINDNER? Ernest August, 1, s
HENSEL, Johann Gottlieb, 35, gardener   Rodstock
HENSEL, Anna Rosina, b KOTHE, 32, w
HENSEL, Johanne Christiane, 8, d

From: Brandenburg, Kreis Kottbus
To: Australia, 1844

SCHENK, Wilhelm, 40   Town of Kottbus
SCHENK, --, w
SCHENK, Ernst, 15, s
KRUEGER, --, 34   Town of Kottbus
KRUEGER, --, w
KRUEGER, Karl, 9, s
KRUEGER, Gustav, 5, s
KRUEGER, Theodor, 4, s
DUEHRING, --, 30   Town of Kottbus
DUEHRING, --, w
DUEHRING, Hermann, 2-1/2, s
DUEHRING, Paul, 1, s
DUEHRING, --, 6 months, d
DUEHRING, Christian, 23   Town of Kottbus
STUMMANN, --, 57   Town of Kottbus
STUMMANN, --, w
STUMMANN, --, 24, d
STUMMANN, --, 22, d
STUMMANN, --, 17, d
STUMMANN, --, 9, s
STUMMANN, --, 6, s
PINTER, Wilhelm Mathaeus, 20   Town of Kottbus
MESSNER, Karl Friedrich August, 41,   Crossen
   shoemaker
MESSNER, Karoline, b HENNICKE, 37, w
MESSNER, Karoline Marie, 7, d
MESSNER, Karl Friedrich August, 5, s
MESSNER, Rudolf Otto, 4, s
MESSNER, Marie Elisabeth, 1, d

From: Provinz Posen, Kreis Meseritz
To: Australia, 1844

KLEMM, Gottfried, 44   Kuschten
KLEMM, --, w
KLEMM, --, 16, s
KLEMM, --, 14, s
KLEMM, --, 20, d
KLEMM, --, 10, d
KUTSCHKE, Thomas, 45   Gross-Dammer
KUTSCHKE, --, w
KUTSCHKE, Ludwig, 16, s
KUTSCHKE, --, 23, d
KUTSCHKE, --, 20, d
KUTSCHKE, --, 13, d
KUTSCHKE, --, 11, d
KUTSCHKE, --, 8, d
WALANDT, Lorenz, 46   Gross-Dammer
WALANDT, --, w
WALANDT, Karl, 6, s
WALANDT, Simeon, 3, s

WALANDT, --, 18, d
WALANDT, --, 16, d
WALANDT, --, 10, d
STANITZKI, Nicolaus, 38   Gross-Dammer
STANITZKI, --, w
STANITZKI, --, 6, d
STANITZKI, --, 3, d
STANITZKI, --, 6 months, s
KROLL, Johann, 37   Gross-Dammer
KROLL, --, w
KROLL, --, 2-1/2, d
KROLL, --, 1/2, d
PSCHYBILLA, --, 38   Gross-Dammer
PSCHYBILLA, --, w
PSCHYBILLA, Andreas, 9, s
PSCHYBILLA, Anton, 3, s
PINETZKI, Simeon, 46   Gross-Dammer
PINETZKI, Andreas, 20, s
MODISDACH, Simeon, 28   Gross-Dammer
MODISDACH, --, w
GIDDA, Anton, 26   Gross-Dammer

Out of the 421 Lutheran emigrants of the year
1844, a total of 411 have been identified by
name, as follows:

To America
    From Provinz Brandenburg   157
    From Provinz Pommern   43
To Australia
    From Provinz Schlesien   113
    From Provinz Brandenburg   59
    From Provinz Posen   <u>39</u>

            Total   <u>411</u>

1845

From: Provinz Brandenburg, Kreis Crossen
To: Australia, 1845

METZENTHIN, Karl August, 30,   Town of Crossen
   journeyman clothmaker
SCHULZ, Auguste, w
METZENTHIN? Albertine, 7, s
METZENTHIN? Emma, 5, d
METZENTHIN? Auguste, 2, d
METZENTHIN? Karl, 1, s
HOFFRICHTER, Karl Heinrich Friedrich, Town of Crossen
   32, master shoemaker
NOACK, Dorothea, 31, w
HOFFRICHTER? Pauline, 6, d
HOFFRICHTER? Karl, 2, s
HABERMANN, Friedrich Wilhelm, 53,   Town of Crossen
   cloth manufacturer
KOEHLER, Johanne Christiane, w
HABERMANN? Friedrich Wilhelm, 23, s
HABERMANN? Florentine Agnet, 21, d
HABERMANN? Berthold Roland, 19, s
HABERMANN? Christiane Wanda, 17, d
FORBITZKI, Johanne Wilhelmine, 14, maid
ALTMANN, Friedrich August, 39,   Town of Crossen
   master cabinetmaker
TIETZ, Johanna Wilhelmine, 26, w
ALTMANN? Johanne Auguste Wilhelmine, 7, d
ALTMANN? Marie Luise Mathilde, 6, d
ALTMANN? Johann Otto, 1, s
REYHER, Gottlob, 58, strap tailor   Town of Crossen
   [*Leistenschneider*]
WERNER, Anna Rosina, 50, w
REYHER? Silvius, 15, s
BLUME, Karl August, 49, owner of a   Town of Crossen
   vineyard
BLUME, --, w

BLUME, --, 18, c
BLUME, --, 14, c
BLUME, --, 11, c
BLUME, --, 9, c
BLUME, --, 7, c
BLUME, --, 4, c
BLUME, --, 1, c
DRIECHE1, Friderike Wilhelmine,   Town of Crossen
    27, unmarried
ALTMANN, Gustav Adolf, 23, jour-   Town of Crossen
    neyman tanner
PILZ, Josef, journeyman cloth cutter Town of Crossen
SCHULZ, Friedrich Wilhelm, 26, land- Town of Crossen
    scape gardener
HOFFRICHTER, Karl Ludwig, 30, journey-   Merzwiese
    man mason
FISCHER, Dorothea Elisabeth, 31, w
HOFFRICHTER? Ernestine Wilhelmine, 9, d
SCHMIDT, Wilhelm, cabin boy   Merzwiese
HOFFMANN, Johann Samuel, 26, journey-   Boberstag
    man potter
MEINKE, Auguste Karoline Luise, 23, un-   Boberstag
    married
JACOB, Gottfried, 43, cottager, with   Treppeln
    three children

From: Provinz Brandenburg, Kreis Zuellichau
To: Australia, 1845
BOTHE, Karl, 35, day laborer   Klemzig
BOTHE, Eleonore, b JENTSCH, w
SCHULZ, Christian, 36, gardener   Klemzig
GRADE, Karoline, 36, w
SCHULZ? Ernestine, 6, d
SCHULZ? Luise, 4, d
SCHULZ? Ernest August, 1, s
HIRTE, Friedrich, 30, cottager   Kay
EDLICH, Helene, 34, w
HIRTE? Friedrich Wilhelm, 8, s
HIRTE? Johanna Helene, 6, d
HIRTE? Johanne Maria, 3, d
HIRTE? Karl August, 1, s
EDLICH? Maria Rosina, b BURKERT, widowed mother-
    in-law
STOIKE, Dorothea, 35, unmarried day laborer   Kay
PAECH, Johann Gottlob, 40, gardener   Moestchen
BARTELT, Dorothea Elisabeth, 40, w
PAECH? Johanna Luise, 14, d
PAECH? Maria Elisabeth, 11, d
PAECH? Friedrich Wilhelm, 6, s
PAECH? Johann Josef, 3, s
PAECH? Johann Gottfried, 1, s
BARTELT, Johann Gottfried, 80, father-in-law
BARTELT, Anna Rosina, b LAENGER, 68, mother-in-law
KUCHEL, Johann Gottfried, 33, hired hand   Lochow
KUCHEL, Anna Dorothea, b KUCHEL, 33, w
KUCHEL, Johanne Luise, 5, d
KUCHEL, Johanne Dorothea, 4, d
KUCHEL, Johanne Eleonore, 2, d
KUCHEL, Anna Rosina, 3 weeks, d
KUCHEL, Daniel, 70, foreman   Lochow
SCHUBERT, Johann Gottfried, day laborer   Niedewitz
BALDERMANN, Dorothea Elisabeth, 29, w
SCHUBERT? Johanne Luise, 6, d
SCHUBERT? Karl August, 3, s
SCHUBERT? Johann Heinrich, 1, s

From: Provinz Schlesien [Silesia], Kreis Liegnitz
To: Australia, 1845
BOEHM, Georg Friedrich, 29, day laborer Pohlschildern
KRUSCHE, Johanne Elisabeth, 25, w

JOHN, Johann Gottlieb, 66, journeyman   Gross-Tinz
    carpenter
HAEUSLER, Maria Rosina, 59, w
JOHN? Johanne Eleonore, 30, d
JOHN? Johann Gottlieb, 24, s
JOHN? Traugott Benjamin, 22, s
DIETRICH, Johann Karl, 46, journeyman   Gross-Tinz
    mason
REICHELT, Anna Rosina, 41, w
DIETRICH? Johann Christian, 19, s
DIETRICH? Dorothea Luise, 15, d
DIETRICH? Johanne Ernestine, 13, d
DIETRICH? Johanne Eleonore, 10, d
DIETRICH? Maria Rosina, 6, d
DIETRICH? Karl Ernst Traugott, 3, s
DIETRICH? Karl Wilhelm August, 6 months, s
OTTE, Johann Wilhelm, 26, journeyman   Gross-Tinz
    mason [probable emigrant]
HAEUSLER, Karl, 26, inhabitant   Campern
JOHN, Johanne Christiane, 28, w
HAEUSLER? Wilhelm, 3, s
HAEUSLER? Karl, 4 weeks, s
OBST, Johann Karl Friedrich, 24, journey- Merschwitz
    man mason
HEIDRICH, Anna Rosina, w
OBST? Johanne Maria, 6 months, d
OBST, Ernst Wilhelm, 17, apprentice mason, brother
HEIDRICH, Gottlieb, 32, farmer   Merschwitz
    (brother-in-law of J. K. F. Obst)
SCHMIDT, Anne Susanna, w
HEIDRICH? Anna Christiane, 3 months, d
OBST, Gottlob, 29, journeyman mason   Parchwitz
HAMPEL, Johanne Elisabeth, w
OBST? Heinrich August, 6, s
OBST? Ernst Gottlieb, 1, s
    (The mother, Marie Elisabeth OBST, b SCHAEGE, had
    to remain behind temporarily, due to sickness.
    Probably, she followed them during the heavy emi-
    gration wave of the forties and fifties. Among
    the emigrants to Australia in 1848, without a
    declaration of religious affiliation, was the
    mason Gottlob SCHAEGE and family from Gross-Tinz,
    Kreis Liegnitz; it is possible that he was a
    relative of Mrs. OBST and that she accompanied
    them to Australia.)
HEIDRICH, Johann Christian, 58, day   Alt-Laest
    laborer
NEUMANN, Marie Eleonore, 54, w
HEIDRICH? Johanne Elisabeth, 30, d
HEIDRICH? Karl Wilhelm, 16, s
SCHOLZ, --, maid
KNUSCHKE, Johann Christian, weaver   Heidau
KNUSCHKE, Maria Rosina, b KLANT, 43, w
KNUSCHKE, Anna Elisabeth, 8, d
JUNGFER, Ernst, cottager   Royn
HAEUSLER, Johanne Eleonore, 30, w
JUNGFER? Ernst, 5, s
JUNGFER? Johann Gottfried, 1, s
KRIEBEL, Johann Christian, 57,   Klein-Jaenowitz
    gardener
POHL, Johanna Elisabeth, 48, w
KRIEBEL? Gottlieb, 26, s
KRIEBEL? Wilhelm, 19, s
KRIEBEL? Johanne Eleonore, 17, d
KRIEBEL? Ernestine, 10, d
HAMPEL, Heinrich, 34, day laborer   Klein-Jaenowitz
PUTZKER, Anna Rosina, w
HAMPEL? Karl Heinrich, 8, s
HAMPEL? Johanna Christiane, 6, d
HAMPEL? Anna Rosina, 4, d
HAMPEL? Johanna Ernestine, 6 months, d

From: Provinz Schlesien [Silesia], Kreis Lueben
To: Australia, 1845

JOHN, Karl, 35, master blacksmith	Buchwaeldchen
OBST, Dorothea Susanna, 35, w	
JOHN, Wilhelm, 26, journeyman black-smith	Buchwaeldchen
WOGISCH, Gottlieb, 75	Buchwaeldchen
WOGISCH, Marie Eleonore, 36, w	
LINDNER, Gottlob, 50 stall owner? [Freistellenbesitzer] livery stable?	Buchwaeldchen
JOHN, Maria Rosina, 40, w	
LINDNER? Johanna Elisabeth, 19, d	
LINDNER? Friedrich Ernst, 17, s	
LINDNER? Johann August, 3, s (twin)	
LINDNER? Wilhelm Traugott, 3, s (twin)	

(The oldest daughter, Johanna Eleonore LINDNER? 20, will stay in Germany, as she wishes to marry in Silesia.)

SEIDEL, Gottfried, 51	Buchwaeldchen
SEIDEL, Johanna Christiane, 22, d	
SEIDEL, Johanna Karoline, 14, d	
JUNGFER, Anna Rosina, b SEIDEL, 20, divorced, d of Gottfried SEIDEL	Buchwaeldchen
SCHOLZ, Gottlieb, 39, livery stable owner [Freistellenbesitzer]	Koslitz
MUMMERT, Johanna, 31, w	
SCHOLZ? Wilhelm Heinrich, 17, s	
SCHOLZ? Johanna Christiane, 15, d	
SCHOLZ? Charlotte Henriette, 14, d	
SCHOLZ? Ernst Hermann, 9, s	
SCHOLZ? Pauline Auguste, 8, d	
SCHOLZ? Johanna Pauline, 3, d	
SCHOLZ? Hermann Eduard, 2, s	
JURECK, --	Lueben

From: Provinz Schlesien [Silesia], Kreis Steinau
To: Australia, 1845

(Two unidentified families of at least four members in total.)

From: Provinz Posen, Kreis Buk
To: Australia, 1845

SCHUPELIUS, Christian, 49, shoemaker	Sontop
SCHUPELIUS, Anna Elisabeth, w	
SCHUPELIUS, Wilhelm, 13, s	
SCHUPELIUS, Johann Heinrich, 8, s	
SCHUPELIUS, Johanna Juliane, 6, d	
ECKERT, Gottlieb, 46, property owner	Sontop
MUSTER, Anna Dorothea, 47, w	
MUSTER, Johanna Wilhelmine, 15, foster daughter	
BRADTKE, Wilhelm, 41, blacksmith	Cichagora
SCHLIPKE, Rosina Dorothea, 44, w	
BRADTKE? Johanna Luise, 22, d	
BRADTKE? Ernst Heinrich, 15, s	
BRADTKE? Amalie Ottilie, 10, d	
BRADTKE? Adolf, 4, s	
BRADTKE? Wilhelm Gustav, 3, s	
FISCHER, Gottfried, 46, property owner	Cichagora
DEUTSCHMANN, Anna Dorothea, 29, w	
FISCHER? Gottfried, 3, s	

From: Provinz Posen, Kreis Kosten
To: Australia, 1845

PIETSCH, Samuel, 40, day laborer	Rensko
PIETSCH, Anna Dorothea, 32, w	

(There may have been 3 children also, but the manuscript is defectively printed and they are not named.)

PANKOW, Karl Friedrich, 49, property owner	Rensko

BEISE, Sophie Elisabeth, 61, w	
PANKOW? Elisabeth, 9, d	
PANKOW? Gottfried, 6, s	
PANKOW? Anna Rosina, 4, d	

From: Brandenburg, Kreis Neu-Ruppin
To: America, 1845

LANDON (or LAUDON), Karl Friedrich, 36, master tailor	Gransee
ACHTERMANN, Karoline Friderike Henriette, w	

(Stated to have been Old Lutherans.)

From: Brandenburg, Kreis Angermuende
To: America, 1845

HERZBERG, Wilhelm, farmer, with w and 4 children	Lunow
FLUEGGE, Ephraim, master linen weaver, with w and 6 children	Lunow
FISTLER, --, cabinetmaker	Luetzlow
DAMEROW, Anna Dorothea, 42, w, with 6 children, as follows:	
SCHROEDER, Wilhelmine, 17, stepdaughter, from the wife's first marriage, plus her own children:	
SCHROEDER? Karl, 14, wife's s by first marriage	
SCHROEDER? Hermann, 11, wife's s by first marriage	
SCHROEDER? Emilie, 8, wife's d by first marriage	
SCHROEDER? Hanna, 7, wife's d by first marriage	
SCHROEDER? Rosalie, 1, wife's d by first marriage	

(The manuscript may be somewhat ambiguous, but apparently the wife brought 1 stepdaughter and 5 children of her own into her marriage with Herr FISTLER.)

SACK, August, fisherman	Liepe
GOLDBECK, Wilhelmine, w , plus 2 children, her parents, and 2 sisters-in-law, 19 and 16 years	
NEUMANN, --, cottager, plus 2 children	Liepe

(He is divorced from his wife.)

GRENZ, --, farmer, with w and 5 children	Chorinchen
WOLTER, Daniel Friedrich, 24, fisherman's assistant (Brother of Mrs. -- SCHROEDER, b WOLTER, who emigrated in 1844 from Fiddichow, Kreis Greifenhagen.)	Schwedt
WESENICK, --, 32, tailor, with wife (39) and their children, number unknown; the stepchildren remain in Germany	Meichow
HOFFMEISTER, --, 58, widow, with 2 unmarried daughters, age 23 and 20	Meichow
CASTILLON, Johann, journeyman miller, with w and 7 children, 13 to 1 years	Meichow

From: Brandenburg, Kreis Prenzlau
To: America, 1845

JAGERITZ, Christian Friedrich, 29, shoe-maker	Bruessow
GENSOW, Albertine Wilhelmine, 24, w	
ELLMANN, Erdmann Friedrich, 42, sadler	Rossow
WERK, Marie Luise, 38, w	
GRASMANN, Wilhelm, 27, weaver	Fahrenwalde
ZABEL, Helene, 31, w	
SCHROEDER, Johann Wilhelm Lorenz, 45, weaver, unmarried	Hammelstall
FAEHRMANN, Karl Friedrich Wilhelm, 27, shepherd boy, unmarried	Eickstedt
BOENING, Michael, 24, farmer's son	Menkin
IKE, Karl Friedrich Wilhelm, 27, master brickmaker	Schenkenberg
IKE, --, b STUEDEMANN, w, plus 1 son	

DAEHN, Christian Fredrich, 35, master   Schenkenberg
   weaver
UECKS, --, 41, w, plus 1 son, plus
   wife's mother, aged 63, plus mother's
   4 other children [all unnamed]

From: Provinz Pommern [Pomerania], Kreis Naugard
To: America, 1845
NEITZEL, Friedrich Wilhelm, 27, far-   Trechel
   mer's son
UTECH, Friderike, 23, w
   (Parents and brothers and sisters remain in
   Germany but follow in 1846.)
MAASS, Karl, farmer   Trechel
UTECH, Wilhelmine, 28, w
MAASS? Ernestine Friderike, 5, d
MAASS? Henriette, 3, d
MAASS? August Karl Friedrich, 2, s
UTECH, Christian, farmer   Trechel
BUBLITZ, Christine, 51, w
UTECH? Henriette Luise, 20, d
UTECH? Christian Friedrich August, 16, s
UTECH? Johann Friedrich August Ferdinand, 14, s
SUELFLOW, Johann Friedrich, cottager   Trechel
   and wheelwright
VIERGUTZ, Dorothea Christine, 35, w
SUELFLOW? Christian Ferdinand, 16, s
SUELFLOW? Luise Christine Wilhelmine, 13, d
SUELFLOW, Joachim Friedrich, 75, father   Trechel
   [of Johann Friedrich SUELFLOW]
   (The 17 persons listed above gave religion
   as their reason for emigrating, while the
   58 listed below either give no reasons or
   their reasons have been contested.)
BUETOW, Karl Friedrich Wilhelm, 32, journey- Trechel
   man tailor
BUETOW, Luise, b WILCKE, 61, his mother
NEITZEL, Johann Friedrich August, 21,   Trechel
   applicant for school position [Schul-
   amtsbewerber]
NEITZEL, Karl Friedrich Gottlieb, 24,   Trechel
   journeyman miller
   (The two NEITZEL boys were sons of
   Christian NEITZEL, a teacher, probably
   deceased, for whom farmer Christian
   NEITZEL was guardian; the guardian
   wished to accompany his wards but
   delayed his emigration until 1846.)
HOEFS, Karl Friedrich, master blacksmith   Maskow
WARMBIER, Dorothea Maria, w
GOETSCH, Karl Friedrich August, laborer Klein-Sabow
BRAUN, Luise Henriette, w plus 3 children
GOETSCH, Friedrich Wilhelm, tailor   Bernhagen
LIERMANN, Dorothea Marie Charlotte, w
QUANDT, Karl Friedrich, 25, hired hand,   Pflugrade
   unmarried
DEGENER, Johann Friedrich Wilhelm, 27,   Pflugrade
   laborer
SCHNUR, Wilhelmine, 30, w, plus 2 children
DEGENER, Christian Friedrich, 42, farmer Pflugrade
MOESCH, Dorothea Luise, 49, w, plus 5 children
ZASTROW, Martin Friedrich, 42, property Pflugrade
   owner
BOHLMANN, Dorothea Luise, 40, w, plus 8 children
ZASTROW, Gottlieb Friedrich, 48, property Pflugrade
   owner
ZUELSDORF, Anna Sophie, 44, w, plus 4 children
PASEWALK, August, 24, cottager   Pflugrade
POLZMANN, Friderike, 23, w, plus 2 children
KORTH, Wilhelm, 31, cottager   Pflugrade
ZASTROW, Wilhelmine, 36, w, plus 3 children

ZASTROW? --, b WERNER, 71, mother-in-law
CALLIES, Friedrich Wilhelm, 26, laborer Pflugrade
GOETZ, Johanna Friderike, w, plus 2 children
   (It is possible that CALLIES, PASEWALK, Gottlieb
   Friedrich ZASTROW, and QUANDT did not emigrate
   until 1846.)
SCHERPING, Friedrich Christian, shoemaker Gollnow
SCHERPING, Charlotte, b MAASS, w
SCHERPING, Eduard Wilhelm Friedrich, 1, s

From: Provinz Pommern [Pomerania], Kreis Regenwalde
To: America, 1845
Note: Information taken from files on sects [Kon-
   ventikelwesen]
STREY, Johann Gottfried Emanuel, 31, butcher Plathe
PLANTZ, Charlotte Sophie, 26, w
STREY? Marie Karoline Luise, 5, d
STREY? Johanna Wilhelmine Sophie, 3, d
STREY? Friedrich Wilhelm, in first year, s

From: Provinz Pommern [Pomerania], Kreis Saatzig
To: America, 1845
Note: Information taken from files on sects [Kon-
   ventikelwesen]
SCHWANTES, Christlieb, 51, farmer   Lenz
KLUG, Karoline Sophie, 49, w
SCHWANTES? Karl Friedrich Wilhelm, 22, s
SCHWANTES? Marie Karoline Erdmuthe, 15, d
SCHWANTES? Johanna Christiane Wilhelmine, 12, d
SCHWANTES? Justine Wilhelmine, 8, d
SCHWANTES? Daniel Ferdinand, 3, s
KOLLATH, Henriette, 24, maid
   (The father, Christlieb SCHWANTES gives reli-
   gious belief as motive for emigration.)
BREHMER, Christian, 54, laborer   Uchtenhagen
NASS, Dorothea Charlotte, 48, w
   (BREHMER was the brother-in-law of [Martin
   Friedrich] CHRISTIAN from Damerow, Kreis
   Saatzig, who emigrated in 1843.)
BRUESSOW, Gottlieb, tailor   Uchtenhagen
HANKE, Dorothea Luise, w
BRUESSOW? Ernst Friedrich Wilhelm, 6, s
BRUESSOW? Ernestine Friderike Luise, 3, d

From: Provinz Pommern [Pomerania], Kreis Randow
To: America, 1845
HOUDELETTE, Luise, 29   Ploewen
HOUDELETTE, Johanna, 18
   (Daughters of farmer Johann HOUDELETTE; they
   were specifically stated to have been Old Lu-
   therans.)

From: Provinz Pommern [Pomerania], Kreis Kammin
To: America, 1845
Note: Although not individually identified as Old
   Lutherans, all of the following persons are thought
   to have been members, because the names have been
   taken from a file entitled "Regarding Sectarian
   Affairs and Resulting Emigration to America" for
   the period 1 April 1843 to 1 May 1846.
EHLKE, Wilhelm Christian, 53, lessee   Betzlaff
KANNENBERG, Sophie Friderike Luise, 50, w
EHLKE? Hanna Sophie Friderike, 24, d
EHLKE? Johann Karl Christlieb, 22, s
EHLKE? August Friedrich Wilhelm, 17, s
EHLKE? Ferdinand Friedrich Wilhelm, 14, s
EHLKE? Hermann Wilhelm Gottfried, 8, s
KOEPKE, Wilhelm Friedrich, 41, farmer   Betzlaff

LANGE, Maria Friderike Wilhelmine, 32, w
KOEPKE? Auguste Wilhelmine Henriette Albertine, 11, d
KOEPKE? Berta Friderike Albertine, 9, d
KOEPKE? Auguste Em[ilie?] Friderike, 6, d
KOEPKE? Emilie Albertine, 2, d
KRAUSE, Anna Regina, 74, mother
   [It is not clear who Frau Krause is the
   mother of, but from the usual context in
   this manuscript, she would have been the
   mother of Wilhelm Friedrich KOEPKE.]
RADLOFF, Johann Michael, 37, day laborer   Betzlaff
KRUEGER, Friderike Christiane, 35, w
RADLOFF? Karl Friedrich Ferdinand, 6, s
RADLOFF? Wilhelmine Albertine Friderike, 2, d
KOEPKE, Johann Gottlieb, 31, day laborer   Betzlaff
GAULKE, Wilhelmine Auguste Friderike, 23, w
KRAUSE, Christian Wilhelm Friedrich, 48,   Betzlaff
   farmer
MOLZ, Friderike Dorothea Tugendreich, 32, w
KRAUSE? Ferdinand Friedrich Wilhelm Eduard, 15, s
KRAUSE? Hanna Wilhelmine Charlotte Sophie, 12, d
KRAUSE? Berta Sophie Marie Henriette, 11, d
KRAUSE? August Friedrich, 9, s
KRAUSE? Karl Julius Eduard, 5, s
MOLZ, Karl Friedrich Hermann, 16, stepson
KRAUSE, Katherine Luise, b HANNEMANN, 79, widow,
   mother of Christian W. F. KRAUSE
MOEGENBURG, Karl Sigismund, 51, peasant   Betzlaff
WENDORFF, Marie Elisabeth, 43, w
MOEGENBURG? Johann Friedrich Wilhelm, 18, s
MOEGENBURG? Karl Wilhelm Ludwig, 17, s
MOEGENBURG? Karoline Friderike Luise, 15, d
MOEGENBURG? Ernestine Wilhelmine Luise, 13, d
MOEGENBURG? Karl August Friedrich Bogislav, 10, s
MOEGENBURG? Friderike Wilhelmine Ernestine, 8, d
MOEGENBURG? Wilhelmine Albertine Henriette, 5, d
MOEGENBURG? Henriette Luise Friderike, 3, d
KRAUSE, Gottlieb Friedrich, 45, property   Cretlow
   owner
VOIGT, Maria Luise, 41, w
KRAUSE? Karl Friedrich Bogislav, 15, s
MAAS, Johann Gottlieb, 67, property owner   Cretlow
SCHMIDT, Wilhelmine Sophie Karoline, 34, w
MAAS? Karl Friedrich Wilhelm, 8, s
MAAS? Karoline Henriette Auguste, 5, d
MAAS? Martin Gottlieb Severus, 3, s
MAAS? Gotthilf Johann Wilhelm, 1, s
SCHMIDT, Anna Dorothea, 31, wife's sister
KRAUSE, Karl Friedrich Bogislav, 47, proper-   Cretlow
   ty owner
GAHNZ, Ernestine Luise, 37, w
KRAUSE? Ernestine Rosalie Wilhelmine, 9, d
PANKOW, Karl Friedrich, 49, property owner   Cretlow
BEISE, Sophie Elisabeth, 61, w
PANKOW? Johann Friedrich, 27, s
PANKOW? Maria Ernestine Friderike, 24, d
PANKOW? Karoline Luise Ernestine, 21, d
GAHNZ, Marie Ernestine, b TRITTIN, 37,   Cretlow
   widow of a day laborer
GAHNZ? Charlotte Karoline Henriette, 17, d
KANNENBERG, Johann Friedrich, 43, cot-   Dieschenhagen
   tager
HENSELING, Hanne Charlotte, 37, w
KANNENBERG? Hanne Karoline Alwine, 9, d
KANNENBERG? Johann Friedrich Wilhelm, 7, s
KANNENBERG? Emilie Henriette Friderike, 4, d
KANNENBERG? August Gotthilf Hermann, 1, s
WISKOW, Karoline Christine, b EHLKE, 45,   Rachitt
   widow of an inhabitant
WISKOW? Marie Luise, 12, d
WISKOW? Johann Karl Friedrich, 9, s

From: Provinz Pommern [Pomerania], Kreis Usedom-
     Wollin
To: America, 1845
OTTO, --   Rehberg
KUCKAHN, --, w, plus 5 children
   [The entry is ambiguous and could also read
   Otto KUCKAHN, with w, and 5 children.]
EHMKE, --   Rehberg
STREGE, --, w, plus 3 children
GNEWUCH, --   Rehberg
KOHLMEY, --, w, plus 5 children
OTT, --   Rehberg
SCHUETT, --, w, plus 3 children
BUDAHN, --, farmer   Dannenberg
SCHULZ, --, w, plus 6 children
KRAUSE, --   Dannenberg
NEUMANN, --, w, plus 5 children
KUCKAHN, --, property owner   Dargebanz
MUESCH, --, w, plus 4 children
BAASS, --   Lebbin
BANKE, --, w, plus 5 children
BRAUNSCHWEIG, Jakob Friedrich   Fernowsfelde
BUDAHN, --, w, plus 4 children
BRAUNSCHWEIG, Johann Gottfried Ludwig   Fernowsfelde
WERGIN, --, w, plus 4 children
BRAUNSCHWEIG, Johann Friedrich Wilhelm   Fernowsfelde
VOELTZ, --, w, plus 2 children
BORKENHAGEN, --   Fernowsfelde
BUDAHN, --, w, plus 6 children
ERDMANN, --   Fernowsfelde
ERDMANN, --, b ERDMANN, w, plus 5 children
MAGNITZ, Johann Heinrich Ferdinand, cottager Warnow
MAGNITZ, Karl Heinrich
   [Relationship not given.]
WENDLAND, --   Codram
BERNDT, --, w, plus 6 children

   Recapitulation of 1845 emigration:

To Australia from	Provinz Brandenburg	84
" "	"	Provinz Schlesien	80
" "	"	Provinz Posen	23
To America	from	Provinz Brandenburg	79
" "	"	Provinz Pommern	284
		Total	550

1846

From: Provinz Pommern [Pomerania], Kreis Randow
To: America, 1846
Note: For the following persons, there were def-
      inite declarations of religious motivation
      for their emigration.
WOLFF, Ludwig Ferdinand, 21, farmer's son   Ploewen
GOERS, Christian, 23, farmer's son   Ploewen
GOERS, Charlotte, 25, unmarried
GOERS, Karoline Wilhelmine, 20, unmarried
   (The three were brother and sisters.)
HASENBANK, Gottfried, 39, journeyman car-   Ploewen
   penter
GERLOFF, Dorothea Friderike, 39, w
HASENBANK? Wilhelm Karl Gottfried, 2, s
JAGOW, Michael, 39, weaver   Ploewen
RIECK, Marie Dorothea, 35, w
JAGOW? Friedrich Ferdinand Ludwig, 8, s
JAGOW? August Friedrich Albert, 6, s
JAGOW? Wilhelm Christian Friedrich, 1, s
STROHFELD, David Wilhelm, 41, day laborer   Ploewen
KOLPIN, Charlotte Auguste, w
STROHFELD? Friedrich Wilhelm Martin Erdmann, 11, s

STROHFELD? Johann Friedrich David, 8, s
STROHFELD? Karoline Friderike Wilhelmine, 5, d
GOMBERT, Jaques, restaurateur   Ploewen
KRUEGER, Karoline, w
GOMBERT? Friedrich Wilhelm, 22, s
GOMBERT? Johann, 19, s
GOMBERT? August Friedrich, 13, s
GOMBERT? Karoline Wilhelmine, 11, d
RUBBERT, Johann, 65, inhabitant   Boock
BRUST, Dorothea, w
ZIEM, Joachim, 25, inhabitant   Boock
ROGGOW, Christian, 45, inhabitant   Boock
BOLION, Charlotte, w
ROGGOW? Minna, 18, d
ROGGOW? Wilhelm, 17, s
ROGGOW? --, 11, s
ROGGOW? Karl, 2, s
HELLERT, Gottfried, 45, inhabitant   Boock
LEMKE (also LIMPKE), Maria Dorothea, w
HELLERT? Luise, 19, d
HELLERT? Karl, 16, s
WERTH, Joachim, 30, inhabitant   Boock
BEHM, Minna, w
WERTH? Henriette, 8, d
WERTH? Karl, 6, s
WERTH? Ernestine, 4, d
STENGEL, Christian, inhabitant   Boock
SPERLING, Sophie, w
STENGEL? Wilhelmine, 4, d
STENGEL? Wilhelm, 2, s
BROECKER, Joachim, 35, inhabitant   Boock
BEHM, Maria Dorothea, w
BROECKER? Ernestine, 9, d
BROECKER? Johann, 8, s
BROECKER? Wilhelmine, 3, d
ELLMANN, Friedrich, 35, inhabitant   Boock
RUBBER, Christine, w
ELLMANN? Wilhelm, 5, s
ELLMANN? Karoline, 2, d
VOGEL, Friedrich, 36, inhabitant   Boock
WERTH, Friderike, w
VOGEL? Wilhelmine, 8, d
MOLL, Karl, 49, inhabitant   Mewegen
ELLMANN, Friderike, w
MOLL? Philippine, 17, d
MOLL? Albert, 14, s
MOLL? Heinrich, 10, s
MOLL? Karl, 6, s
WERTH, Martin, 70, inhabitant   Mewegen
LEMKE, Marie, w
WERTH, Johann, 35, inhabitant   Mewegen
WERTH, Christiane, b WERTH, w
WERTH, Wilhelm, 16, s
WERTH, Wilhelmine, 14, d
WERTH, Karoline, 11, d
WERTH, Karl, 1-1/2, s
WERTH, Johann, 6 months, s
WERTH, Martin, 44, inhabitant   Mewegen
ZIEM, Maria Dorothea, 32, w
WERTH? Friderike, 14, d
WERTH? Wilhelm, 6, s
WERTH? Karl, 2, s
BEHM, Regine, b BEHM, 60   Mewegen
ROHDE, Christian, 44, inhabitant   Mewegen
ROHDE, Regine, b WERTH, w
ROHDE, Wilhelmine, 15, d
ROHDE, Friderike, 13, d
ROHDE, Philippine, 11, d
ROHDE, Karl, 7, s
ROHDE, Karoline, 5, d
ROHDE, Luise, 2, d
MOLL, Regine, b ZIEHM, married   Mewegen

MOLL, Karl, 6, s
MOLL, August, 4, s
   (Her husband emigrated in 1843, and his family
    is to rejoin him [in America].)
WITTKOPF, Christian, 45, inhabitant   Mewegen
ROLDE, Maria, w
WITTKOPF? Gustav, 10, s
WITTKOPF? Wilhelm, 4, s
WERTH, Johann, 30, inhabitant   Mewegen
KRIENKE, Dorothea, w
WERTH? Wilhelmine, 9, d
WERTH? August, 3, s
WERTH? Berta, 1, d
KRIENKE, Friderike, 14, sister-in-law
BEHM, Joachim, 32, inhabitant   Mewegen
WITTKOPF, Anna Sophie, w
BEHM? Karoline, 9, d
BEHM? Karl, 6, s
BEHM? Albertine, 5, d
MUELLER, August, 25, inhabitant   Mewegen
SCHULZ, Friderike, w
WERTH, Karl, 35, inhabitant   Rothen Clempenow
ELLMANN, Regine, w
WERTH? Karl, 13, s
WERTH? Wilhelm, 11, s
WERTH? August, 4, s
KRAUSE, Christian Friedrich, 36, shoemaker Loecknitz
MERTEN, Charlotte Friderike, 39, w
KRAUSE? Henriette Friderike Charlotte, 9, d
KRAUSE? Hulda Julie Auguste, 13, d
STOLZENBURG, Friedrich, 36, peasant   Zedlitzfelde
BECKER, Elisabeth, 37, w
STOLZENBURG? Friedrich Wilhelm, 6, s
STOLZENBURG? Christian Friedrich, 3, s
STOLZENBURG? Johann August, 1, s
WOLANSKY, Karl Friedrich, 44, laborer   Salzow
ZUEHLSDORFF, Maria Christine, w
BRETSCH, Karl Ludwig Friedrich August, 8, adopted
   child

From: Provinz Pommern [Pomerania], Kreis Kammin
To: America, 1846
Note: Data taken from a file entitled "Concerning
       Sectarian Affairs and Resulting Emigration
       to North America" [for 1845]. Of the 113
       emigrants for the year, only 46 can be iden-
       tified by name.

BRENDEMUEHL, Joachim, former property owner   Nitzow
MITZLAFF, Dorothea Marie, w
BRENDEMUEHL? Dorothea Friderike, 23, d
EICHHORST, August Ferdinand, journeyman   Nitzow
   blacksmith
STECHOW, Karl Gottlieb, day laborer   Nitzow
BROCKHUSS, Luise Charlotte, w
STECHOW? Karoline Ernestine Friderike, 1, d
KOEPKE, Johann Friedrich Bogislav, 38, cot-   Batzlaff
   tager
KOEPKE, Friderike Karoline Ernestine Luise, b LANGE,
   35, w
KOEPKE, Hermann Friedrich Wilhelm, 9, s
KOEPKE, Hanna Wilhelmine Friderike, 6, d
KOEPKE, Karoline Wilhelmine Ernestine, 5, d
KOEPKE, Karl Albert Friedrich, 3, s
KRAUSE, Christlieb, 44, day laborer   Duenow
JAEGER, Karoline Sophie, 43, w
KRAUSE? Friderike Wilhelmine Henriette, 13, d
KRAUSE? Karl Friedrich Wilhelmine, 8, d
KRAUSE? Friedrich Wilhelm, 5, s
KRAUSE? August Friedrich Wilhelm, 2, s
PROCHNOW, Pauline Em[ilie?] Albertine,   Langendorf
   b OTTO, 48, widow

PROCHNOW, August Karl Friedrich, 26, s
PROCHNOW, Hermann Friedrich Anton, 21, s
PROCHNOW, Pauline Emilie Albertine, 19, d
HOFEMEISTER, Karl Friedrich Gottlieb, 27,   Morgow
   day laborer
LEMCKE, Karl Friedrich Wilhelm   Drewitz
LEMCKE, August Ferdinand Leberecht
   [The relationship of these two persons is
   not given.]
KNALL, Johann Gottfried, farmer   Jassow
EGGERT, Dorothea Sophie, 40, w
KNALL? Wilhelmine Albertine, 12, d
KNALL? Karoline Marie Luise, 8, d
KNALL? Berta Marie Elise, 6, d
KNALL? Emilie Sophie, 5, d
KNALL? Johann Heinrich Wilhelm, 2, s
KNALL? Rosalie Albertine Henriette, 2 months, d
EGGERT, Johann Eggert, 69, inhabitant, father-in-law
EGGERT, Charlotte Sophie, b TEWS, 78, mother-in-law
KNOLL, Heinrich Wilhelm, 41, inhabitant   Denthin
VOLKMANN, David, 56, farmer   Kohlen
KOEPSELL, Marie Elisabeth, 45, w
VOLKMANN? Wilhelmine Friderike Sophie, 19, d
VOLKMANN? Karoline Ernestine Tugendreich, 17, d
VOLKMANN? Johann Friedrich, 13, s
VOLKMANN? Hanna Marie Elisabeth, 11, d
VOLKMANN? Wilhelm August, 7, s
VOLKMANN? David Ferdinand, 4, s
KOEPSELL, Joachim Gottfried, 32, hired hand
   (With regard to the last three families in the
   above list, it is specifically stated that they
   are emigrating because of hindrances to their
   religious beliefs, whereas for the other fam-
   ilies no reasons for their emigration are given.)

From: Provinz Pommern [Pomerania], Kreis Greifenberg
To: America, 1846
Note: According to a governmental list, dated 7 Feb
       1847, no less than 63 persons identified as
       Old Lutherans emigrated in 1846, but only 9
       thereof are identifiable by name.
ARNDT, Gottlieb, former land owner   Zitzmar
CRANTZ, Marie, w
FICK, Wilhelmine Karoline, unmarried stepdaughter
FICK, Konradin, 24, stepson
FICK, Martin Ferdinand, 16, stepson
MUELLER, --, widow   Zitzmar
   (Emigrated without permit.)
KRESSIN, Julie, b SEEGEBARTH, widow of   Holm
   farmer Johann KRESSIN
KRESSIN, Martin Wilhelm, 21, s
KRESSIN, --, unmarried woman   Holm
   (Emigrated without permit.)

From: Provinz Pommern [Pomerania], Kreis Naugard
To: America, 1846
Note: Just as in other Kreisen (townships), there
       were in Kreis Naugard to distinct groups of
       Old Lutherans: the first group gave religi-
       ous beliefs as the motive for their emigra-
       tion; the second group typically stated "by
       no means for religious reasons" but who,
       nonetheless, belonged to the Old Lutheran
       persuasion.
Group I:
BRAASCH, Joachim Georg, 59   Gollnow
BRAASCH, Wilhelm Friedrich August, 21, s
BRAASCH, Wilhelmine Henriette, 17, d
BRAASCH, Wilhelm Friedrich Theobert, 15, s
BRAASCH, Helene Auguste Marie, 12, d

RACKOW? Dorothea Friderike Tugendreich, 32, d,
   (she was the illegitimate daughter of Joachim
   Georg BRAASCH by the unmarried Sophie RACKOW)
BRAASCH, Wilhelmine, 24, d of Joachim G. BRAASCH's
   brother
BRAASCH, Karl Friedrich August, 22, s of Joachim G.
   BRAASCH's brother
BRAASCH, Amalie Florentine, 18, d of Joachim G.
   BRAASCH's brother, the policeman Christian Fried-
   rich BRAASCH of Neumassow
[It is not clear that all the nieces and the nephew
   were children of Christian Friedrich BRAASCH.]
FETTGENHAUER (also FETTCHENHAUER), Karo-   Gollnow
   line Math[ilde?], b BRAASCH, 37, widow
FETTGENHAUER, Auguste, 19, d
FETTGENHAUER, Robert, 14, s
FETTGENHAUER, Karl, 10, s
FETTGENHAUER, Hulda, 7, d
   (Karoline Mathilde FETTGENHAUER, b BRAASCH, was
   also a niece of Joachim Georg BRAASCH.)
HAMMEL, Martin Friedrich, 45, farmer and   Gollnow
   shoemaker
GOETSCH, Charlotte Luise Friderike, 43, w
HAMMEL? Hermann Karl Ferdinand, 20, s
HAMMEL? august Franz Ludwig, 17, s
HAMMEL? Luise Marie Wilhelmine, 12, d
HAMMEL? Elisabeth Marie, 6, d
HAMMEL? Marie Anna Charlotte, 4, d
HAMMEL? Lydia Wilhelmine Karoline, 2, d
Group II:
EHLERT, Karl Friedrich, 36, master cabinet-   Gollnow
   maker
EHLERT, --, b LAWERENZ, 29, w, plus 3 children
NEITZEL, Christian, 58, farmer and deacon   Trechel
BUBLITZ, Sophie, 58, w
NEITZEL? Johann Friedrich, 19, s
NEITZEL? Gotthilf Friedrich, 17, s
NEITZEL? August Friedrich, 15, s
LEGRAND, Johann Gottfried, 29, inhabitant   Langkofel
LEGRAND, --, b MUEHLENBECK, 28, w, plus 2 children
ZASTROW, Karl Friedrich, 37, farmer   Pflugrade
BRUMMUND, Charlotte, 34, w, plus 5 children
PANKOW, Karl Friedrich   Neufanger
PANKOW, --, b KAMMRADE, w, plus 4 children
WASENBERG, Karl August, 31, inhabitant   Wismar
WASENBERG, --, b VIERGUTZ, 28, w
ROEHL, Karl Friedrich August, farmer   Gross-Benz
ROEHL, --, b WOLFRAM, w, plus 4 children
GENNRICH (or JENNRICH), Peter Friedrich,   Gross-Benz
   fisher
GENNRICH, --, b LIERMANN, w, with 8 children,
   only one of whom is mentioned by name:
GENNRICH, Hermann, 21, shepherd boy
   (A daughter, Luise GENNRICH, remained in Ger-
   many, as she could not bring herself to leave.)
BORCHHARDT, Karl Friedrich August, shep-   Gross-Benz
   herd boy
GRIESBACH, Christof, shepherd   Wangeritz
GRIESBACH, --, b HOEFS, w, plus 5 children
   from 11 to 2 years of age
DRAEGER, --, [charcoal?] burner   Kniephoff
DRAEGER, --, b KRUEGER, w, plus 1 child
KAHN, Johann Christian, 68, day laborer   Gross-Sabor
GRAUSENICK, --, 59, w, plus 2 sons
BACKHAUS, Michael Friedrich, 33   Falkenberg
LUEBCKE, Johann Martin, journeyman mason   Falkenberg
LUEBCKE, --, KEIBLER, w, plus 9 children

   (The above 94 emigrants from Kreis Naugard are
   those upon which there was a governmental report, dated 7 Feb 1847. It may be that there
   were other persons who should have been included
   among the Old Lutherans, but for whom the permits

for emigration give no indication of their religious motivation. Since such motivation might
become clear from other sources, they are included
in the following list:

GERBITZ, Gottfried, farmer, with unnamed Graevenhagen
  family members
KEMPFERT, Heinrich, journeyman tailor   Graevenhagen
HAUNKE, Karoline Sophie Marie, unmarried   Parlin
  d of school teacher HAUNKE, who will
  emigrate with the family of farmer
  SCHWANDT from Kreis Saatzig
BORCHHARDT, Johann Joachim, 56, farmer   Rothenfier
BORCHHARDT, --, 17, s

From: Provinz Pommern [Pomerania], Kreis Regenwalde
To: America, 1846
Note: Information taken from a file concerning sec-
  tarian affairs
WACHS, Johann Christian, 54, peasant   Neu-Labuhn
SCHMECKEL, Marie Luise, 50, w
SCHMECKEL, Henriette Ernestine, 27, illegitimate d
  of Marie Luise SCHMECKEL
WACHS, Johanne Emilie, 25, d
WACHS, Friderike Luise Florentine, 23, d
WACHS, Johanna Karoline Charl..e, 17, d
WACHS, Luise Henriette Karoline, 15, d
WACHS, Karl Gottlieb Hermann, 11, s
WACHS, Johann August Gotthilf, 6, s
WACHS, Friedrich Wilhelm Leopold, 5, s
WACHS, Johann Ferdinand, 21, s of   Neu-Labuhn
  Johann Christian WACHS, a soldier separated
  from the Army
LAWERENZ, Charlotte, w
  (Another daughter, Albertine Karoline Sophie
  PLAUTZ, b WACHS, married to a soldier, was re-
  quired to remain in Germany.)
SPIERING, Karl Friedrich Gottlieb, super-   Neu-Labuhn
  visor and interim school teacher, 45
MANKE, Friderike Wilhelmine, 27, w [second w?]
SPIERING? Auguste Ernestine Wilhelmine, 18, d
SPIERING? Johann Wilhelm Heinrich, 16, s
SPIERING? Ernestine Wilhelmine Friderike, 14, d
SPIERING? Emilie Luise Wilhelmine, 3, d
SPIERING? Karl Gotthilf, 1, s
WENDORF, Wilhelm, 27, laborer   Heiglitz
SCHMIDT, Johann Gottlieb, 42, day   Ruebenhagen
  laborer
  (He states that he will go with the WACHS
  and SPIERING families to America and gives
  "religious grounds" as his reason for emi-
  grating.)

From: Provinz Brandenburg, Kreis Prenzlau
To: America, 1846
SCHMIDT, Karl Friedrich, 31, master Town of Prenzlau
  cabinet maker
SCHMIDT, --, b HANSTEIN, plus 2 legitimate children
  and 1 illegitimate child
HUCK, August Wilhelm Ferdinand, 43, Town of Prenzlau
  mechanic
BOOS, --, housekeeper
BOOS, --, their illegitimate child
SCHAEKER, Rudolf Ferdinand, 29,   Town of Prenzlau
  cabinetmaker
PFLUGRAD, --, w, plus 3 children
STECHLITZ, Johann Jakob Friedrich,   Town of Prenzlau
  33, cabinetmaker
HARTWIG, --, w
HOH, Karl, 42, butcher   Town of Prenzlau
THOMAS, --, w, plus 6 children

SUHR, Joachim, 34, laborer   Town of Prenzlau
SY, --, w, plus 3 children
MILLEVILLE, Philipp, 29, blacksmith   Bergholz
SCHULZ, --, w, plus 3 children
PFUHL, Johann Friedrich August, 45, farmer   Bergholz
SUCKOW, --, w, plus 3 children
WILLIAM, Philipp, 36, farmer   Bergholz
SUCKOW, --, w, plus 2 children
RUBBERT, Christian, 36, day laborer   Bergholz
BECKER, --, w, plus 3 children
RUBBERT, Karl, 26, day laborer   Bergholz
STRASSBURG, --, w, plus 3 children
MIETZNER, Karl Friedrich, 57, day laborer   Bergholz
BEHM, --, w, plus 1 child
MOLL, Wilhelm, 35, day laborer   Bergholz
WOLDT, Marie, w, plus 4 children
LUESCHOW, Christof, 64, former property   Bergholz
  owner
SCHULZ, --, w
STEGEMANN, Michael, 34, laborer   Wallmow
RIEK, --, w, plus 3 children
WIESE, Johann, 32, shepherd boy   Wallmow
BARTEL, --, w, plus 2 children and parents-
  in-law
BANDELOW, Gottlieb, 32, weaver   Wallmow
DUROW, --, w, plus 2 children
SCHULZ, Gottlieb, 47, laborer   Wollin
SCHROEDER, --, w, plus 3 children
BEUTEL, Johann, 41, laborer   Wollin
BONNIN, --, 43, w, plus 2 children
ZUEHLSDORFF, Christine Luise, 20, maid   Wollin
KOEHN, Johann Friedrich, 42   Wollin
KOEHN, --, w, plus 1 son
MEYER, Wilhelm, 66, cabinetmaker   Wollin
CAPLIK, --, w,
MEYER? --, 25, s
WENDT, Michael, 38, laborer   Kleinow
KUEKEN, --, w, plus 2 children
SCHULZ, Gottlieb, 24   Kleinow
  (His w and 1 child remain in Germany;
  she gave permission for his emigration.)
JUDISCH, Friedrich, 25, hunter   Cremzow
WEISS, --, w, plus 2 children
MEWES, --, 30, hired hand   Cremzow
STOLLHOFF, --, 31, w, plus children
STOLLHOFF, --, 77, father-in-law
  (Mewes had difficulties with his wife's em-
  ployer [*Dienstherrschaft*, apparently she was
  a serf employed by a nobleman] who did not
  want her to leave before completing her period
  of service, but in the end allowed her to emi-
  grate. The number of children accompanying
  her is not given.)
DETLOFF, Karl Friedrich, 28, journeyman   Falkenwalde
  blacksmith
MEYER, Karl Ludwig, 33, shoemaker   Falkenwalde
MUELLER, --, w, with 2 children
MUELLER, --, weaver, father-in-law
MUELLER, --, b DETLOFF, mother-in-law
MUELLER, Henriette, 20, sister-in-law
SY, --, 25, shoemaker   Bruessow
MERKEL, Friedrich Wilhelm, 23, clerk   Bruessow
ZABEL, Wilhelm, 29, peasant's son   Fahrenwalde
PUESCHELBERT, Friedrich Wilhelm, 40,   Fahrenwalde
  shoemaker
SCHULZ, --, w, plus 3 children
MAERTEN, Johann Friedrich, 45, day   Fahrenwalde
  laborer
NEUMANN, --, w, plus 5 children
COLLIER, Johann, 45, cottager   Fahrenwalde
PAGEL, --, w
JUDISCH, Ludwig Ferdinand, 48, merchant   Roggow

FRIEDRICH, --, w, plus 4 children
DUROW, Christian David, 50, cottager   Zerrenthin
DUROW, --, w, plus 5 children
MEYER, Wilhelm, 27, hired hand   Menkin
PROEFROCK, --, 32, hired hand   Menkin
WENDT, Martin, 48, laborer   Damme
SPRENGER, --, w, plus 4 children
KNOPF, --, 61, "separated"   Strasburg
   (His destination was given as North Carolina.)
JAGOW, Samuel Friedrich, 42, farmer   Grimme
SUCKOW, --, w, plus father's 5 children
ZIEMENDORF, Peter, 45, farmer   Grimme
DUCHOW, --, w, plus 2 children
BILLEAU, Peter, 60, tailor   Grimme
GOMBERT, --, w
KRUEGER, Christof, 37, journeman sadler   Nieden
SCHROEDER, Ludwig, 41, master tailor   Fuerstenwerder
PETRAN, --, w, plus 5 children

From: Provinz Brandenburg, Kreis Neu-Ruppin
To: America, 1846
Note: Files regarding Old Lutheran emigration to
   America
ZANTKE, Christian Friedrich, 45, shepherd   Guehlen
BUTH, Anna Maria, 44, w
SALOMON, Luise, foster daughter, housekeeper
   (They acknowledged their memberships as Old
   Lutherans in a hearing [with governmental
   officials].)
STOECKENIUS, Eugen, 26, s of Major   Wulckow
STOECKENIUS

From: Provinz Brandenburg, Kreis Angermuende
To: America, 1846
Note: From the same files as the above
HERMANN, Martin Friedrich, potter   Verkehrt Gruenow
HERMANN, --, w, plus 4 children
HAGEN, Christof, day laborer   Greifenberg
HAGEN, --, w
WILCKE, Michael Friedrich, horse herder   Welsow
WILCKE, --, w, plus 2 children
SCHMIDT, Friedrich, shepherd   Welsow
SCHMIDT, --, w, plus 7 children
WALTER, Marie Elisabeth, b GROSSKOPF,   Welsow
   farmer's widow
MUELLER, Christian, farmer   Frauenhagen
MUELLER, --, w, plus 2 children
MANTKE, Ephraim Friedrich, master black-   Frauenhagen
   smith
MANTKE, --, w, plus 6 children
BEITZ, Johann Friedrich, shepherd   Frauenhagen
BEITZ, --, w, plus 3 children
BOLDT, Johann Friedrich, weaver   Meichow
HAASE, --, w, plus 3 children, 19-15 years
BOLDT, Karl Friedrich   Kolonie Poessen
NEUMANN, Wilhelmine, w, plus 1 son
   (Karl F. BOLDT was the son of Johann F. BOLDT
   above.)
PORTH,--, shepherd   Wedellsberg
HASE, --, w
PORTH? --, married son
GEBAUER, Henriette, son's wife
PORTH? --, s
PORTH? --, s

From: Provinz Brandenburg, Kreis West-Priegnitz
To: America, 1846
Note: From the same files
SCHULZE, Karl Gottlieb, 31, cabinetmaker   Havelberg

HEIMGRAEBER, --, w
SCHELLER, --, silver worker   Perleberg
WAGNER, Tobias, postoffice helper   Perleberg

From: Schlesien [Silesia], Kreis Liegnitz
To: America, 1846
GLOR, Philipp, grocer   Kroitsch
GLOR, --, w, plus 4 children

From: Schlesien, Kreis Prenzlau
To: Texas, 1846
Note: From the same files
FIEBIGER, Friedrich, 40, Candidate   Fuerstenwerder
   for a theological degree

From: Schlesien, Kreis Westpriegnitz
To: Texas, 1846
MUECKE, --   Stessow
GIESE, --, clerk   Lenzen
EGGERT, --   Lenzen
PALM, --, master blacksmith   Perleberg
PALM, --, w, plus 6 children
   (E.U. of 4.8--meaning unknown.)
GRAF, --, journeyman carpenter   Perleberg
ERDMANN, --, sadler   Saaslich
PALM, --, master blacksmith   Saaslich
   (E.U. of 10.9.--meaning unknown.)
von GAUVAIN, Oswald   Brandenburg

From: Schlesien [Silesia], Kreis Nieder-Barnim
To: Texas, 1846
KUEHNE, Karoline   Wensickendorf

From: Provinz Brandenburg, Kreis Sorau
To: Australia, 1846
WEIDNER, Gottlob, 43, gardener   Fielitz
HERMANN, Johanna Christine, 38, w
WEIDNER? Johanna Auguste, 7, d
WEIDNER? Johanna Clementine, 4, d
   (Give acknowledgment as Old Lutherans.)

From: Provinz Brandenburg, Kreis Westpriegnitz
To: Australia, 1846
Note: From the same files as for Kreis Neu-Ruppin
   and Kreis Prenzlau
KURTH, Christian Friedrich, 35, shoe-   Wusterhausen
   maker
FRENZ, Dorothea, 25, w
KURTH? Karl August, 5, s
KURTH? Berta Maria, 3, d
KURTH? Wilhelm Gottlob, 1, s
   (Acknowledged as Old Lutherans.)

From: Provinz Schlesien [Silesia], Kreis Breslau
To: Australia, 1846
OSSIG, Gottfried, 58, gardener, widower   Peterwitz
OSSIG, Gottfried, 25, s from second marriage
OSSIG, Gottlob, 21, s from second marriage
OSSIG, Christof, 17, s from second marriage
OSSIG, Karl, 12, s from second marriage
   (His two children from the first marriage did not
   wish to accompany their father. He declared him-
   self to be an Old Lutheran and wished to go to his
   coreligionists in Lobethal.)

From: Provinz Schlesien [Silesia], Kreis Freistadt
To: Australia, 1846
GIERSCH, Johann August, 26, journeyman   Lindau
  tailor
SELLGE, Anna Elisabeth, 30, w

From: Provinz Posen, Kreis Kosten
To: Australia, 1846
Note: It has been impossible to identify most of
     the large number of emigrants from Provinz
     Posen for the year 1846; however, the fol-
     lowing persons are named, although it is not
     known certainly that they were Old Lutherans.
SCHULZ, Wilhelm, farmer   Pruszkowo
SCHULZ, Juliane, 20, w
SCHULZ, --, 1, d

    To recapitulate the Lutheran emigrants for the
    year 1846, a total of 789 persons, the follow-
    ing have been identified by name:

To America from Pomerania	293	
	Brandenburg	253
	Silesia	6
To Australia from Brandenburg	9	
	Silesia	7
	Posen	3
	Total	571

1847

From: Pommern [Pomerania], Kreis Randow
To: America, 1847
Note: Data from files on Sectarian Affairs. The
     religious motivation for emigration was al-
     so attested to by the Landrat (governmental
     official).
HASENBANK, Johann Friedrich, 49, farmer   Ploewen
SÉNÉCHAL, Wilhelmine, 34, w
HASENBANK? Christine Wilhelmine, 15, d
HASENBANK? Charlotte Friderike Wilhelmine, 13, d
HASENBANK? Johann August Friedrich Wilhelm, 11, s
HASENBANK? Christine Wilhelmine, 8, d
HASENBANK? Charlotte Karoline Auguste, 6, d
HASENBANK? Justine Dorothea Wilhelmine, 2, d
BROECKER, Johann, 28, lessee [Vorwerks-   Neuenhagen
  paechter]
WITTKOPF, Anna Sophie, 23, w
BROECKER? Alwine Auguste Luise, 3, d
BROECKER? Berta Therese Karoline, 1, d
WITTKOPF, Wilhelmine Ernestine, wife's illegitimate d
  [age not given]
ZIEHM, Karoline, 23, maid, unmarried   Neuenhagen
MOLL, Johann Heinrich Ferdinand, 26, car-   Mewegen
  penter
BEHM, Friderike, 23, w
MOLL? Rudolf Albert Julius, 1, s
TESSENDORF, Georg Wilhelm Friedrich,   Unknown
  barge helmsman
RIEBOW, Johanne, w
TESSENDORF? Dorothea Friderike Emilie, 4, d
TESSENDORF? Friedrich Wilhelm, 2, s
TESSENDORF? Rosa Bertha Dorothea Friderike, 1, d
RIEBOW, Veronika Henriette Karoline, 14, sister-in-
  law
RIEBOW, Friedrich Wilhelm August, 23, hired hand,
  [relationship not stated]
TESSENDORF, Georg Friedrich, 68, barge
  helmsman [relationship not stated]

From: Mark Brandenburg, Kreis Lebus
To: America, 1847
Note: Files of the Oberkirchenkolleg [church files]
ROSSIN, Martin, 49, tailor   Langsow
RASCHKE, Anna Sophie, 48, w
ROSSIN? Gottlieb, 16, s
ROSSIN? August, 10, s
ROSSIN? Anna Sophie, 17, d

From: Schlesien [Silesia], Kreis Liegnitz
To: America, 1847
KIRSCHKE, --, houseowner and blacksmith   Weissenleipe

From: Schlesien [Silesia], Kreis Lueben
To: Australia, 1847
KNAUERHASE, Johann Gottfried, 38, gardener   Gugelwitz
BEYER, Anna Rosina, 34, w
KNAUERHASE? Johann Karl, 8, s
KNAUERHASE? Johanna Christiane, 6, d
KNAUERHASE? Johann Ernst, 4, s
KNAUERHASE? Johann Hermann, 1, s
KANUERHASE, Maria Rosina, sister
  (Separatist views given.)

From: Schlesien [Silesia], Kreis Sagan
To: Australia, 1847
HOFFMANN, Samuel, 52, farmer   Reichenau
HOFFMANN, Dorothea, b WALTER, w
HOFFMANN, Johanna Rosina, 26, d
HOFFMANN, Friedrich Karl, 18, s
HOFFMANN, Johann Friedrich Wilhelm, 15, s
HOFFMANN, Johann Heinrich, 13, s
HOFFMANN, Johann Samuel, [age unknown], s
HOFFMANN, Christian, 3, s
  (Two other sons, Johann Gottlieb HOFFMANN and
  Johann Gottfried HOFFMANN remained behind to
  complete their military? service period, but emi-
  grated in 1849.)
LAUBE, Gottlieb, 52, houseowner   Tschirskau
REIMANN, Anna Elisabeth, 48, w
LAUBE? Christian, 18, s
LAUBE? Karl Benjamin, 11, s
LAUBE? Gottlob, 6, s
FECHNER, Samuel, 48, day laborer   Cosel
NIPPE, Gottfried, 36, unmarried, s of
  the farmer -- NIPPE, brother of -- NIPPE
  who emigrated in 1844
WUNDERLICH, Gottlieb, 35 or 33,   Klein-Dobritsch
  gardener's son, unmarried

From: Schlesien [Silesia], Kreis Gruenberg
To: Australia, 1847
SCHULZ, Gottlob, foreman [Lohnfuhrmann]   Town of
PEITZ, Juliane Christiane, 2   Gruenberg
  (Doubtful whether they were Old Lutherans.)
ROSENBERG, --, master tailor, widower   Town of
ROSENBERG, Franz Josef Ehrhard, 23, s   Gruenberg
ROSENBERG, Henriette Elisabeth, 21, d
ROSENBERG, Auguste Berta, 19, d
ROSENBERG, Josef Adolf, 17, s
  (Doubtful whether they were Old Lutherans. The
  oldest daughter, Maria Josefa ROSENBERG, was mar-
  ried and remained in Germany.)

From: Schlesien [Silesia], Kreis Liegnitz
To: Australia, 1847
HANUSCHKE, Heinrich, journeyman   Prinkendorf
  cabinetmaker

From: Brandenburg, Kreis Sorau
To: Australia, 1847
GROSS, Johann Traugott, 32, citizen and   Sorau
    linen weaver
NASCH, Johanna Christiane, w
GROSS? --, 6, s
    (Specifically stated to be Old Lutherans.)
RUSS, Johann Gottlieb, 26, hired hand   Rodtstock
    (Specifically stated to be Old Lutheran.)

From: Brandenburg, Kreis Zuellichau
To: Australia, 1847
DOLLING, Gottfried, 36, owner of a   Keltschen
    farm
DOLLING, --, b WOYDT, plus 4 children and parents
[of husband or wife not stated]
HEINRICH, Friedrich Wilhelm, 39,   Klein-Dammer
    cabinetmaker
HEINRICH, --, w, plus 4 children
HIRTHE, Andreas, gardener   Klein-Dammer
HIRTHE, --, w, plus son
MATTNER, Gottlob, 49, cottager   Kranschow
MATTNER, --, w, plus 3 children
THIELE, Georg, 52, shoemaker   Zuellichau
THIELE, --, w, plus 3 children
GUTSCHE, Wilhelm, 25, master tailor   Zuellichau
GUTSCHE, --, w
KROSCHEL, Gottfried, 40, owner of a   Padligar
    farm
KROSCHEL, Elisabeth, b SCHULZ, 40, w, plus 4 children
TSCHIPPIG, Gottfried, 35, gardener   Padligar
TSCHIPPIG, Johanna Luise, b FECHNER, 31, w,
    plus 4 children
FECHNER, --, b KLUGE, mother-in-law
FECHNER, --, 35, sister-in-law
VORWERK, Karl Ernst, laborer   Friedrichs-Laesgen
VORWERK, --, w, plus 7 children
GROCKE, Johann Christof, 46, gardener   Moestchen
GROCKE, --, w, plus 3 children

From: Provinz Posen [kreis not known]
To: Australia, 1847
Note: Only seven emigrants can be identified by
      name from the heavy emigration of 1847 from
      Posen.
OSTER, Philipp? pastor   Unknown
OSTER, Sophie Emilie, b STAMM
OSTER, --, 17, s
STREMPEL, Adolf, son of Stromaufseher   Posen?
[river administrator] Strempel
KALM, Johann Gottlieb, property owner   Preuschwitz,
SCHULZ, Auguste Wilhelmine, w   Kreis Kosten
KALM? Auguste Wilhelmine, 8 weeks, d
    (J. G. KALM was the brother-in-law of -- SCHULZ
    who emigrated in 1846.)
WOLLMANN, --, mason   Preuschwitz, Kreis Kosten

    From a total of 381 emigrants in 1847, the number
    identified by name above has been:

    To America   31
    To Australia   99

            Total   130

                        1848

From: Pommern [Pomerania], [kreis not given]
To: America, 1848

Note: Persons who stated that they were emigrating
      for reasons of their religious beliefs
HASEMANN, Karl Friedrich, day laborer   Cardemin
HASEMANN, Hanna Wilhelmine Friderike, d
HASEMANN, Friedrich Gottlob, day laborer   Cardemin
MUEGGENBURG, Karoline Wilhelmine, w
GRUETZMACHER, Gottlieb Friedrich, hired hand Cardemin

From: Brandenburg, [Kreis not given]
To: America, 1848
ALBERTS, Marie Luise, 19, unmarried   Nieder-Finow
    (Stepdaughter of Johann Friedrich August SCHULZE,
    of Kietz, who emigrated in 1843. She was born in
    Wuschewire.)

From: Schlesien [Silesia], Kreis Liegnitz
To: Australia, 1848
HUEBNER, Johann Gottfried, inhabitant   Gross-Tinz
HUEBNER, --, b SIEGERT, plus 4 children
SCHAEGE, Karl Gottlob, mason   Gross-Tinz
SCHAEGE, --, b VOGEL, plus 3 children
BLUEMEL, Johann Gottlob, gardener   Alt-Beckern
HOFFMANN, --, w, plus 3 children
BAUMGART, Karl, hired hand   Alt-Beckern
HABEL, --, w
ERNST, Anna Rosina, b WEINHOLDT, widow   Alt-Beckern
ERNST, --, d
GLATZ, August, inhabitant   Berndorf
SEIFERT, --, w, plus 2 children, 3 and 1 years
MUELLER, Karl Gottlieb, weaver   Berndorf
    (He leaves his wife, -- MUELLER, b HIRSCH, in
    Germany.)
PURRMANN, Johann Gottfried, 44, livery   Kummernick
    stable owner
GOEBEL, --, w, plus 3 daughters
HETTNER, Johann Gottlieb, 37, inhabitant,   Panten
    unmarried
TEUSNER, --, owner of a farm not a part   Wildschuetz
    of a nobleman's estate [Freibauerguts-
    besitzer]
HOFFMANN, --, w, plus 3 children, 15, 9, 8 years
FIEDLER, Karl Gottlieb, master tailor,   Kunitz
    plus 3 children, ages 22, 18, and 8 years
HOFFMANN, --, w, tailor, plus 4 children   Kunitz
    [The entry is somewhat ambiguous and does
    not mention her husband or whether she was
    a widow.]
HOFFMANN, Gottlieb, gardener   Neudorf
BAUER, --, w, plus 1 daughter, age 6
JOPPICH, Johann Gottlieb, wheelwright   Parchwitz
JOPPICH, --, w, plus 3 children, 6, 2, and 10 months
    (It was stated specifically that this family
    emigrated because of their separatist views.)
FIEBIG, Karl Heinrich, room polisher   probably from
STEINCHEN, --, 42, w   Parchwitz
FIEBIG? --, 6, d
SCHUBERT, Karl Heinrich, former soap   Liegnitz
    maker
    (Schubert was an activist for the Silesian
    "Mission Congregation" of emigrants in 1848.
    According to a brief from Schubert in Bremen
    to his wife and daughter, dated 10 March 1848,
    it is clear that his family did not accompany
    him, as he states that it is uncertain whether
    they will ever see each other again but that
    he would do everything possible to see to it
    that they followed him to Australia.)
SAELGE, Johann Christian, journeyman   Scheibau,
    miller   Kreis Freistadt

From: Provinz Posen, Kreis Kosten
To: Australia, 1848
PIETSCH, Johann Georg, house owner   Remsko
REDLICH, Maria, w
PIETSCH? Johann Gottlob, 14, s
PIETSCH? Anna Rosina, 11, d
PIETSCH? Johann Georg, 7, s
PIETSCH? Elisabeth, 4, d
REDLICH, Johann Christian, house owner   Remsko
   (The above listed persons were called Separat-
   ists. The follow persons were probably also
   of the same religious views.)
WUTTKE, Johann Georg, day laborer   Remsko
WITTKEN, Johanna Elisabeth, w,
WUTTKE? Karl, 8, s
WUTTKE? Wilhelm, 6, s
WUTTKE? Juliane, 2, d
DUEMKE, Gottlieb, day laborer   Remsko
WUTTKE, Gottfried, day laborer   Remsko

From: Schlesien [Silesia], Kreis Jauer
To: Australia, 1848
UEBERGANG, Samuel, livery stable owner   Merzdorf
UEBERGANG, Rosina, b LANGER, w
UEBERGANG, Anna Rosina, d
UEBERGANG, Dorothea, d
UEBERGANG, Wilhelmine, d [or Wilhelm, s]
UEBERGANG, Karoline, d
FRITSCH, Friedrich Wilhelm, day laborer   Skohl

           Recapitulation
      To America   6
      To Australia   83

           Total   89

1849

From: Brandenburg, Kreis Zuellichau
To: Australia, 1849
Note: A total of 87 persons from Kreis Zuellichau
      emigrated in 1849 but, in the absence of in-
      formation regarding their religious beliefs,
      they are not listed herein.

From: Schlesien [Silesia], Kreis Sagan
To: Australia, 1849
HOFFMANN, Johann Gottlieb, 23,   Reichenau
HOFFMANN, Johann Gottfried

From: Posen, Kreis Bomst
To: Australia, 1849
Note: Listed as Lutheran Separatists
GRUNWALD, Johann Christian, 54   Neu-Tuchorze
SCHILLER, Maria Dorothea, 56, w
GRUNWALD? Juliane, 23, d
GRUNWALD? Gottfried, 18, s
GRUNWALD? Juliane Beate, 4, illegitimate daughter
    of Juliane GRUNWALD?
LESKE, Rosina Dorothea, 40, widow   Neu-Tuchorze
LESKE, Johann Gottfried, 22, s
LESKE, Johanna Beate, 5, d
LESKE, Anna Dorothea, 2, d
ARNDT, Johann Gottlieb   Bomst
ARNDT, --, w, plus 1 son
   (Old Lutheran beliefs uncertain.)
SCHROEDER, Eduard Wilhelm, plus wife   Bomst

(Old Lutheran beliefs uncertain.)
REIMANN, Karl Friedrich Eduard   Bomst
REIMANN, --, w, plus 1 daughter
   (Old Lutheran beliefs uncertain.)
FIETZ, --, tailor   Karge
FIETZ, --, w, plus 3 children
   (Old Lutheran beliefs uncertain.)
BRUSE, Andreas   Karge
   (Old Lutheran beliefs uncertain.)
GREGOR, Christian   Unruhstadt
GREGOR, --, w, plus 1 son
   (Old Lutheran beliefs uncertain.)
STORCH, Heinrich   Unruhstadt
KRUEGER, Karl   Unruhstadt
NOAK, Karl   Unruhstadt
FRANKE, --, master miller   Wollstein
FRANKE, --, w, plus 3 children
GEIER, Wilhelm, property owner   Alt-Kramzig
GEIER, Johanna, b ECKERT, w
   (Note further members of this family emi-
   grating in 1854.)

From: Posen, Kreis Meseritz
To: Australia, 1849
Tamm, --, wind and water miller   probably Meseritz

1850

From: Posen, Kreis Meseritz
To: Australia, 1850
SCHULZ, Gottlieb, property owner   Tirschtigel
SCHULZ, --, b PENSKE, plus 2 sons, 19, 17
ROY, Ferdinand, farmer   Tirschtigel
KAHL, --, w, plus 1 daughter
RICHSTIEG, Georg, property owner   Kuschten
RICHSTEIG, Luise, w, plus 4 children
KURZ, Samuel, carpenter   Brausendorf
KURZ, --, b SCHILLER, w, plus 1 son
KURZ, Wilhelm   Chlastawe
KURZ, --, w, plus 1 child, 9 months
MUELLER, Samuel, 47, property owner   Ziegelscheuner-
BRAUNAK, Juliane Eleonore, 29, w   Hauland
MUELLER? Anna Maria Erdmuthe, d
MUELLER? Karl Heinrich, s
MUELLER? Karl Samuel, s
MUELLER? Karl Eduard Andreas, s

From: Posen, Kreis Bomst
To: Australia, 1850
ROESLER, Johann Wilhelm, 41   Neu-Borui
ROESLER, --, w
ROESLER, Wilhelm August Dienegott, 13, s
ROESLER, Friedrich Wilhelm, 11, s
ROESLER, Johann Dienegott, 9, s
ROESLER, Wilhelmine, 6, d
ROESLER, Ernst Heinrich, 3, s
ROESLER, Auguste, 1, d

From: Brandenburg, Kreis Zuellichau
To: Australia, 1850
Note: The names of 98 emigrants from this Kreis
      have not been found.

From: Brandenburg [Kreis not given]
To: America, 1850
Note: Files and family book of the Old Lutheran
      congregation of Kiehnwerder, Kuestrin

FREUND, Karl Friedrich, baker   Alt-Friedland
WOICKE, Dorothea Elisabeth, 44, w
FREUND? Karl Julius, 17, apprentice baker, s
FREUND? Karoline Emilie, 15, d

1851

From: Schlesien [Silesia], Kreis Rothenburg
To: Australia, 1851
URBAN, --, head of the Old Lutheran con-   Weigersdorf
   gregation

From: Posen, [kreis not given]
To: Australia, 1851
STREMPEL, --, *Stromaufseher* [river   City of Posen
   administrator]
STREMPEL, --, w, plus all remaining sons and
   daughters, at least 6 persons in total
   (Note that the son Adolf STREMPEL emigrated
   with Pastor OSTER in 1847.)

From: Posen, Kreis Bomst
To: Australia, 1851
Note: The following emigrants were called Lutheran
      dissidents
HAEUSLER, Wilhelm, 41, former restaurant   Borui
   and innkeeper
HAEUSLER, --, w
HAEUSLER? Beate, 11, d by first marriage
HAEUSLER? Rosina, 6, d by second marriage
HAEUSLER? Wilhelm, 4, s by second marriage
HAEUSLER? Traugott, 1, s by second marriage
LEHMANN, Wilhelm, 36   Borui
HOFFMANN, Karoline, 31, w
LEHMANN? Johann August, 9, s
LEHMANN? Johanna Beate, 7, d
LEHMANN? Rosina, 4, d
LEHMANN? Johann Wilhelm, 1, s
HAEMMERLING, Christian, gardener   Chlastawe
HAEMMERLING, --, b MATTNER, w
HAEMMERLING, Georg   Chlastawe
HAEMMERLING, --, b FECHNER, w
LINKE, Johann Georg   Chlastawe
HAEMMERLING, Dorothea Elisabeth, w, plus
   3 children
PILZ, Johann, journeyman carpenter   Gross-Dammer
PILZ, --, b MASUR, w

From: Pommern [Pomerania], [Kreis not given]
To: New Bergholz, New York, U.S.A.
Note: From a detailed letter from the year 1852
      there is news of a family of craftsmen,
      surname unknown, who emigrated from the
      Lutheran congregation of Saatzke. The
      family members were father, mother, and
      at least five children, of whom we have
      two names, August (who died) and Wilhelm.
      They joined a relative by the name of
      KRUEGER in New Bergholz.

1852

From: Brandenburg? [Ober-Lausitz], Kreis Rothenburg
To: America, probably Texas, 1852
URBANG, Mathes, subject to military duty   Tzschellen
   (Since the entire emigration movement from

Kreis Rothenburg was comprised of Old Lutherans,
URBANG is identified as the first of the emigrants.)

From: Brandenburg, Kreis Zuellichau
To: Australia, 1852
Note: According to the *Hengstenbergschen Zeitung*
      [newspaper], there were said to have been
      about 70 emigrants from the Zuellichau and
      Posen regions, all of whom were said to have
      been Old Lutherans or *schwaermerisch* [religi-
      ous enthusiasts].
MEISSNER, Karl Wilhelm, 28,   Town of Zuellichau
   manager
STUBE, Karl August, winemaker   Town of Zuellichau
STUBE, --, w, plus 1 son
KUBERNE, Karl, 19, hired hand   Schmoellen
LABSCH, Martin, 47, and wife   Schmoellen
TUNACK, Wilhelm, 38, day laborer   Schmoellen
TUNACK, --, w, plus 4 children
BOEHM, Friedrich, 26, day laborer,   Schmoellen
   with wife

From: Posen, [Kreis not given]
To: Australia, 1852
RUDOLPH, Gottfried, property owner   Borui
RUDOLPH, --, w, plus 3 children

1853

From: Brandenburg, Kreis Zuellichau
To: Australia, 1853
Note: There were 137 emigrants from Kreis Zuellichau
      during the year 1853, but it is not known which
      of them were Alt Lutherans; as a consequence,
      no names are listed herein.

From: Posen, Kreis Bomst
To: Australia, 1853
POELCHEN, Christian, property owner   Borui
POELCHEN, --, w, plus 4 children
KLITSCHKE, --, property owner   Karge
KLITSCHKE, --, w, plus 2 sons

From: Pommern [Pomerania], [Kreis not given]
To: Buffalo, New York, U.S.A., 1853
Note: Although not identified, there was one Old
      Lutheran family, consisting of father, mother,
      seven children, and a maid, who emigrated.

From: Brandenburg, Kreis Lebus
To: Buffalo, New York, U.S.A.
HECKMANN, Elisabeth, 54, widow   Langsow
KRANZ, Eva Maria, b LEMMERMANN, 42, widow   Langsow
   of Martin Kranz

From: Schlesien [Silesia], Kreis Rothenburg
To: Texas, U.S.A., 1853
THOMASCHKE, --, head of the Old Lutheran   Klitten
   congregation
KIESSLING, Andreas, farmer   Weigersdorf
KIESSLING, --, b PIETSCH, w
HOTTAS, Johann, 25, s of a houseowner   Reichwalde
KRAUSE, Christof, 36, inhabitant   Muecka

MICHALK, Maria, w
KRAUSE? Johann, 9 months, s
WAGNER, Anna, maid (from Weigersdorf)
SCHMIDT, Johann, 16   Kringelsdorf
  (accompanied by children of the siblings
  of Maria MATJETZ's father from Kaschel--
  indefinite data given.)
GRUSCHE, Georg, 63, windmiller   Moholz
GRUSCHE, Anna Rosina, w
GRUSCHE, Karl August, 24, s
GRUSCHE, Henriette, d
GRUSCHE, Ernestine, d
GRUSCHE, Johanna, d
NEUMANN, Johann Traugott, 41, cabinet- Nieder-Horka
  maker and inhabitant; son-in-law of Georg
  GRUSCHE
GRUSCHE, Johanna Rahel, w
NEUMANN? Johann Wilhelm, 10, s

From: Schlesien? [Silesia], Kreis Hoyerswerda
To: Texas, U.S.A., 1853
WILKE, Andreas, day laborer, plus w   Amtsanbau
KOINER, Mathes, 32, plus w and 3 children Amtsanbau
SIELOW, Gottlieb, 37, bricklayer, with   Amtsanbau
  w and 4 children
KASPER, Johann, houseowner, plus w and   Colpen
  4 children

1854

From: Brandenburg, Kreis Zuellichau
To: Australia, 1854
Note: There were a total of 70 emigrants from Kreis
      Zuellichau in 1854, but the Old Lutheran mem-
      bers are not identifiable, just as in 1853.

From: Posen, Kreis Bomst
To: Australia, 1854
BRAUN, Christian   Schwenten
TIETZ, --, w, plus 3 children
ZEPPEI, Gottlieb, farmer   Kuelpin
ZEPPEI, --, w, plus 2 children
FABIUNKE, Karl Wilhelm, houseowner   Ruden
FABIUNKE, --, w, plus 3 children
ECKERT, Josef   Alt-Kramzig
  (His sister, Johanna GEIER, b ECKERT, emigrated
  in 1849 to Southern Australia and sent her bro-
  ther £30 to join her there.)

From: Schlesien [Silesia], Kreis Rothenburg
To: Australia, 1854
VOGEL, Andreas, tailor   Dauban
ROSTOCK, Anna Christiane, w
VOGEL? Maria, d
KOOTZ, Johann Gottlob, machineshop owner Noes
KOOTZ, Christiane Auguste, b WOLFF, w
KOOTZ, Karl Ernst August, 10, s
KOOTZ, Ernst Leberecht, 8, s
KOOTZ, Karl Hermann, 7, s
KOOTZ, Maria Rosalie, 4, d
KOOTZ, Karl Bernhard, 1, s
TESCHNER, Johann Traugott, houseowner   Horka
ROEHL, Johanna Christiane, w
ROEHL, Christiane Auguste, stepdaughter
RICHTER, Johann Gottlieb, 30   Spree
WERNER, Johann Karl Gotthilf, cabinet- Tormersdorf
  maker, unmarried

TIETZE, Friedrich August   Tormersdorf
  (He is divorced from his wife.)
LIEDE, Friedrich Gustav, 23,   Nieder-Seiffersdorf
  journeyman mason
  (His sister, -- SCHALLER, b LIEDE, had already
  emigrated to Southern Australia where she was
  living in very good circumstances. Her emigra-
  tion has not been previously reported herein.)
SCHORAT, Matthaeus, 26, machinist   Niesky
  [Metaldreher]

From: Schlesien [Silesia], Kreis Rothenburg
To: Texas, U.S.A., 1854
TUPPACH, Karl   Gebelzig
STEPHAN, Magdalena, w
TUPPACH? August, 9, s
TUPPACH? Karl, 2, s
GREULICH, Johann, 32, rural policeman   Gebelzig
BRAEUER, Johanna Christiane, w
GREULICH? Johanna, d
GREULICH? Maria, d
GREULICH? Johann, s
BRAEUER, Auguste, b SCHUSTER, widow, mother-in-law
TUP[P]ACK, Andreas, 31, gardener   Gebelzig
KAISER, Magdalena, w
TUPPACK? August, 4, s
TUPPACK? Johann, 5 months, s
GREULICH, Andreas, 33   Gebelzig
MUELLER, Magdalena, w
HAULISCHKE, Johann Gottfried, 45   Creba
KOPPATSCH, Johanna Maria, w
HAULISCHKE? Christiane Luise, 14, d
HAULISCHKE? Henriette Marie, 12, d
HAULISCHKE? Ernestine Emilie, 10, d
HAULISCHKE? Friedrich Ernst, 2, s
LOWKE, Georg, houseowner   Klein Radisch
KIANK, Anna, w
RECK, Matthaeus, 27, houseowner   Klein Radisch
JENKE, Johann, 46, farmer   Klein Radisch
RICHTER, Anna, w
JENKE? Matthaeus, 10, s
JENKE? Hanna, d
JENKE? Maria Rosina, d
SCHIEWARTH, Christof, 26, inhabitant Klein Radisch
SCHUSTER, Anna, w
SCHIEWARTH? Marie, d
KASPER, Andreas, 39   Klein Radisch
GREULICH, Maria, w
SCHMIDT, Johann, 43   Sand Foerstgen
SCHLENKER, Johanna, w
SCHMIDT? Johanna Christine, 16, d
SCHMIDT? Agnete, 13, d
VOGEL, Andreas, houseowner   Sand Foerstgen
HANSKE, Agnes, w
VOGEL? Johann, 14, s
VOGEL? Ernst, 11, s
VOGEL? August, 6, s
VOGEL? --, d
SCHUSTER, Matthaeus   Sand Foerstgen
EBERT, Johanna Eleonore, w
SCHULZE, Johann, 53, fertilizer   Sand Foerstgen
  owner [Gartennahrungsbesitzer]
BRADE, Maria, w
SCHULZE? Johann, 32, s
SCHULZE? Matthaeus, 22, s
SCHULZE? Magdalena, d
ZWAR, Andreas, houseowner   Sand Foerstgen
ZWAR, --, w, 1 son (7 years) and 4 daughters
NOACK, Christof, 41, houseowner   Sand Foerstgen
PURSCHE, Johanna Christiane, 31, w
HOCKER, Georg, 49, shoemaker   Sand Foerstgen

SCHULZE, Magdalena, w
KIESLING, Johann, inhabitant — Weigersdorf
HANSKE, Anna, w
KIESLING? Johann 22, s
KIESLING? Magdalena, d
KIESLING? Ernst, 15, s
NEUMANN, Eduard, 38, inhabitant — Weigersdorf
URBAN, Maria, w
NEUMANN? Johann, 13, s
NEUMANN? August, 8, s
NEUMANN? Maria, d
NEUMANN? Maria Magdalena, d
SIMMANK, Johann, 58, houseowner — Weigersdorf
PROCHNO, Magdalena, w
SIMMANK? Anna Maria, d
MICKAN, Anna, stepdaughter
MICKAN, 9, stepson
MICKAN, Peter, 5, stepson
MIERSCH, Georg, houseowner — Weigersdorf
KILIAN, --, Pastor — Weigersdorf
GROESCHEL, Maria, w
KILIAN? Gerhard August, 2, s
KIESSLING, Andreas, farmer — Weigersdorf
PIETSCH, Johanna, w
KIESSLING? Maria, d
BARTHEL, Andreas, 31, mason — Petershain
BARTH, Johann Adolf, 29 — Petershain
KOLLATSCH, Johanna Luise, 25 — Neusaerichen
KOLLATSCH, Ernestine, 21
KOLLATSCH, Adolf Oskar, 1, s
KOLLATSCH, Christine Rosamunde, 18
   (The three young women were sisters; it is
   not clear which was the mother of the boy,
   but apparently Ernestine may have been.)
BALZER, Gottlieb — Saenitz
RICHTER, Ernst Julius, 25, journeyman — Oedernitz
   butcher
MAIDORN, Johann Christian, 47 — Oedernitz
RAUPACH, Christiane Rosina, w
MAIDORN? Ernst Wilhelm, 9, s
NOCKE, Georg, tailor — Reichwalde
SCHMIDT, Matthaeus, houseowner — Reichwalde
SCHNEIDER, Rosina, w
SCHMIDT? Johann, 23, s
SCHMIDT? Maria, d
SCHMIDT? Johanna, d
SOWKE, Andreas, gardener — Reichwalde
KRAUTSCHICK, Anna, w
SOWKE? Christof, 14, s
SOWKE? Johann, 5, s
SOWKE? Matthaeus, 1, s
SOWKE, Maria, d
SOWKE, Johanna, d
ANDERS, Georg, gardener — Reichwalde
MALTICK, Johanna, w
MALTICK? Henriette Friderike, stepdaughter
ANDERS? Christof, 5, s
ANDERS? Ernst, 4, s
ANDERS? Karl August, 1, s
KOEBEL, Christof, houseowner — Reichwalde
SCHNEIDER, Maria, w
KOEBEL? Christiane, d
ANTON, Gotthelf [so spelled] houseowner — Reichwalde
   (He will send for his wife later.)
PEHSE, *genannt* [*alias*] FRANKE, Andreas, — Reichwalde
   35
KUNZE, Johanna, widow of FRANKE
FRANKE, Andreas, 14, stepson
FRANKE, Johannes, stepson
PEHSE, Andreas, 9, his own son
LORENTICH, Georg, 38, houseowner — Reichwalde
KASPER, Elisabeth, w

LORENTICH? Johann, 16, s
LORENTICH? Mathes, 15, s
LORENTICH? Andreas, 10, s
LORENTICH? Magdalena, 6, d
LORENTICH? Johanna, 1, d
JURACK, Magdalena, 17, unmarried
   (Accompanies her sister, name unknown or not clear)
PETER, Mathias, 65, serf — Reichwalde
LUSCHUETZ, Rosina, 62, w
RIPPACH, Ernst, houseowner — Reichwalde
KOPACK, Johanna, w
RIPPACH? Ernst, 7, s
RIPPACH? Johann, 6, s
RIPPACH? August, 4, s
RIPPACH? Helene, d
RIPPACH, Elisabeth, mother
NOWKE, Johann, 56, houseowner — Reichwalde
MATUCK, Johanna, 49, w
NOWKE, Johann, 20, s
LUSCHUETZ, Johanna, b NOWKE, d
LUSCHUETZ, Andreas, 5, s of Johanna
   (The husband of Johanna LUSCHUETZ, b NOWKE, is of
   no account and has lived apart from his wife for
   years; he remains in Germany but has no objection
   to his wife's emigration.)
HOTTAS, Johanna, 21, unmarried — Reichwalde
RICHTER, August, her fiancé — Kachel
LORENTZSCH, Johanna, unmarried — Reichwalde
LORENTZSCH, --, 17, her daughter
   (Two sons, aged 30 and 24 years, remain in Ger-
   many.)
LEHMANN, Karl, 40, mill owner — Dauban
BASCHE, Magdalena, w
HANDRICK, Johann, 37, farmer — Dauban
SCHAEFER, Maria, w
HANDRICK? Johann, 13, s
HANDRICK? Johann August, 11, s
HANDRICK? Johann Karl, 8, s
HANDRICK? Andreas, 4, s
HANDRICK? Anna, d
HANDRICK? Magdalena, d
TEINERT, Johann Karl, 38, fertilizer owner — Dauban
SCHNEIDER, --, w
TEINERT? August, 17, s
TEINERT? Johann, 12, s
TEINERT? Ernst, 11, s
TEINERT? Hanna, d
TEINERT? Maria, d
TEINERT? Magdalena, d
KOERK, Johann, 55, fertilizer owner — Dauban
MROS, --, w
KOERK? Johann, 21, s
KOERK? Anna, d
KOERK? Magdalena, d
KOERK? Agnes, d
SCHKADE, Christof, 61, houseowner and shoe- — Dauban
   maker
HEINICK, Agnes, w
SCHKADE? Marie, d
VOGEL, Johann, 46, fertilizer owner — Dauban
SCHLESE, Anna, 29, w
VOGEL? Marie, 5, d
VOGEL? Anna, 2, d
SCHARRAT, Johann Gottlieb, 49, inhabitant — Dauban
DOMANN, Johanna, w
SCHARRAT? Wilhelmine Otilie, 9, d
SCHARRAT? Ferdinand Paul, 6, s
SCHARRAT? Emilie Auguste, 1, d
LEHMANN, Johann Traugott, 35, journeyman — Dauban
   miller, brother of Karl LEHMANN listed above
BUETTNER, Georg, 48, houseowner — Dauban
SCHLEZE, Maria, w

BUETTNER? Andreas, 16, s
BUETTNER? August, 10, s
BUETTNER? Anna, d
BUETTNER? Maria, d
BUETTNER? Magdalena, d
NOACK, Andreas, 40, houseowner   Dauban
DUMKE, Anna, w
KIESCHNIK, Johann, 58, houseowner   Dauban
KIESCHNIK, Agnes, w
KIESCHNIK, Andreas, 25, s
KIESCHNIK, Magdalena, 20, d
KIESCHNIK, Johann, 20, s
KIESCHNIK, Maria, d
KIESCHNIK, Agnes, d
MOERBE, Maria, b HETSCHIK, widow   Dauban
MOERBE, Anna, 22, d
   (A son, Johann MOERBE, 24, apparently remained
   in Germany.)
KULLING, Franz Albert, 16, houseowner's son   Dauban
VOGEL, Christof, inhabitant   Dauban
ROTHE, Gottlieb, 32, shepherd boy   Leippa
RICHTER, Karl Heinrich, 25, rural policeman   Spree
SCHATTE, Johann, 29, houseowner   Kliffen
KIESETZ, Rosina, w
SCHATTE? Matthaeus, 8, s
SCHATTE? Johann, 6, s
SCHATTE? Anna, d
BARTSCH, Maria, houseowner   Kliffen
BARTSCH, Hanna, d
BARTSCH, Maria, d, illegitimate
BARTSCH, Rosina, d, illegitimate
BARTSCH, Johanna, b born in 1854, illegitimate
MIESNER, Ernst, 21, salesman   Kliffen
ISELT, Georg, 39, inhabitant   Kliffen
RAMSCH, Rosina, 43, w
ISELT? Hanna, 7, d
ISELT? Johann, 2, s
PAULICK, Jakob, 54, houseowner, with w   Kliffen
DONATH, Christiane Karoline, 22, unmarried   Kliffen
SCHUBERT, Johanna, 48   Kliffen
PETRICK, Magdalena, w
SCHUBERT? Hanna, d
SCHUBERT? Rosina, d
SCHUBERT? Mathaeus, 13, s
SCHUBERT? August, 12, s
SCHUBERT? Agnes, d
SCHUBERT? Johann, 2, s
SCHUBERT, Anna, b KRAUTSCHICK, mother
   [It is thought that the name Johanna, which is
   feminine, should read Johann SCHUBERT, thus mak-
   ing the emigrant the father of the family.]
MERTING, *genannt [alias]* BARTHEL,   Thomaswaldau
   Johann, 30, houseowner
HOHLE, Hanna, w
MERTING? Johann, 4, s
MERTING? Mathes, 1, s
MERTING, Georg, 24, brother
MERTING, Johann, 69, father
MERTING, Anna, b SCHATTE, mother
MARTSCHINK, Mathes, 30, day laborer   Duerrbach
SCHUBERT, Christof, 37, farmer   Duerrbach
SCHUBERT, Dorothea, w
SCHUBERT, Maria, d
SCHUBERT, Hanna, d
TZSCHORMAKK, Johann, 39, houseowner   Duerrbach
HERENZ, Hanna, w
TZSCHORMAKK? Maria, d
TZSCHORMAKK? Johann, 10, s
TZSCHORMAKK? Hanna, d
TZSCHORMAKK? Rosina, d
TZSCHORMAKK? Agnes, d
SCHOELLING, Mathes, 39, farmer   Duerrbach
MATZ, Anna, w

SCHOELLING? Johann, 16, s
SCHOELLING? Mathes, 6, s
SCHOELLING? Maria, d
SCHOELLING, Johann, 61, retired
SCHOELLING, Anna, b BRIDDE
   (The relationship of these two emigrants to
   the rest of the family is not given.)
SCHOELLING, Johann, 34, hired hand, brother
SCHOELLING, Maria, sister
SWOIBE, Rosina, 23, maid
MROSK, Mathes, 40, houseowner   Duerrbach
SCHOELLING, Hanna, w
MROSK? Maria, d
MROSK? Johann, 14, s
MROSK? Rosina, d
MROSK? Agnes, d
MROSK? Magdalena, d
RANESCH, Georg, 41, houseowner   Duerrbach
PAULICK, Rosina, w
RANESCH? Johann, 2, s
KUBITZ, Johann, 42, farmer   Duerrbach
KUBITZ, Hanna, 43, w
KUBITZ, Johann, 20, s
KUBITZ, Mathes, 17, s
KUBITZ, Christof, 8, s
KUBITZ, Maria, 15, d
TZSCHIEDER, Johann, 77, father-in-law
HOHLE, *genannt [alias]* KRUPPER, Johann, 29,   Jahmen
   gardener
KOCKUL, Rosina, 24, w
HOHLE? Johann, 1, s
HOHLE, Anna, 57, widow, mother
BECKER, Georg, 31, gardener   Jahmen
DROSCHE, Rosina, 27, w
BECKER? Johann, 1, s
DROSCHE, Mathes, 68, father-in-law
HOTTAS, *genannt [alias]* KASPER, Johann, 62,   Jahmen
   houseowner
BRIDDE, Maria, w
HOTTAS? Johann, 16, s
SCHATTE, *genannt [alias]* MROSKE, Matheus,   Jahmen
   62, houseowner
SCHAUTSCHICK, Rosina, w
SCHATTE? Hanna, d
SCHATTE? Johann, s
KRUPPER, *genannt [alias]* HOHLE, Mathes,   Jahmen
   hired hand
KRUPPER, Christof, 20
   (These two young men, as well as [Johann] Merting,
   geb. HOHLE [probably means *genannt* BARTHEL] from
   Thomaswaldau, were sons of the widow Anna HOHLE,
   who was also called the widow KRUPPER, b SCHAUT-
   SCHICK.)
ISELT, Rosina, b SCHUSTER, 46, widow   Jahmen
ISELT, August, 18, s
ISELT, Johann, 16, s
ISELT, Andreas, 12, s
ISELT, Mathes, 7, s
RICHTER, August, 21, journeyman brewer   Kaschel
RICHTER, Luise, sister
MUELLER, Karl Ernst, 41, houseowner   Kaschel
WELLMANN, Maria, 44, w
MUELLER? Wilhelmine, 11, d
MUELLER? Friedrich, 8, s
JANETZ, *genannt [alias]* PECH, Johann, 42,   Kaschel
   houseowner
KOATNY, Rosina, w
JANETZ? Johann, 17, s
JANETZ? Mathes, 14, s
JANETZ? Hanna, d
JANETZ? Maria, d
DOMASCHKA, Mathes, 36, gardener   Kaschel
JURZ, Hanna, w

DOMASCHKA? Rosina, d
DOMASCHKA? Maria, d
JURZ, Hanna, b BUETTNER, mother-in-law
SOCKE, Georg, 42   Kaschel
SCHIEWARTH, Anna, w
SOCKE, Maria, d
SONSEL, Anna, unmarried   Kaschel
SONSEL? Anna, d
    (Her husband? is said already to be in America.)
RICHTER, Johann Gottfried, 52, master brewer Kaschel
MICHLER, Charlotte, w
RICHTER? Christiane, d
RICHTER? Amalie, d
RICHTER? Selma, d
RICHTER? Ernst Moritz, 8, s
RICHTER? Friedrich Adolf, 6, s
SCHUBERT, Johann, 29, gardener   Kaschel
MITSCHKE, Hanna, w
MITSCHKE? Rosina, 7, stepdaughter
SCHUBERT, Hanna, 1, d
MITSCHKE, Marie, mother-in-law
BECKER, Johann Gottfried, 43, gardener   Cunnersdorf
SCHWARZ, Maria Rosina, w
BECKER? Maria Auguste Ernestine, d
BECKER? Johann Karl August, 6, s
BECKER? Karl Ernst, 1, s
TSCHOPPE, Johann Karl, baker,
    (Accompanies the BECKER family.)
MICHALK, Hann, 29, maid   Oelsa
SCHULZ, Matheus, 47, gardener   Wunscha
JURITZ, Johanna, w
SCHULZ? Rosina, d
SCHULZ? Maria, d
SCHULZ? Johann, 14, s
SCHULZ? Matheus, 11, s
SCHULZ? Christof, 7, s
BEHLOW, August Robert, 41, shoemaker   Neuhof
BEIER, Ernestine Luise, w
BEHLOW? Gustav, 5, s
BEHLOW? Pauline, d
BEHLOW? Auguste, d
LEHMANN, Andreas, houseowner   Gross-Saubernitz
MEHLE, Anna, w
LEHMANN? Johann August, 17, s
LEHMANN? Andreas Eduard, 13, s
LEHMANN? Karl August, 11, s
LEHMANN? Karl Ernst, 9, s
LEHMANN? Karl, 6, s
LEHMANN? Maria, d
ZIESCHANZ, Johann, 44, mill owner   Gross-Saubernitz
HOMMEL, Anna, w
NOACK, Karl Ernst, 21, journeyman   Gross-Saubernitz
    miller
STEPHAN, Andreas, carpenter and   Gross-Saubernitz
    houseowner
KAISER, Anna, 59, w
STEPHAN? Anna, 25, d
STEPHAN? Karl, 19, s
ISELT, Matheus, day laborer   Muehlrose
ZELT, Johanna, w
RICHTER, Christof, 56, master wheelwright   Viereichen
SCHUSTER, Maria, 56, w
RICHTER? Johann Karl Ernst, 23, s
RICHTER? Johanna Karolina, d
RICHTER? Henriette, d
RICHTER? Johann Karl August, 15, s
JANNACK, Christof, houseowner   Tschellen
JANNACK, Georg, 25, s
JANNACK, Christian, 22, s
JANNACK, Johann, 20, s
JANNACK, Michael, 16, s
SCHULZE, Johann, master brewer, unmar-   Kringelsdorf
    ried

SUCKER, August, unmarried   Mueckenhein
TSCHOPPE, Traugott, houseowner   Thiemendorf
TSCHOPPE, Anna Rosina, w
TSCHOPPE, Karl Traugott, 16, s
TSCHOPPE, Friedrich August, 14, s
TSCHOPPE, August Heinrich, 3, s
TSCHOPPE, Johanna Ernestine, 8, d
HOEMPEL, Johann Gottfried, 29, gardener   Quitzdorf
GROSSMANN, Johanna Luise, w
HOEMPEL? Karl August, 3, s
HOEMPEL? Karl Wilhelm, 11 months, s
FRIEDRICH, Karl August, 14   Quitzdorf
    (Accompanies the HOEMPEL family.)
WILLE, Theodor Waldemar, 18, journeyman   Niesky
    mechanic
WILBRICH, Karl, 22   Neusorge
LEISCHNER, Johann Karl, former   Nieder-Seifersdorf
    houseowner
BERGEL, Johanna Christiane Rahel, w
SCHUBERT, Georg, 36, gardener   Unknown
BORN, Rosina, w
SCHUBERT? Mathes, 15, s
SCHUBERT? Andreas, 10, s
SCHUBERT? Johann, 7, s
WILBRICH, Karl August, 22, peasant   Unknown
WILBRICH, Heinrich, 18
    [Note, however, a Karl WILBRICH from Neusorge
    above.]

From: Schlesien [Silesia], Kreis Hoyerswerda
To: Texas, U.S.A., 1854
Note: Although most of the following emigrants only
      state that their destination is "Amerika,"
      they are known to have accompanied the emi-
      grants from Kreis Rothenburg to Texas. Ac-
      cording to the Landrat [government official]
      nearly all of them were Old Lutherans.
FRENZEL, Hermann, journeyman weaver   Amtsanbau
HAENTSCH, August, journeyman linen weaver   Amtsanbau
WUCKASCH, Mathes, room polisher   Buchwalde
WUCKASCH, --, w, plus 4 children
KNIPPER, Johann, houseowner   Buchwalde
KNIPPER, --, w, plus 3 children and mother-
    in-law
ZOCH, Christian, farmer   Spreewitz
ZOCH, --, w, plus 3 children
SCHNEIDER, Johann, hired hand, plus   Spreewitz
    his fiancée [otherwise unnamed]
KOLBA, Christian, farmer   Neudorf
KOLBA, --, w, plus 2 children, father, and
    mother-in-law
CASPER, Chrisitan, houseowner   Neudorf
CASPER, --, w, plus 1 son
PATSCHKE, --, day laborer   Colpen
PATSCHKE, --, w
CASPARICK, --, journeyman cabinetmaker   Zerre
CASPARICK, --, w, plus 5 children
LIENACK, Mathes, hired hand   Zerre
PAULS, Mathes, journeyman carpenter   Seidewinkel
PAULS, --, plus 2 children
WIERICK, Hans, houseowner and master   Seidewinkel
    tailor
WIERICK, --, w, plus 2 chilren
KLETZKE, Heinrich, houseowner   Weiss-Collm
KLETZKE, --, w, plus 2 children
PRELLOP, Mathes, houseowner   Geisslitz
PRELLOP, --, w, plus 1 son
LIESCHKE, Johann Traugott, fish dealer   Ruhland
LIESCHKE, --, w, plus 2 children
MATUSCH, Johann, gardener's son   Driewitz
    Recapitulation: 33 to Australia; 477 to America;
        totaling 510 emigrants for the year 1854

FAMILY SEPARATIONS

In Chapter XIV of Herr Iwan's study of the Old Lutheran emigration from Prussia, a number of instances are recorded in which there were separations of family members, some emigrating, others remaining in Prussia. Since these cases are of considerable genealogical interest, the data presented therein are translated in their entirety hereinafter, beginning at Volume 2, page 215, et seq. He summarizes his study of these separations in the following manner:

Causes	Total Cases	Number of Actual Separations
Marriage disagreement	47	18
Children's guardianships & similar	92	42
Military service obligation	42	10
Total	181	70

From a total of 1,083 families emigrating to America and Australia, only 70 families suffered actual separation of immediate family members, about 6.3%.

KLEMTKE   Anna Rosina Klemtke, from Stentsch near Schwiebus, wished to emigrate to Australia with her coreligionists. Her husband emphatically opposed this plan. She applied to the *Patrimonialgericht* [civil court] for a divorce, which was denied, and she was advised to apply to the *Regierung* [Executive branch of the government]. She then applied to the *Regierung* Frankfurt/Oder, asking that her husband's opposition be overruled on the grounds that they had no children. The *Regierung* denied her appeal on 5 Jul 1836; ". . . it would be evidence of her Christianity, if she were to submit to her husband's will." *Regierung Frankfurt/Oder. Zuellichau & Sternberg Kreise, 1836-1837. [Files on Emigration Applications].*

ZEDLER   On 11 Jul 1838 the police president of Breslau referred the application of journeyman tailor Karl Benjamin Zedler to the *Regierung* [Executive branch of the government], inasmuch as Zedler's wife did not wish to accompany her husband to America. The couple had been interrogated on 9 Jun 1838 as to how the wife was to be supported, if Zedler were to leave her behind. The couple declared that they had agreed privately thereon, as she had long supported herself as a laundress, and they were already separated. There were no children, and the wife would receive all the furniture. A suit for legal separation had been filed three years previously, but decision thereon had been suspended. The husband's application for emigration was denied, and he was advised either to obtain a legal divorce or to make arrangements to support his wife by remittances from America. On 5 Oct 1838 Zedler submitted a divorce decree and was granted an emigration permit. He emigrated. *Staatsarchiv Breslau. Rep. 14 P.A.X. 28a [Files on Emigration Applications of Separatists].*

ULBRICHT   In 1838 the coachman Christoph Ulbricht from Reichenau, Kreis Sagan, refused to permit his wife, Anna Elisabeth Ulbricht, b RAETEL, to emigrate to Australia and would not give her money for the trip. He demanded that she remain with him in Germany. In the event that the *Regierung* [Executive branch of the government] gave her an exit permit, he would require her to divorce him before leaving. He was a member of the Landeskirche [the official state church] and had tried his best to persuade his wife and stepchildren to join him therein. A great deal of domestic discord had resulted. His wife insisted on emigrating with her children. If the husband would not provide money for the trip, she hoped to obtain it from her own coreligionists. In a hearing on 17 Jul 1838 the wife was found to be persistent in her demands and could not be persuaded otherwise. The record does not say whether an exit permit was granted or whether she was granted a divorce. Her children emigrated in 1844, but she is not listed with them. She either died in the meanwhile or remained in Germany. *Regierung Liegnitz, Kreis Liegnitz, 1835-1857, 4 volumes [Files on the Emigration of Prussian Subjects and Their Naturalization in Foreign Countries].*

HOFFMANN   Divorce was planned in the Hoffmann family of Harthe, Kreis Zuellichau, in 1838. In the file on the gardener Johann Friedrich Hoffmann, aged 61, it was stated that the husband of his daughter, Maria Elisabeth ADAM, and the wife of his son, Johann Christian Hoffmann, refused to emigrate with the family. With regard to these proposed divorces and the disposition of the minor children no decision was reached. Permits were not issued for the young people; they were required to remain in Germany, and no divorces were granted. *Regierung Frankfurt/Oder, Kreis Zuellichau-Schwiebus, 1838, Volume 1 [Files on Emigration Applications to Australia].*

JORDAN   Gottlieb Jordan from Polnisch-Hammer, Kreis Trebnitz, who was not himself a Separatist, made application for the emigration of his wife Rosina. In a hearing on 3 Jun 1839 the husband stated his willingness to allow his wife to emigrate. Although there were no children, the marriage was not dissolved. The wife was granted an exit permit, however. *Staatsarchiv Breslau. Rep. 14 P.A.X. 28g, Vol. 1, 1836-1838 [Files on Emigration Applications from Separatists].*

SCHMALIAN   As a detail of the group emigrating with Pastor Grabau in 1839, it was stated that the wife of the clothmaker -- Schmalian from Osterwieck, Bezirk Magdeburg, applied for divorce as a consequence of his emigration. The Magdeburg governmental files, under date of 4 Mar 1839, contain a query as to whether the husband had given up his emigration plan. Further data in the files are not clear as to whether a divorce was granted. *Staatsarchiv Magdeburg. Rep C 28 Polizeiregistratur, 1838-1843 [Files of the Regierung Magdeburg on Emigration Applications from Lutheran Separatists].*

SEELIGER   Of a certain tailor's wife, -- Seeliger, from Schabenau, Kreis Guhrau, there is evidence that she wished to emigrate with her seven children, leaving her husband, who was a drunk and neglected his family. When told that she could not emigrate unless divorced, and that she would be given no control over her children, her husband gave permission for her to leave. However, nothing came of the entire Schabenau emigration project [and it is not known whether she emigrated]. *Staatsarchiv Breslau. Rep 14 P.A.X. 28g, Vol. II, 1839-1845 [Files on Emigration Applications from Separatists].*

EICHHORST Dorothea Eichhorst, b GUST, wife of fisherman — Eichhorst, from Klein Dievenow [Kreis Kammin], wished to emigrate with her children, inasmuch as she could no longer live without her Lutheran faith. Her father also wished to emigrate for religious reasons. Her husband, on the other hand, declared, "I do not wish to be divorced from my wife, nor do I wish to be separated from my children. I am convinced that it is possible for my wife and children to live in a Christian manner and to die at peace here [in Germany]." Since it was not possible for the couple to reach an accord in Kammin, the matter was referred to the next higher instance in Stettin. The final decision is unknown, but apparently not in favor of the wife, as her name does not appear in the list of persons to whom emigration permits were granted. *Staatsarchiv Stettin. Landratsamt Kammin. Vol. II, May-Jul 1839 [Special Files on Emigration of Dissidents from Kreis Kammin to America].*

FLEISCHFRESSER The wife of farmer — Fleischfresser, from Benz, Kreis Kammin, was a member of a dissident group and hoped to emigrate to America with her two married daughters. The husband did not wish to leave Germany, however, and would give no consent to his wife's emigration plan. The couple was called before Landrat v. Voeltz on 1 Jun 1839. The two sons-in-law, — HELM from Scharchow and — GAHNS from Kammin, also appeared. After lengthy discussion, the wife, — Fleischfresser, b TRITTIN, stated as follows: "As a matter of conscience, I cannot remain in Germany, and will leave my husband, accompanied by my children of the same religious opinions." The children and sons-in-law declared themselves in agreement with her statement, and further stated that they would pay the mother's passage to America, if she accompanied them. The husband declared: "I will not give consent to my wife's emigration nor to a divorce, and I will not permit a division of our joint properties." A decision in the matter was required of the *Regierung* [Executive branch of the government]. It appears that, despite her husband's opposition, she was allowed to emigrate, as her name, as well as those of her sons-in-law, appear in the list of persons granted exit permits by the administration of Kreis Kammin. *Staatsarchiv Stettin. Landratsamt Kammin. Vol. II, May-Jul 1839 [Special Files on Emigration of Dissidents from Kreis Kammin to America].*

THIELE Mrs. Dorothea Maria Thiele, b HAACK, 58 years old, from Nipperwiese, Kreis Greifenhagen, wished to emigrate to America with her son Gottfried Heinrich Thiele. The husband, although willing that the wife emigrate, did not wish to do so himself. He did not believe a legal divorce to be necessary, since both were old, and he had no intention ever to remarry. In the event that his wife were granted an exit permit, and he did not decide later to follow her, he would go to live with [another] son, the schoolteacher in Bernau. In the list of 1 Jun 1843, mother and son, but not the husband, were listed as having received exit permits. Divorce was not required here, but the separation did not appear to have been a difficult one. (Regarding the necessity for a divorce, the Landrat was unclear.) *Staatsarchiv Stettin. Regierung Stettin, Abt. I, Tit. XI, Sekt. 1, Nr. 8, Vol. 4, 1839-1847 [Files on Sectarian Matters in Kreis Greifenhagen].*

REICHBERG With regard to the wife of cablemaker — Reichberg, from Zielenzig, Kreis Steinberg, who emigrated to America in 1841 with her brother,

the butcher — SCHMIDT, for clearly religious reasons, the files disclose that she was divorced from her husband. *Staatsarchiv Magdeburg. Regierung Magdeburg, Rep C 28, Polizeiregistratur, 1844 [Files on Emigration Applications of Lutheran Separatists].*

SCHMIDT A long controversy occurred in 1843 between the cabinetmaker Georg Schmidt, of Prenzlau, and his wife, Ottilie Schmidt, b BUCHHOLZ. The husband wished to emigrate for religious reasons, but the wife wished to remain in Germany, because their entire assets had been brought into the marriage by her and would be expended entirely by the trip, with the consequence that they would arrive in the new country penniless. She had no objection to her husband's emigration, because he had neglected his business and lost his customers by going to pray for days on end. Their business had been hurt, and he had assigned all the assets to her, which, she assumed, gave her the right to divorce him. Upon being informed that this was not the case, she took back her consent to his emigration and protested the exit permit, which had been issued to him in the meanwhile, until such time as he should divorce her. She stated that she was unable to tend to the business with the help of hired journeymen cabinetmakers and would have to remarry. She was then informed that she could only ask for his arrest. She refused to take this step, and her husband emigrated. However, the controversy apparently ended well, as the wife then emigrated in 1844 to rejoin her husband abroad. *Regierung Potsdam. [Files on the Intended Emigration of Old Lutheran Separatists to America, Vol. I, 1843 to end of May].*

NEUMANN — Neumann, a cottager, from Liepe, Kreis Angermuende, submitted a certificate of divorce in 1845 and was thereupon granted an exit permit. *Regierung zu Potsdam. [Files on the Intended Emigration of Old Lutheran Separatists to America], Vol. II, June 1843 to end of 1845.*

TIETZE The last of this group of cases pertains to the emigration of — Kilian in 1854. Herein, it is stated that a certain Friedrich August Tietze from Tormersdorf, wishing to emigrate to Australia, intended to divorce [his wife], and that, upon completion thereof, there was no impediment to his exit. Since he received his exit permit on 13 May 1854, it must be assumed that he received the divorce. [No explanation of any relationship to — Kilian is given.] *Regierung zu Liegnitz. Kreis Rotenburg [Files on the Emigration of Prussian Subjects and Their Naturalization in Foreign Countries], Vol. 9/10, 1853-1854.*

TETZLAFF The Pomeranian commissioners for 1836, — von Heyden and Pastor — Stricker, reported to the Oberpresidenten [higher governmental authorities] in Stettin on 14 Nov 1836 that three women and one man wished to emigrate for reasons of religious conviction. One of them was Frau — Tetzlaff, daughter of — KLUETZ and his wife — RADTKE, from Hackenwalde, Kreis Naugard, all of whom wished to emigrate. Frau Tetzlaff had married at the beginning of the year and was quite a few months pregnant. She wished to go with her parents and other relatives, but her husband would not emigrate and refused to give consent for her emigration. The young couple stated that they had married of their own accord, and it seemed clear that the government would not grant her an exit permit alone. There is no evidence that either she or her parents emigrated. Among the list of would-be emigrants prepared by von Heyden in 1836 there is the name of farmer

Johann RADTKE, from Marsdorf, whose wife, Luise RADTKE, b TETZLAFF, did not wish to emigrate (perhaps the sister of the above TETZLAFF?). Johann Radtke's name does not appear among the actual emigrants, and it is assumed that this marriage did not break up. The other woman, listed by von Heyden as wishing to emigrate, was -- HUELSBERG, from Gollnow. She, likewise, was not granted an exit permit, because her husband refused permission for her departure. [no citation given]

ZILLNER   Frau Dorothea Zillner, from Gollnow, was also refused an exist permit, even though her husband was willing to allow her emigration and gave her 100 Thaler [dollars] travel money. He wished, however, to keep two of five children. The separation of the children seems to have weighed heavily upon her, and she did not go. *Former Ministry of Spiritual and Similar Affairs. [Files on Sectarian Affairs, as well as on Separatists and Pietists and the Management of Separatist Affairs and Measures Taken Regarding Emigration], Vol. II, 1836 to August.*

HAAS   According to report number 46, from Landrat -- von Poser [of Trebnitz] on 27 May 1838, one member of a couple named -- Haas wished to emigrate (it is not clear whether husband or wife). The husband demanded custody of the minor children. Since no one of this surname appears in the Trebnitzer list of emigrants, it appears that emigration permits were denied, because of the question of the children's custody. *Staatsarchiv Breslau. Rep 14 P.A.X. 28g [Files on the Applications of Separatists for Emigration], Vol. I, 1836-1838.*

WEBER   The brewer Christian Weber, age 42, from Golzen, Kreis Zuellichau, stated that he intended to leave his wife, also a member of the brewers' guild, and his children behind, because she did not belong to his confession and would not agree to join. He was granted an exit permit for himself alone on 20 Feb 1838. *Regierung zu Frankfurt/Oder. [Files on the Applications of Individuals from Kreis Zuellichau-Schwiebus and the Granting of Exit Permits for Australia], Vol. I, 1838.*

SCHULZ   The farmer Johann Georg Schulz, age 56, from Graeditz, Kreis Zuellichau, stated in a hearing on 30 Apr 1838 as follows: "My wife Eleonore [Schulz], b. PAECH, and my son Johann Georg [Schulz], age 11, remain behind, and I have transferred ownership of my farm to her already two years ago." He received an exit permit for Australia on 26 May 1838. *Ibid.*

KNUTH   On 31 Oct 1838 the ministers [of government] von Altenstein and von Rochow reported to the government in Stettin: Doubts regarding the permissibility of granting an exit permit to former landowner -- Knuth from Schwessow, Kreis Greifenberg, without his wife, seem to have been resolved after a hearing, since the wife's means of support appears to have been assured. Nothing seems to stand in the way of his emigration; he received an exit permit in May 1839. *Former Ministry of Spiritual and Similar Affairs. [Files on Sectarian Affairs, as well as on Separatists and Pietists and the Management of Separatist Affairs and Measures Taken Regarding Emigration] Vol. II, 1836 to August.*

EHRHOFF   The shoemaker Christian Ehrhoff from Wernigerode, Bezirk Magdeburg, wished to emigrate with [Pastor] Grabau in 1839. His wife Charlotte SCHULTE refused to accompany him with their nine-month-old son. The husband stated that, when four years old, he would demand that the son be sent to him. Since the husband had provided for the wife's support, and was said to have adequate funds, he was given an exit permit on 17 Mar 1839. *Staatsarchiv Magdeburg. [Files of the Regierung zu Magdeburg on Applications for Emigration of Lutheran Separatists, 1838-1843]. Rep C 28, Polizeiregistratur.*

WOLFF   The butcher's wife, Elisabeth Wolff, b SIMON, from the Eimergasse [street name] in Erfurt, requested on 18 Jul 1839 an expedited exit permit in order to accompany a last group of emigrating Pomeranian Lutherans to Hamburg [and overseas]. She had 1000 Thaler [dollars] and would emigrate alone; her husband would remain behind in order to sell the house. The magistrate discovered that the husband had gone to Frankfurt/Main ten days previously, and that the wife intended to leave him during his absence. His permission for her emigration was not to be had for, although he was a member of the Lutheran dissidents, he had already declared to area official -- Vogel that he did not then approve of her emigration. The surname Wolff does not appear in the list of emigrants. *Staatsarchiv Magdeburg. [Consistory for Provinz Saxony Regarding the Separation of United Evangelical Congregations], Vol. IV, to December 1838.*

HOERNLEIN   Juliana Hoernlein, b. SANDER, wife of a weaver, of Erfurt, stated in 1839 during a hearing, as follows: "I am not opposed to my husband's emigration to North America, taking our two oldest children with him. I have reached an amicable agreement with him and remain behind with our youngest child, who is less than four years old." The husband was granted an exit permit on 15 Apr 1839. After the youngest child reached four years of age, Hoernlein applied to have the child accompany him [he apparently had not yet left Germany] and on 5 Jun 1839 it was decided that the matter would be heard by the court, since the mother was opposed to giving up the child. The decision of the court is unknown. *Ibid.*

PARLOW   The property owner Karl Friedrich Parlow, from Coesenthin, Kreis Wollin, was granted an exit permit on 10 May 1839 for himself alone. His wife and stepchildren were denied exit permits and had to remain behind. *Staatsarchiv Stettin. Regierung Stettin. Abt. I, Tit. XI, Sekt. 1, Nr. 8, Vol. 4 [Sectarian Matters in Kreis Greifenhagen].*

DAMEROW   The day laborer Gottfried Damerow, from Wallmow, Kreis Prenzlau, was legally separated from his wife and granted an exit permit on 7 Jun 1843 for himself alone. There were no children. *Regierung zu Potsdam. [Files on the Intended Emigration of Lutheran Separatists to America], Vol. II, June 1843 to end of 1845.*

BRENDEMUEHL   -- Brendemuehl, b. BENZ, wife of a day laborer, from Gansken-Pribbernow, Kreis Greifenberg, wished to emigrate with her children, although her husband and father were opposed thereto. Her application was denied on 7 Feb 1843. *Staatsarchiv Stettin. Regierung Stettin. Abt. I, Tit. XI, Sekt. 1, Nr. 8, Vol. 3 [Files on Sectarian Matters in Kreis Greifenberg].*

TRIPPENSEE   A most ugly case is that of tailor --
            Trippensee, from Broellin near Bruessow,
Kreis Prenzlau. On 1 Aug 1843 he sold his home and
took his wife and seven minor children to Garz in
order to begin the trip to Hamburg. In Garz his wife
became ill, refused to go further because of the tales
of inhabitants, and returned to her mother in Bruessow
with the seven children. Her husband continued the
journey taking with him all their money. The wife
was refused her former job by the estate lessee --
DUDY, and she was forced to go to the poorhouse
[*Landesarmenhaus*]. Certainly, it was an evil act for
the husband to abandon his sick wife and seven children. *Regierung zu Potsdam. [Files on the Intended
Emigration of Old Lutheran Separatists to America]
Vol. II, Jun 1843 to end of 1845.*

WARMBRUNN   A contrary case, displaying submissiveness,
            insight, and respect, is that of the family
Warmbrunn [from] Guben. Frau Luise Auguste [Warmbrunn]
b. Sagitz, wife of the journeyman clothmaker Traugott
Warmbrunn, stated in an affidavit, dated 4 Jun 1838,
that, although she did not agree with her husband's
religious views, she believed it to be her duty to
accompany him, as he wished to emigrate to Australia
with his coreligionists from the Zuellichau region.
She had tried to return to her parents in Zibelle, due
to her failing health and the tender ages of her children, but had encountered difficulties with her husband thereby. In the meanwhile her mother had died,
which made it easier for her to emigrate with her husband. Exit permits were granted for the entire family
on 8 Jun 1838. *Regierung zu Frankfurt/Oder. [Files
on the Applications of Individuals from Kreis Guben
for Emigration Permits to Australia, 1838-1856].*

WILCKE   The tailor Johann Christian Wilcke, from Mag-
         deburg, wished to emigrate in 1839 with [Pas-
tor] von Rohr. His wife stated that she wished to remain in Germany. On 5 Mar 1839 the husband was told
that he could not emigrate without his family. *Staatsarchiv Magdeburg. [Files of the Regierung zu Magdeburg
on Applications for Emigration of Lutheran Separatists,
1838-1843]. Rep C 28, Polizeiregistratur.*

TUCHEN   The basketmaker -- Tuchen, from Gommern, Bez-
         irk Magdeburg, wished to emigrate for reasons
of religion. In 1838 his wife stated in an affidavit
that she did not intend to accompany him; he could do
what he wished, but at age 63 she would not go. Herr
Tuchen was denied an exit permit, because his wife
would become a public charge without him, and he took
back his application. *Ibid.*

HILDEBRANDT   The journeyman roofer Gottlob Hildebrandt
              in Potsdam, from Bohnau near Weissenfels,
wished to emigrate with [Pastor?] Kindermann, and received his release from [Prussian] citizenship. He had
been married for seven years; his wife, Dorothea [Hil-
debrandt], b SPECK, did not belong to his faith, nor
did she wish to emigrate. She would not stand in the
way of his departure and would support herself. Since
Hildebrandt had missed his opportunity for a free passage overseas, he reported that he would give up his
emigration plan temporarily. His permit was placed in
the files. *Regierung zu Potsdam. [Files on the Intended Emigration of Old Lutheran Separatists to Amer-
ica] Vol. I, 1843 to end of May.*

KUTZER, ZANDER   -- Kutzer and -- Zander, wives of day
                 laborers, from Beauregard, Kreis Ober-
barnim, stated to the Landrat [area official] that they

did not wish to emigrate with their husbands and ur-
gently requested that exit permits not be granted to
them. On 13 May 1843, nonetheless, releases from
citizenship were granted to both men and their wives;
apparently, the husbands had convinced their wives to
accompany them. *Ibid.*

HOEFS   The carpenter -- Hoefs, from Ruebenhagen,
        Kreis Regenwalde, did not wish to emigrate,
but his wife Charlotte Dorothea [Hoefs] b. PFLUGHOEFS,
begged him daily with tears in her eyes to go. They
had had a happy marriage and three children, and he
intended to give in to his wife's wishes. Exit permits were made out on 6 Apr 1843, but, since he had
many debts and had been sentenced to six weeks in jail
for constructing a building without a permit, the exit
permits were cancelled, and he was arrested. Even
though the Landrat [area official] intervened on his
behalf--mainly because he wished to be rid of the
fanatical wife, since she would influence many others
to emigrate--the government refused to grant exit permits. *Staatsarchiv Stettin. Regierung Stettin. Abt. I,
Tit. XI, Sekt. 1, Nr. 8, Vol. 4? Kreis Regenwalde,
1828-1847.*

THIELE, SCHULZ,   Further examples of marital sep-
MUELLER, LUSCHUETZ   arations caused by emigration are
                    the following cases:
Laborer Gottfried Heinrich THIELE, from Nipperwiese,
remained in Germany, while his wife emigrated in 1843
[with their children].
The wife of Gottlieb SCHULZ, from Kleinow, Kreis Prenzlau, remained in Germany, when her husband emigrated in
1846.
The wife of Gottlieb MUELLER, from Berndorf, Kreis
Liegnitz, remained in Germany, when her husband emigrated in 1848.
The wife of -- LUSCHUETZ, from Reichwalde, Kreis
Rothenburg, Silesia, remained in Germany, when her
husband emigrated in 1854, and was happy to be rid of
him, as he had neglected his family.
None of the above persons remaining in Germany had any
objections to the emigration of their marriage part-
ners. *[No citations given.]*

GROTTKE   The cottager Karl Grottke, from Polnisch-
          Hammer, Kreis Trebnitz, with his son Karl,
was granted an exit permit in 1839. His wife Christiane Dorothea [Grottke] b. STOBER, stated that she
would remain behind for the time being but would rejoin them later. *Staatsarchiv Breslau. Rep 14 P.A.X.
28g [Files on Applications for the Emigration of Sep-
aratists] Vol. II, 1839-1845.*

GROBENGIESSER   Frau -- Grobengiesser, b. RIBCKE, from
                Bruessow, age 67, was granted an exit
permit with her two daughters, age 26 and 24, with the
agreement of the husband and father, on 7 Jun 1843, to
go to America. The husband, Johann Justus Grobengiesser, age 56, was to remain in Germany only until he had
straightened out the affairs of his son, liable to military service, and a third daughter. The son's military obligation was dissolved by an appeal to the Minister of War. On 29 Jun [1843] he and the son were
granted special exit permits, so that they probably
accompanied the wife and two daughters. [Nothing is
said about the third daughter's case.] *Regierung zu
Potsdam. [Files on the Intended Emigration of Old Lutheran Separatists to America] Vol. II, Jun 1843 to
end of 1845.*

WEGNER   A similar case was that of -- Wegner, from
         Falkenwalde, Kreis Prenzlau. The wife Chris-
tiane was granted a release from citizenship for herself and four children on 12 Jun 1843 after the husband gave his permission [for her to emigrate]. He
remained behind to attend to the affairs of his son
who was subject to military service. This matter was
speedily resolved, as in the Grobengiesser case above,
so that it is unlikely that there was a long separation of the family. *Ibid.*

BORCHARDT   Similar to the Wolff case, *supra*, in which
            the wife wished to leave her husband sur-
reptitiously, there was a parallel case in 1846. The
second wife of farmer Johann Joachim Borchardt, from
Rothenfier, Kreis Naugard, absconded with 400 Thaler
[dollars] and, he stated, sneaked away to America
without a passport. Since he could not bear to be
separated from her, he applied for a release from citizenship for himself and a son of his first marriage,
age 17-1/2 years. On 28 May 1846 he was told that his
release would be granted as soon as he had settled his
affairs with three other children of his first marriage and had been released from his duties as guardian
of his brother's children. It is probable that he was
able to settle these matters, since he had a farm
worth 4000 Thalers. *Staatsarchiv Stettin. Landratsamt Naugard. [Special Files on Applications for Emigration Permits to North America for Members of Lutheran Separatism, 1842-1846].*

GRAEBE   The master cablemaker Ernst Graebe, from Wer-
         nigerode, Bezirk Magdeburg, emigrated to
America in 1837 with his oldest son and settled in
Pittsburgh. In 1839 he returned to Germany to get his
wife and four other children, who had been left behind.
Although he had not settled in [Pastor] Grabau's American colony, he had emigrated for reasons of religious
conviction and was shown in the German records as a
Lutheran separatist. *Staatsarchiv Magdeburg. [Files
of Regierung Magdeburg on Applications for Exit Permits from Lutheran Separatists, 1838-1843]. Rep. C 28
Polizeiregistratur.*

SALINGRE   A particularly interesting case is that of
           farmer Johann Salingre, from Bergholz,
Kreis Prenzlau. He was allowed to emigrate in 1843
after having been legally separated from his wife.
In 1844 he returned [to Prussia] to get his former
wife, Frau [-- Salingre], b. Hourtienne. Buechsel,
in his memoirs, at page 169, writes as follows regarding this case:
"The farmer Salingre and his had lived peacably together. Their farm was successful. The husband
was examined by -- Ehrenstroem very carefully, because Salingre was rich. The wife, although extremely pious, had been unable to agree to emigrate
and had remained in Germany. She had no peace, however, and ate her bread in tears; nor could the husband in America forget his wife. Day and night he
felt pangs of guilt for having left her. On a Sun-
day evening after the wife had already gone to bed,
there was a knock on the window. She asked who it
was and recognized her husband's voice. A noble
discussion took place: the wife wished to return to
America with him; the husband, on the other hand,
was willing to remain in Germany, if she found it
impossible to part with her parent's estate.
Shortly thereafter, they sold everything, and the
wife received an exit permit on 27 Mar 1844. They
returned to America reunited." *Regierung zu Potsdam. [Files on the Intended Emigration of Old*

*Lutheran Separatists to America] Vol. II, Jun 1843 to
1845.*

MOLL   A Lutheran Separatist journeyman carpenter, --
       Moll, from Mewegen, Kreis Randow, Pomerania,
emigrated to America in 1843 leaving his wife and family behind. He returned for them in 1846. [His case
is significant and is reported in some detail as follows in Volume I of Iwan's study.]

A certain -- Moll, from Boock parish, Mewegen, Kreis
Randow, Pomerania, returned from America in the fall
of 1845 to get his wife and children. He had emigrated first in 1843 and is the only person from Kreis
Randow for whom we have the name, because the Kreis
files for 1843 are missing. The lucky receipt of the
files for 1846 makes it possible to obtain insight into the emigration of that year, in which Moll played
the most important role. Despite the progressively
more successful steps to mitigate the religious motivation for emigration, it is interesting to note here
the purely religious character of the Randow emigration. The first authorities to report Moll's agitation for emigration among Evangelical parishioners
were a local pastor, -- Harmisch of Boock and Superintendent -- Oelgarte in Loecknitz (both Kreis Randow),
both of whom made reports to the Consistory. Quoting
the Superintendent's report of 2 Jan 1846 to the Consistory it is to be seen quite clearly how a smoulder-
ing spark could be fanned into a renewed flame spread-
ing all around, as in the first years of emigration:
"Several weeks ago, journeyman carpenter -- Moll,
a Lutheran Separatist of Boock Parish, Mewegen, returned from North America, where he had emigrated
three years ago. He stated that he had come for
the purpose of getting his family to return with
him to America. His visit to Mewegen, his tales of
conditions in America, the letters he brought with
him from overseas, his oral and written arguments
against the State Church, were all meant to reach
the attention of dissidents living in the neighborhood. It must be that this man intentionally is
trying to stir people up once again. He goes
around to all the villages on Sundays and holidays
calling forth the people of his persuasion to gather
round him, and seeks to incite persons of means to
emigrate, thereby causing divisions within families.
His efforts apparently are not without some success,
for he has persuaded some dissidents to go. A particular theater for his activities appears to be in
my two branch congregations in Ploewen (Kreis Randow) and Bergholz (Kreis Prenzlau). Since he came,
the Lutheran dissidents have moved to Mewegen or to
one of the branches in order to make their defiance
known, arm in arm. I do not yet know whether he has
been able to make new proselytes for his sect. In
the event that he is allowed to continue, proselytes
are to be expected, however. How far the worldly
authorities should allow such agitation, I shall
leave to them to decide. As for me, I believe it my
duty to the Church to counteract his growing influence. If he cannot be forced to leave the Prussian
State immediately, I suggest that the Consistory
undertake the following:
1. To prohibit Moll from leaving his immediate
   place of temporary residence;
2. To prohibit him from meeting for worship with
   dissidents outside Mewegen.
Moll, being now a foreigner, and matters of religious conscience not being at stake since Lutheran
dissidents are not allowed to go from village to
village for the purpose of worship, I request that
the appropriate measures be undertaken."

Pastor Harmisch clearly stated that Moll alternately held cult meetings in his, or rather his wife's, house, and in Boock and Bergholz. These meetings were attended not only by long-time Separatists, but also by 17 to 20 new families, and that all of the participants intended to emigrate to America. These people gave the greatest credence to Moll, who preached that the State Church was wrong, and that no one would go to Heaven who remained in it.

The Consistory transmitted this report to the government, which passed it along to Landrat -- von Puttkamer for consideration. His reports of 30 Jan 1846 and 16 Feb 1846 are important in several respects.[1] With regard to Moll's activities, the truthfulness of the pastors was affirmed, and Puttkamer gave orders that Moll be warned regarding illegal incitement to emigration and forbidden religious services. There is nothing to show that there were any proceedings against him, however. After the General Concession [made by the government to the Separatists] there would have been no grounds for prosecution, excepting for the event of an order of the government against private religious services of Separatists. [Puttkamer] found it understandable that America, with its civil and religious freedom, would be very attractive to dissidents; he stated prophetically that the United States would draw many immigrants and their money from Germany in the future; that it was fortunate that such a country was on the other side of the ocean; and that it would also be attractive to Germans who were not religious fanatics, as were the Lutherans. He reported that 30 Lutherans had already applied for their exit permits and that another 100 applications were anticipated. He thought probable that all the Lutherans of the region would then be gone. Puttkamer warned that action against Moll should be cautious, because the latter had a passport from the United States, and that any action against him might have international repercussions. In the meanwhile, by the end of March no less than 123 applications for release from citizenship had been received in Kreis Randow.

The movement had also spread to Kreis Uckermuende, where Moll had influence through his brother Karl. As a consequence, Moll was forced to leave the country precipitously and without terminating his affairs. He went to Hamburg, probably to make arrangements for passage overseas, but complained to the American chargé d'affaires and applied to [the Prussian government] to make a short return to Mewegen to complete his business there. As a consequence, the Prussian Ministry of Foreign Affairs requested a further report from the authorities in Stettin. These authorities reported that Moll's application was to be denied, because his affairs could be completed by his brother Karl, who was also to emigrate. They also let it be known that, if Moll were to be found again within their jurisdiction, they would banish him over the borders of the province. The Ministry of Foreign Affairs expressed itself as being in accord with the Stettin authorities. But Moll had already completed his labors. On the fifth, twelfth, and 28th of March [1846] 123 persons from Kreis Randow were granted releases from citizenship. Everyone of them stated that they were leaving for reasons of religious conviction. Two other governmental lists[2] give totals of 119 and 96 respectively for the Randow religious emigrants. One no longer was so concerned with the exact number of emigrants.

Files from Kreis Uckermuende are missing. From the Kreis Randow files, we learn that the villages of

Ziegenort, Althagen, and Warlang (where Karl Moll lived) were affected with the emigration idea, and that two persons in Althagen wavered in their resolve. Since the general reports of the Stettin government and those of the Oberpraesident contain no mention of emigration from Kreis Uckermuende, it seems probable that none took place from this Kreis.[2]

On the other hand, the great emigration of 1846 from the Mark [Pomerania] was a consequence of Moll's activities. According to Superintend Oelgarte's report, Moll was influential over the Pomeranian border as far as Bergholz, which had been a wellknown source of emigrants in previous years. Two files of the Potsdam Regierung [government] are entitled "Regarding the Emigration of Old Lutheran Separatists to America."[3] Although only two families are specifically identified as Old Lutherans, the title to the files are good evidence of the status of persons listed therein. Only three families, composed of 19 persons, are labeled as Evangelical [State Church] or Not Separatist, so that of 277 emigrants from the Mark [Pomerania] a total of 258 remain as Separatists, five of whom went to Australia and 253 to the United States. For 17 of these persons Texas was given as the immediate destination; for the remainder only the destination "North America" or "America" is given; only once Wisconsin and Milwaukee.

1. *Staatsarchiv Stettin. Regierung Stettin. Abt. I, Tit. XI, Sekt. 1, Nr. 8, Vol. 3 [Conventicle (Sectarian) Affairs in Kreis Randow, 1846-1849].*
2. *Staatsarchiv Stettin. Regierung Stettin. Acc.1911, Nr. 156 [General Files on Conventicle Affairs] Vol. III, 1843-1847;* also *Staatsarchiv Stettin. [Files of the Royal Higher Presidency for Pomerania Including Summaries of Emigration from Pomerania] Vol. I, 1844-1847; Vol. II, 1847-1855.*
3. *Regierung zu Potsdam. [Files on Emigration from the Prussian States and the Granting of Certificates of Citizenship], 1840-1848.*

ANTON   Cottager -- Anton, from Reichwalde, Kreis Rothenburg, Silesia, emigrated in 1854 leaving his wife behind. He expected to return for her later. *Regierung zu Liegnitz. [Files on the Emigration of Prussian Subjects and Their Naturalization in Foreign Countries] Kreis Rothenburg, Vol. 9-10, 1853-1854.*

EMIGRATION DIFFICULTIES CAUSED BY THE LEGAL GUARDIANSHIPS OF CHILDREN

In accordance with the law, persons under the care of guardians were not allowed to emigrate without the express permission of the *Vormundschaftsbehoerden* [Guardianship Authorities]. And, since there were a great many such cases among the Old Lutheran emigrants, these Authorities often played a crucial part in the emigration proceedings. Indeed, guardianship problems, often not clearly recognized in advance by the would-be emigrants, were among the most serious hindrances, particularly since the government, being very negative toward emigration itself, insisted upon carrying out the regulations precisely. A particular complication of the Old Lutheran emigration was the fact that governmental authorities considered all children born of marriages celebrated outside the State Church as being illegitimate and, therefore, as being in need of guardians. However, no cases are found in which the government actually proceeded to the logical legal conclusion in emigration cases. In 1841, for example, millowner

KLAR,
KRAUSE,
WALK

-- Klar from Deutsch-Kassel, was given an exit permit without difficulties together with his "illegal" wife and a daughter of their marriage; the same occurred in the case of cottager Gottfried Krause, from Sawade, with his "illegal" wife and the two children of their marriage. In the case of farmer's son Christian Walk, from Wallmow, who had been married by an Old Lutheran minister, the wife was called a "concubine;" but even in this case there was no hesitancy in allowing the children of the "concubinage" to emigrate without requiring that the Guardianship Authorities give their consent to the exit permits.

There were many cases in which the Guardianship Authorities gave permission for the emigration of their wards; but there were also many cases in which the Authorities made difficulties. Such cases could only be resolved by granting or denying emigration permits. In the event of a denial, there were three possibilities: The guardians, being unable to make further provision for their ward, remained in Germany; or the ward emigrated with his guardians without having legal permission to do so, as occasionally happened. In these two cases, there occurred no separation of the family. The third possibility was to leave the ward behind in Germany, after providing for his care. There are numerous cases of parents who did this; but there are also many cases where the children emigrated later after the guardianship had been dissolved. Denial of exit permits to stepchildren, a frequent case before the Guardianship Authorities, caused a number of anomalies. Emigration without permit, flight, or falsification of the children's papers, as will be seen in cases set forth hereinafter, also occurred. The Guardianship Authorities justified their denial of exit permits to wards on the following grounds:
1. The Authorities did not wish to expose the ward to possible death in foreign countries;
2. There was insufficient reason for emigration;
3. It would be impossible to settle the ward's estate and make the guardian accountable in the event that the ward were to die during the trip to, or in, America (Justizamt Gramzow, Kreis Angermuende). *Regierung zu Potsdam. [Files on the Intended Emigration of Old Lutheran Separatists to America] Vol. II, June 1843 to End of 1845.*

PAECH   Governmental officials told farmer Johann Georg Paech, from Kay, Kreis Zuellichau, that he must have the permission of the Guardianship Authorities in order for the children of his first marriage to be given exit permits to emigrate to Australia in 1838. The *Patrimonialgericht* [domestic affairs court] for Kay declared that Paech did not need such permission. His oldest son, having military difficulties, remained behind, as will be related in the section on military cases. *Regierung Frankfurt/Oder. [Files on the Applications of Individuals from Kreis Zuellichau Schwiebus for Exit Permits to Australia] Vol. I, 1838.*

HOFMEISTER,   In the case of master butcher Johann
KANT   David Hofmeister, from Hakenwalde, Kreis Naugard, the Pomeranian Commission for 1836 under von Heyden determined that, due to the decision of the Guardianship Court regarding the four Kant stepchildren from Frau Hofmeister's first marriage, exit permits were denied. As a consequence of this decision, Hofmeister had had temporarily to abandon his intention to accompany the large Pomeranian emigration group of 1839. In 1843 he again sought to emigrate, but the *Land- und Stadtgericht* [provincial

and city court] in Gollnow again denied permission for the settling of the children's estate and for exit permits. The court held itself duty-bound to oppose the emigration of its wards on the grounds that everyone could practice the religion of his or her choice in Germany and could have a good income, whereas one had heard evil things of America. Hofmeister did not give up, however. Together with others, he applied directly to the King for relief. The Minister of the Interior replied by instructing the court in Gollnow to grant permission for all the stepchildren to emigrate, with the exception of the oldest stepson Johann Friedrich Kant, who was in military service. Later, in 1843, Hofmeister wrote from America encouraging this stepson to follow them, as he would like it in America and could practice his trade (more on this matter is given among the military cases, *infra*). *Staatsarchiv Stettin. Regierung Stettin, Abt. I, Tit. XI, Sekt. 1, Kreis Naugard [Files on Conventicle (Sectarian) Affairs].*

HEPNER,   A similar case is that of carpenter Heinrich
DICKON   Hepner, from Freistadt, Silesia. Hepner had put off his emigration to Australia until 1844, because the Silesian Commissioner for 1836, *Regierungsrat* [Councillor of Government] Naumann, said he must have the permission of the Guardianship Authorities and the court for his stepdaughter -- Dickon to emigrate. Hepner, his wife, and stepdaughter were given exit permits in 1844. *Regierung zu Potsdam. [Files of the Commission of Regierungsrat Naumann on the Emigration of a Number of Separatists from the Kreisen of Liegnitz, Gruenberg, Freistadt, Sagan, and Sprottau, 1836].*

WEIMANN   The journeyman mason -- Weimann, from Schoenborn, Kreis Zuellichau, was refused permission by the Guardianship Authorities for his two stepsons to accompany him to Australia on the grounds that there was not the slightest grounds for emigration. Weimann appealed to the *Obervormundschaftsgericht* [appellate court for guardianship matters] which granted permission on 25 May 1838, and the family was able to remain united. *Regierung Frankfurt/Oder. [Files on the Applications of Individuals from Kreis Zuellichau and the Granting of Permission to Emigrate to Australia, March-May 1836].*

KLUGE   A case to the contrary is that of the widowed day laborer -- Kluge, from Nickern, Kreis Zuellichau. She wished to emigrate without her two children, aged 19 and 15 years. The guardian gave permission [for the children to leave], but the Guardianship Authorities would give no consent thereto. Her exit permit and passport, already filled out, could not be given to her on 10 May 1838, because she had not made arrangements for the support and care of the children. It is unknown whether she was able to do this; if not, she could not have emigrated. *Ibid.*

TRAPPE,   Another kind of proceeding occurred in the
KRAUSE   case of the shepherd August Friedrich Samuel Trappe, from Wartlow, Kreis Wollin. His stepdaughter Karoline Maria Krause was not granted permission to emigrate by the Guardianship Authorities. Since she was 22 years old, she was declared an adult by the *Patrimonialgericht* [domestic affairs court], giving her the right to dispose of her inheritance and make her own decisions. She was granted an exit permit on 10 Jun 1839 and emigrated with her parents. *Staatsarchiv Stettin. Regierung Stettin. Abt.I, Tit. XI, Sekt.1, Nr.8, Vol.IV [Files on Conventicle Affairs in Kreis Wollin].*

FETTCKENHAUER, A long drawn-out case and controversy
FETGENHAUER, with the Guardianship Authorities oc-
FETTCHENHAUER, curred with regard to the emigration
BRAASCH of the widow — Fettckenhauer (also
Fetgenhauer or Fettchenhauer among
other spellings), b. Braasch, from Neu-Massow, Kreis
Naugard, daughter of the late policeman Christian
Friedrich Braasch. She wished to emigrate with her
four children accompanying her uncles Karl Friedrich
Braasch and Joachim Georg Braasch. The children's
guardian, Sergeant — Beling, and the *Patrimonialgericht* [domestic affairs court] in Jakobshagen refused
permission, since there was no assurance that the
wards would be successful abroad. Only after the
court learned that the mother would be left without
support, if her uncles emigrated, and had received
the assurance of Georg Braasch that the children would
be supported abroad and that they would be returned to
Pomerania, if they did not like it abroad, was the
court's permission given. Frau Fettgenhauer and her
children received their releases from citizenship on
20 Jun 1843.

One of the uncles, Karl Braasch, emigrated to America in 1843 and, according to a letter from Hofmeister,
settled in Wisconsin. A letter from Jaeger states that
Braasch settled next to him at Watertown. The other
uncle, Georg Braasch, who had assured the court that
the children of his niece would be supported abroad,
had to delay his departure, because of other difficulties, and had his exit permit extended until 1844.
However, he was not able to emigrate in 1844 either,
as he was involved in a court case over money with his
own children remaining in Germany. At last in 1846 it
was possible for Georg Braasch to emigrate, requiring
the issuance of new releases from citizenship for him
and for his niece — Fettgenhauer. *Staatsarchiv Stettin. Regierung Stettin. Abt.I, Tit.XI, Sekt.1 [Conven-
ticle Affairs in Kreis Naugard].*

BLIESENER, The stepson of landowner — Bliesener,
RABENHORST the minor Johann Gottlieb Rabenhorst,
from Fanger, Kreis Naugard, wished to
emigrate with his mother and stepfather. The child
received the permission of the Guardianship Court, but
the royal *Pupillengericht* [court for students] refused
to give the mother or stepfather the 100 Thaler [dol-
lars] estate under the court's supervision. Rabenhorst
preferred to give up the money, rather than remain in
Germany. On 12 May 1843 a release from citizenship
was forwarded to him. *Ibid.*

NICOLAUS The landowner — Nicolaus, from Gansken-
Pribbernow, Kreis Greifenberg, had difficulties when he sought to have his daughter from his
first marriage, Hanna Wilhelmine Nicolaus, aged 11
years, emigrate with him. The policeman — Voigt,
her guardian, protested the emigration of his ward
and the payment of her estate. On 30 May 1843 a release from citizenship for the child was granted, however. *Staatsarchiv Stettin. Regierung Stettin. Abt.I,
Tit.XI, Sekt.1, Nr.8, Vol.3 [Files on Conventicle Affairs in Kreis Greifenberg, 1839-1847].*

ZIMDAR, In the case of farmer Johann David Zimdar,
REIMERS from Wisbu bei Greifenberg, also came to a
happy ending. The marital relationship had
to be clarified, because governmental information and
a christening certificate showed a legitimate daughter
of 18 years, an illegitimate one of 15 years, and then
again legitimate children of 14 years and under. It
was shown that the 18-year-old daughter was a child

of Zimdar's first marriage, and that the 15-year-old
daughter was a child born to Zimdar and his second
wife, born Reimers, before their marriage. Therefore, this child was christened under the surname
Reimers. The remaining children, christened Zimdar,
were also by his second wife, born Reimers. After
making this clarification, and after the illegitimate
daughter, Dorothea Reimers, had been given a permission to emigrate by the Guardianship Court, the entire
family was granted their release from citizenship on
23 Jun 1843. *Staatsarchiv Stettin. Regierung Stettin.
Abt.I, Tit.XI, Sekt.1, Nr.8, Vol.3 [Files on Conventicle Affairs in Kreis Regenwalde].*

HOFMEISTER, Widow — Hofmeister, from Meichow, Kreis
ROSSOW Angermuende, 58 years old, already had
her oldest son, cabinetmaker Christian
Friedrich Hofmeister, age 30, and her oldest daughter
Marie, age 29, wife of the tailor — Rossow, and her
two youngest sisters [names not given] in America
since 1844. In 1845 she wished herself to emigrate
accompanied by two unmarried daughters, aged 23 and
20 years. The Guardianship Authorities denied permission, using all three reasons mentioned at the beginning of this section. As a consequence, the widow
Hofmeister made a direct appeal to the King on 12 May
1845, asking that her children be allowed to emigrate.
Whereupon, releases from citizenship were granted to
the daughters but not to her, even though she had applied for it. The mix-up was corrected and all were
allowed to leave together. Whether widow Hofmeister
was a relative of the butcher Hofmeister, from Hakenwalde, who emigrated in 1843 could not be determined.
*Regierung zu Potsdam. [Files on the Intended Emigra-
tion of Old Lutheran Separatists to America] Vol.II,
Jun 1843 to the end of 1845.*

GRUENIG, The widow — Gruenig, from Zoelling, Kreis
HOEPPNER Sprottau, wished to emigrate with her two
daughters. The daughters' guardian, gardener Johann Friedrich Hoeppner, from Zoelling, who
also wished to emigrate, declared himself willing to
continue his guardianship in America. The court in
Zoelling requested of the Landrat that permits be
denied, since the wards would be endangered by the
trip, and because there was not enough money for their
support. The Commissioner for 1836 came to the same
conclusion, and these persons are not to be found in
the lists of emigrants. *Regierung zu Liegnitz. [Files
of Regierungsrat Naumann's Commission Regarding the
Emigration of Numerous Separatists from the Kreisen
of Liegnitz, Gruenberg, Freistadt, Sagan, and Sprottau, 1836].*

PLATTNER, The journeyman shoemaker — Plattner, from
HANTSCHKE Breslau, wished to emigrate in 1838 with
master [shoemaker] — Hantschke. He received his mother's permission and that of his guardian [unnamed], but was required also to get the permission of the Guardianship Authorities. On 28 Oct 1838
the Breslau police president noted that Plattner had
not presented this permission, nor did he have suffi-
cient funds for the trip. The 1839 exit permit for
Hantschke does not list Plattner, and it is assumed
that he remained behind. *Staatsarchiv Breslau. Rep.
14 P.A.X. 28g [Files on Emigration Applications from
Separatists] Vol.I, 1836-1838.*

HEINRICH The intended emigration of Johann Friedrich
Heinrich, 20 years old, gardener's son,
from Wendstadt, Kreis Guthrau, was opposed by his
widowed mother, the Guardianship Authorities, and the

Landrat. Nothing came of his plan, nor would it have been possible, even if the Guthrau-Schabenau emigration of 1839 had taken place, which it did not. [There is a possibility that Heinrich emigrated later, however.] *Ibid.*

HERRLING   Clearly, motives of welfare were important to the Guardianship Authorities, as was their general opposition to the emigration of Separatists. An example is the case of the orphan Maria Herrling, 18 years old. Her guardian and the Guardianship Authorities both opposed her emigration, because both her hands were crippled, and she would have had an uncertain future, if she had emigrated. *Staatsarchiv Magdeburg. Consistory for Provinz Sachsen. [Files on the Dissolution of united Evangelical (State Church) Congregations] Vol.IV, 1838 to December.*

BONDICK   Among the Saxon Lutherans who wished to emigrate with [Pastor] Grabau was the family of linen weaver Ernst Bondick, from Wedringen, Kreis Neuhaldensleben. His four stepchildren needed the permission of the Guardianship Authorities, but it does not appear from the file that they were able to obtain it. The entire family appears to have remained in Germany. *Staatsarchiv Magdeburg. Regierung zu Magdeburg. [Files on Applications of Lutheran Separatists for Exit Permits, 1838-1843] Rep. C28 Polizeiregistratur.*

GELLERT,   An attitude of particularly concerned welfare was taken by the royal Justice Chamber in Schwedt in the case of Anna Sophie Gellert, stepdaughter of shoemaker Franz August Thiede, from Nipperwiese, Kreis Greifenhagen. The judges refused to permit her emigration in 1843 stating that the reasons given for emigration were insufficient to undertake such an adventure. It was not clear that the ward would be happier in America than in Germany, since her ward was poor and would be exposed to penury. The ward should give up her plan, remain at home, industrious and content with her situation in life. She did not need to try her luck abroad and in such a dangerous manner, which would completely exhaust her small estate. As a consequence, none of the Thiede family was able to emigrate. *Staatsarchiv Stettin. Regierung zu Stettin. Abt.I, Tit.XI, Nr.8, Vol.4 [Files on Conventicle Affairs in Kreis Greifenhagen].*

HARTWIG,   An unusual case is that of the laborer --
LUEDEMANN   Hartwig, from Wallmow. He wished to emigrate in 1843 taking with him his stepson Friedrich Luedemann, 11 years old. Hartwig was refused the permission of the Guardianship Authorities, and the judge went so far as to order the child to be taken away from the stepfather and given to his legal guardian, the hired hand -- Luedemann in Trampe. Instead, the child was spirited away and hidden. Hartwig was then arrested and told that he would remain so until the child was returned. The child was then delivered up to the court; Hartwig was released but warned not to emigrate without the court's permission. Hartwig was then forced to work in a road gang and did not receive an exit permit. *Regierung zu Potsdam. [Files on the Intended Emigration of Old Lutheran Separatists to America] Vol.II, Jun 1843 to end of 1845.*

WALTER,   Georg Ferdinand Walter, from Reichenau, Kreis
SEUL   Sagan, applied for emigration but took it back upon the advice of Commissioner Naumann. He renewed the application in 1839. When the family emigrated, they took with them a stepson -- Seul for whom no permission had been obtained from the Guardianship Authorities and, consequently, was without an exit permit. Walter then asked [from abroad] his brother-in-law, the farmer Samuel Hoffmann, to request these papers [from the government]. Whether Hoffmann was able to obtain them is unknown. *Staatsarchiv Breslau. Regierung zu Liegnitz. [Files on Emigration, Etc., from Kreis Sagan] Vol.I, 1836-1842.*

PAGE,   The wheelwright Daniel Page and the cot-
GRAF,   tager Johann Friedrich Graf, from Fiddi-
HOEPNER,   chow, Kreis Greifenhagen, went to great
LOEPERICK efforts in 1843 to take their stepchildren, -- Hoepner and -- Loeperick with them. The Justice Chamber in Schwedt opposed the emigration of the wards. Graff explained the urgency of the situation, inasmuch as he had sold everything and had rented a barge for their transportation [to Hamburg] and said that he would take his stepchildren [Loeperick] without permits, if necessary. The Magistrate noted that Page's two stepchildren, -- Hoepner, being 19 and 16 years old and having funds of their own, probably could take care of themselves, if necessary. Nonetheless, there appears to have been no exit permits issued for these families, even though they had threatened to leave without permits, if this became necessary. *Staatsarchiv Stettin. Regierung zu Stettin. Abt.I, Tit. XI, Nr.8, Vol.4 [Files on Conventicle Affairs in Kreis Greifenhagen].*

WENDT   It should be noted here that in the year 1843 nineteen wards of the Guardianship Authorities were detained at Havelberg, as they sought to reach Hamburg for the purpose of emigration. These wards slipped away and emigrated, nonetheless. A court case was started against them, and the wards submitted from America applications for pardon to the King. At the time of examining the legitimate and illegitimate emigrants at Havelberg, it also occurred that a ten-year-old boy, Wilhelm Wendt, from Wallmow, disappeared entirely, despite diligent search and a public inquiry in Hamburg. In 1848 his name stands first on the list of those who appealed to the King from America. *Regierung zu Potsdam. [Files on the Intended Emigration of Old Lutheran Separatists to America] Vol.II, June 1843 to end of 1845; Vol.III, 1846-1851.*

FIEDLER,   During the first large wave of emigration
TEUSLER   to Australia, forester -- Fiedler, from Klemzig, had difficulties regarding two children of his wife, the widow of Teusler. In his 1836 appeal to the King, he complained that the police had taken the children by force and given them to relatives, where they would not be raised in the fear of the Lord. Their mother mourned their loss continually. In 1838, as the Fiedler family sought to emigrate, the stepchildren's grandfather, businessman -- Teusler, who had been named their guardian, opposed the departure of the children, Bertha Mathilde Teusler and Karl Emil Teusler. From Fiedler's subsequent letters from Australia, it is clear that Bertha accompanied her mother and stepfather, but that Karl Emil did not. Fiedler, in a letter to his brother-in-law -- Koehler asked that the latter do everything possible to help the boy, and Bertha wrote begging that her brother be sent to join them. Emil's name does not appear in any of the lists of emigrants, and it is assumed he never was able to rejoin his family. *Former Ministry for Spiritual and Similar Affairs. [Files on Sectarian and Conventicle Matters, as well as on Separatists and Pietists . . . and Measures to Control the*

Intended Emigration of Separatists] Vol.II, 1835-1836 to August; also see Landeskirche. [Files of the Prittag Congregation, Kreis Gruenberg, Regarding the Lutheran Separation in the Parish]; also see Regierung Frankfurt/Oder. [Files on the Applications of Individuals from Kreis Zuellichau Schwiebus for Emigration to Australia].

LUBASCH   Gottfried Lubasch, from Rissen, Kreis Zuellichau, wished to have his two daughters of his first marriage emigrate with him to Australia. The girls' guardian, court official Samuel Vetter, was agreeable, but not the oldest daughter Johanna Luise Lubasch, age 18. She declared that she did not wish to emigrate, and her guardian was likewise agreeable that she remain in Germany. Exit permits for the Lubasch family did not include her name. *Regierung zu Frankfurt/Oder. [Files on the Applications of Individuals from Kreis Zuellichau Schwiebus for Emigration to Australia].*

KRUEGER,   The lessee of land, Johann Georg Krueger,
RIEMER   from Pribbernow bei Stepenitz, Kreis Kammin, was granted exit permits for himself, his wife -- Krueger, widow of Riemer, born Baehn, and two of their children, but was required to make adequate provision for the support of a stepson, Johann Karl Friedrich Wilhelm Riemer, who was remaining in Germany. This stepson was learning to be a cabinetmaker in Wollin, and the wife's sister (his aunt) became his guardian. *Staatsarchiv Stettin. Regierung Stettin. Abt.I, Tit.XI, Sekt.1, Nr.8, Kreis Kammin.*

SCHWEFEL, Ernst Wilhelm Schwefel, from Neukietz,
KOCH   Kreis Oberbarnim, wished to have two of his wife's children by her first marriage, Friedrich Koch and Maria Koch, emigrate with them in 1843. The Guardianship Authorities protested against the plan. Schwefel then proposed that Pastor Kindermann [an emigrating minister] be made their guardian, or that their inheritance from their father be left behind. The latter alternative was chosen. Schwefel was granted exit permits for himself, his wife, and their own children, but the Koch stepchildren remained behind in Germany. *Regierung zu Potsdam. [Files on the Intended Emigration of Old Lutheran Separatists to America] Vol.I, 1843 to end of May.*

SCHULZE,   The emigration of the -- Schulze family,
ALBERTS   including the children of the marriage, was permitted after the support of Frau Schulze's sister's daughter, Luise Alberts, had been provided for. Luise Alberts then emigrated in 1848 to rejoin the family. *Regierung zu Potsdam. [Files on the Intended Emigration of Old Lutheran Separatists to America] Vol.II, Jun 1843 to end of 1845.*

HENSCHEL   When shoemaker Gottlieb Henschel, from Wuschewire, Kreis Oberbarnim, sought to emigrate in 1844, he was told that his stepson, then in the provincial poorhouse in Strausberg, would be unable to accompany him. *Ibid.*

WESENICK   The stepchildren of the tailor -- Wesenick, from Meichow, Kreis Angermuende, were required to remain behind in 1845, when their mother emigrated. *Ibid.*

SCHMIDT   The master butcher Johann Georg Schmidt, from Gruenberg, wished to take a son with him to Australia and made provision for two other children who were to remain in Germany. However,

Schmidt's name does not appear among the emigrants of 1838 to Australia and it appears that nothing came of his plan. *Regierung zu Liegnitz. [Files of the Naumann Commission on the Emigration of Numerous Separatists from the Kreisen of Liegnitz, Gruenberg, Freistadt, Sagan, and Sprottau, 1836].*

KLOSE   Similarly, in the case of Christian Klose, from Cosel, Kreis Sagan, the father and mother disagreed. The mother did not want the son to emigrate, but the father gave his permission after the fanatical farmer -- Gierach declared that the son no longer belonged to the mother, but to the new congregation. However, Christian Klose's name does not appear in the lists of emigrants. *Ibid.*

GANDT,   Landrat von Voeltz, from Kreis Kammin, re-
CHRISTIAN ported to Oberpraesident von Bonin on 20 May 1837 that during the year four children had been among those emigrating without exit permits. The were as follows: The servant girl Luise Gandt, from Kammin, whose father had not made up his mind regarding her emigration and, from correspondence, was known to be in America. Three young people of the Christian family, from Schmatow, Kreis Kammin, had left without their father's permission. They were journeyman tailor Gottlieb Christian, age 28; servant girl Wilhelmine Christian, age 23; and Karoline Christian, age 21. They may have gone to Australia, as their names are not found in the lists of emigrants to America. *Former Ministry of Spiritual and Similar Affairs. [General Files on Sectarian and Conventicle Matters . . . and the Intended Emigration of Separatists and Measures Thereon] Vol.III, Aug 1836-May 1837; Vol.IV, Jun 1837-Oct 1837.*

SCHULZ,   The widow -- Schulz, born Schmidt, from
SCHMIDT   Schoenborn, wished to have her brother's daughter, Anna Dorothea Schmidt, 18 years, accompany her to Australia in 1838. The girl's father refused permission in February, but then gave permission in May. The girl was given her exit permit on 26 May 1838 and subsequently emigrated. *Regierung zu Frankfurt/Oder. [Files on the Applications from Individuals from Kreis Zuellichau Schwiebus for Emigration to Australia] Vol.I, 1838.*

ULBRICHT, The Ulbricht case has already been men-
RAETEL   tioned among the instances of marriage separation, wherein the wife and her children were not allowed to emigrate in 1838. In 1844, however, her illegitimate son Gottlob Raetel and her legitimate daughter Anna Rosina Ulbricht emigrated, while the son Samuel Ulbricht is not mentioned in the lists. This probably indicates that he remained in Germany. *Staatsarchiv Breslau. Regierung zu Liegnitz. [Files on the Emigration, Etc., from Kreis Sagan] Vol. I, 1836-1842; see also Staatsarchiv Breslau. Regierung zu Liegnitz. [Special Files on the Emigration of Prussian Subjects and Their Naturalization in Foreign Countries, 1844-1849].*

FRANKE   A most unusual case is that of the coachman Samuel Franke, from Laettnitz, Kreis Gruenberg, who emigrated to Australia with his family in 1839. His oldest son, Christian Franke, 18 years, declared: "I have such an inexpressible fear of emigration with my father that I am compelled to remain in Germany. I hope that the law can be employed to my protection and that I shall not be forced to leave the Fatherland against my will. . . ." Since Franke had six children but received exit permits only for himself, his wife, and five children, it must be assumed that the eldest son was able to remain in Germany. *Staatsarchiv Breslau. Rep 201b, Acc 23/24, Nr.40 [Files on the Emigration from Kreis Gruenberg] Vol.I, 1839-1843.*

KLOSE   The oxdriver Christian Heinrich Klose, from Laettnitz, Kreis Gruenberg, 22 years old, would be able to emigrate with others to Australia, the destination given in his application of 1839, only if he got his father's permission and a release from military service obligation. He presented both these permits, and it must be assumed that he was granted an exit permit, although he is not shown on any list of [Separatist] emigrants. *Staatsarchiv Breslau. Rep 201b, Acc. 23/24, Nr. 40 [Files on Emigration from Gruenberg Kreis, etc.] Vol.I, 1839-1843.*

HIRTHE   The coachman Gottfried Hirthe, from Schloin, Kreis Gruenberg, was granted an emigration permit to Australia on 9 Aug 1839 with wife and six children. The two eldest sons, Karl (age 21) and Christian (age 18) remained in Berlin in military service; they did not wish to accompany the family and would remain in the Fatherland. *Ibid.*

BEISSER   The gardener Johann Gottlieb Beisser, from Plau, Kreis Crossen, with wife and two children (15 and 11 years), wished to go to Australia, leaving the two eldest sons, journeyman miller Christoph Valentine Beisser (21 years) and oxdriver Johann Gottlieb Beisser (18 years) in Germany. When asked by government officials whether he had made provisions for these sons and arranged for their guardianship, the father replied that they were old and strong enough to earn their own livelihoods; if a guardianship for them be required, proceedings should be instituted immediately. The father was granted exit permits for himself, wife, and two [younger] children on 20 Sep 1839. His declaration that he wished to accompany Pastor Grabau and to meet up with fellow emigrants from Kreis Gruenberg at the canal near Brieskow, discloses that he [and his family] went to America [instead of Australia]. *Ibid. and Regierung Frankfurt/ Oder. [Files on the Applications of Individuals from Krossen Kreis and Grants of Exit Permits to Australia, 1839-1856].*

ZACHARIAE,   A girl, Rosina Zachariae, age 22, from
PRIESE   Erfurt, was in service with -- Priese, widow of a potter, on Andreas Street [in Erfurt] and was encouraged by the Separatist inhabitants to emigrate in 1839. Her father protested that this girl was too young and inexperienced to emigrate, and she was refused an exit permit. *Staatsarchiv Magdeburg. Konsistorium der Provinz Sachsen. [Files on Separations from the United Evangelical Congregations] Vol.V [January] to 21 Aug 1839.*

PFEIFFER   The illegitimate Karoline Pfeiffer (23-1/2 years) was in service in Erfurt with Pastor Grabau and wished to emigrate with him. The father declared that he had no objection, and she emigrated. *Ibid.*

KRUEGER,   The shepherd boy Friedrich Wilhelm Johann
HEUER,   Krueger, from Schwirsen, Kreis Kammin (19
KOEPSEL   years), wished to emigrate with farmer --
            Heuer, from Justin, and -- Koepsel, from Knurrbusch, in 1839. The father was present at the proceedings and declared himself to be without objections. *Staatsarchiv Stettin. Landratsamt Kammin. Acc. 3/1920, Nr. 410, Vol.II, 1843.*

BORTFELD   The former oboe player Karl Friedrich Wilhelm Bortfeld (25 years old), from Erfurt, was granted an exit permit, even though the parents were having difficulties supporting themselves, and the father was blind. Two other brothers remained in Germany. The would-be emigrant is recorded, on 19 Jun 1839, to have died in the hospital in Magdeburg. [If so, he would not have been an emigrant.] *Staatsarchiv Magdeburg. Regierung zu Magdeburg. [Files on Emigration Applications from Lutheran Separatists, 1838-1843] Rep C 28, Polizeiregistratur.*

DRUDE   Journeyman cabinetmaker Andreas Drude (22 years), in Quedlinburg, wished to emigrate with the Old Lutherans in 1839, but could not obtain parental permission and had to remain in Germany. *Ibid.*

SEELAENDER   Journeyman carpenter Johann Gottlieb Seelaender, from Blumberg, Kreis Crossen, emigrated in 1841 to Australia with his wife and son (2 years), where his father, from Kay, had emigrated in 1838. Thus, the family separation was temporary in nature. *Regierung Frankfurt/Oder. [Files on the Applications of Individuals from Krossen Kreis and Grants of Exit Permits to Australia, 1839-1856].*

UTECH   Day laborer Kaspar Friedrich Utech, from Morgow, emigrated with his family to America in 1843. The wife's mother remained in Germany but received proceeds from the farm [they had left]. *Staatsarchiv Stettin. Landratsamt Kammin. Acc. 3/1920, Nr. 410, Vol.I, 1843.*

EGGERT   Landowner Karl Friedrich Eggert, from Cretlow, emigrated in 1843, but his mother-in-law was provided for in Germany [from property proceeds]. *Ibid.*

EGGERT   J. D. Eggert, from Cretlow, Kreis Kammin, emigrated in 1843 also, and his father-in-law remained behind with his sons. *Ibid.*

VOELZ   The inhabitant Michael Voelz, from Hagen, Kreis Kammin (age 61) emigrated in 1843 with three children, leaving two sons and two daughters in Germany who were either married or provided for. *Ibid.*

KOEPKE   The inhabitant Gottfried Koepke, from Stewen, Kreis Kammin, was permitted to emigrate in 1843 with his wife and children, since his mother was supported by a brother, and all his siblings were provided for. *Ibid.*

HACKBARTH   Former landowner -- Hackbarth (54 years), from Coeselitz, Kreis Kammin, emigrated to America in 1843 with his daughter Dorothea Luise Karoline (28 years), while other children were provided for and left in Germany. *Staatsarchiv Stettin. Landratsamt Kammin. Acc. 3/1920, Nr. 410, Vol.II, 1843.*

HACKBARTH   Another person, Karoline Wilhelmine Friderike Hackbarth (25 years), from Jassow, had her mother's permission to emigrate, inasmuch as six sisters and one brother remained in Germany. *Ibid.*

LEMCKE   Sophie Friderike Lemcke, daughter of the day laborer -- Lemcke, from Hakenwalde, was married to the laborer -- Kronenfeld, in Moratz, and remained in Germany when her father emigrated in 1843. *Staatsarchiv Stettin. Regierung zu Stettin. Abt.I, Tit.XI, Sekt.1, Naugard Kreis [Concerning Conventicle Affairs].*

WURL   Karl Gottlieb Wurl, from Nipperwiese, who was
        blind, emigrated to America in 1843 with the
permission of his father and his siblings who remained in Germany. *Staatsarchiv Stettin. Regierung
zu Stettin. Abt.I, Tit.XI, Sekt.1, Nr.8, Vol.4 [Con-
cerning Conventicle Affairs in Greifenhagen Kreis].*

STOCK   The hired hand Christian Wilhelm Stock, from
        Grambow, Kreis Kammin, emigrated to America
in 1843 to join a brother and sister who had emigrated
in 1842 and who are not listed [among the Separatist
emigrants]. *Staatsarchiv Stettin. Landratsamt Kammin.
Acc. 3/1920, Nr. 410, Vol.II, 1843.*

JAEGER The shepherd Martin Friedrich Jaeger, from
        Maskow, Kreis Naugard, left a 26-year-old
son, Karl Friedrich Jaeger, in Germany, when the father emigrated in 1843 with other children. *Staatsarchiv Stettin. Regierung zu Stettin. Abt.I, Tit.XI,
Sekt.1, Naugard Kreis [Concerning Conventicle Af-
fairs].*

KORTH   The peasant Johann Martin Korth, from Braschen-
        dorf, Kreis Naugard, accompanied by wife and
four children, emigrated to America in 1843, leaving
two married sons, both cottagers, behind. One of the
sons, Wilhelm Korth, then emigrated with wife and
three children in 1845 to rejoin the family. *Ibid.*

MARLOW Johann Wilhelm Marlow (age 23), the son of
        property lessor -- Marlow, from Klein-Leis-
tikow, Kreis Naugard, was in military service and had
to remain in Germany. A second son, Karl August Ferdinand Marlow (18 years) was also hired out to some-
one and was also to remain behind; however, his employer released him, and [Karl] declared: "I wish to
follow my parents, for whom I bear a natural affec-
tion." *Ibid.*

BRAASCH The case of laborer Johann Braasch and his
        wife, from Stettin, is unusual in that they
left two children, 8 and 5 years old, in Germany and
accompanied the grandfather Karl Braasch, from Massow,
Kreis Naugard, to America in 1843. *Ibid.*

BRAASCH The farmer Georg Braasch, already mentioned
        among the Felgenhauer [emigrants], was fi-
nally able to emigrate in 1846, after several delays,
leaving two children behind with whom he had been involved in a court case; one was a married daughter
Alwine Luise, the other was a son Johann Gottlieb Eduard, who intended to marry in Hakenwalde. If Braasch
was able to take a nephew, Karl Friedrich Braasch (age
22) and a niece Wilhelmine Braasch (24 years) with him,
as his application shows, there would also have been a
separation of these young people from their parents.
The records do not state from which brother these
Braasch children were. *Ibid. and Staatsarchiv Stettin.
Landratsamt Naugard. [Special Files on Applications
for and Permissions to Emigrate to America from Persons Who Are Lutheran Separatists, 1842-1846].*

KUHN   The tailor Heinrich Kuhn and his wife, from
        Nipperwiese, Kreis Greifenhagen, will not give
permission for their only son and child, the barge
builder August Wilhelm Kuhn (22 years), to emigrate
under any circumstances. The son had been influenced
by his employer -- Wurl to embrace Separatism and to
emigrate. The parents were old and dependent upon
their son. They desired that the son enter military
service in order to be healed of his fanaticism. By
decision of Regierung Stettin, dated 1 Jun 1843, an

exit permit was denied him. *Staatsarchiv Stettin.
Regierung Stettin. Abt.I, Tit.XI, Sekt.1, Nr.8, Vol.4
[Concerning Conventicle Affairs in Kreis Greifenhagen].*

PYRITZ,   The peasant Martin Pyritz, from Fernowsfelde,
KUCKAHN   Kreis Usedom, would be permitted to emigrate
          in 1843 only if his oldest daughter Alber-
tine (19 years), who is to remain in Germany, is provided for. This condition was apparently met, as the
landowner Michael Kuckahn, in Dargebanz, declared himself ready to take care of her, since the father had
given 40 Talers to him for her support, the remainder
to be given her upon reaching her majority. *Ibid.,
from Kreis Wollin, 1822-1845.*

KUCKAHN   Michael Kuckahn made the same arrangement
HASS   in the case of Robert Hass, the stepson of
          his brother Karl [Kuckahn] in order that
Karl Kuckahn and his family were able to emigrate in
1843. *Ibid.*

GENET   Judith Genet (24 years), unmarried, from Berg-
        holz, needs parental consent to emigrate in
1843, even though she has reached her majority, because she has been living under her father's control.
She was given his permission, and allows her to do as
she wishes. *Regierung zu Potsdam. [Files on the Intended Emigration of Old Lutheran Separatists to America, Vol.I, 1843 to end of May].*

GAEDTKE The farmer Johann Joachim Gaedtke (53 years)
        from Gansken-Pribbernow, Kreis Greifenberg,
had five children, three of whom were stepchildren sur-
named Friede from his wife's first marriage. He emigrated in 1843 with two children, leaving two stepchildren and two of his own children in Germany. The
children were grown, perhaps married. *Staatsarchiv
Stettin. Regierung Stettin. Abt.I, Tit.XI, Sekt.1, Nr.
8, Vol.3 [Concerning Conventicle Affairs in Kreis
Greifenberg, 1839-1847].*

HENNIG The farmowner Johann Hennig, from Welsow,
        Kreis Angermuende, had two sons, aged 19 and
17 years, who refused to emigrate with him in 1843.
Hennig went to court for the purpose of settling affairs with them, but the sons then decided to accompany him. *Regierung zu Potsdam. [Files on the Intended Emigration of Old Lutheran Separatists to Amer-
ica] Vol.II, June 1843 to end of 1845.*

SACK   Former fishery owner Johann Sack, of Liepe,
        Kreis Angermuende, received exit permits for
himself, his wife, and his daughter Wilhelmine. He
and his wife changed their minds and decided not to
emigrate, but the daughter resolved to go, and requested that she be included on her brother's passport,
the cabinetmaker Karl Sack, who had been granted a
release from citizenship with his family on 2 Jun 1843.
She was granted her own release under date of 26 Jun
1843. *Ibid.*

MOLDENHAUER   Sophie Karoline Moldenhauer, from Let-
              schin, daughter of peasant Heinrich Mol-
denhauer and his wife Katharina Moldenhauer, born
Boche, married tailor Erdmann Pankow, from Alt-Levin,
shortly before she was to have emigrated and left the
parents behind. Her mother followed her in 1844; the
father remained in Germany or died. *Regierung zu Potsdam. [Files on the Intended Emigration of Old Lutheran
Separatists to America] Vol.I, 1843 to End of May.
Also Private letter to Herr Iwan from one of the following persons in America: Professor -- Denef, St. Louis;*

Professor -- Fuehrbringer, St. Louis; Pastor -- Engel, Milwaukee; Pastor -- Pankow, Madison; Miss Mathilde Schley, Milwaukee. [Probably the communication was from Pastor Pankow in Madison, Wisconsin, who is likely to have been a descendent.]

KIECKHOEFEL   A sad case of irresponsibility toward a parent is that of the illegitimate Elisabeth Kieckhoefel, from Wallmow, Kreis Prenzlau, 26 years of age and self-supporting. Her mother protested against her intention to emigrate, because the mother would lose her means of support. The Landrat called this wrong to the daughter's attention, pointing out to her that she could demonstrate her true faith by showing love toward the mother [and remaining in Germany]. The daughter seemed to be touched and promised to return to Germany for her mother, but at the same time she complained against the government for not handing out her exit permit. She felt that her rights as an adult were being infringed upon and demanded that she be given her permit. The government in Potsdam immediately directed that the mother had no other recourse but to ask for a court order within 48 hours stopping the issuance of the permit, otherwise the permit would have to be issued. Nothing is to be found regarding such a court order nor of the daughter's emigration. However, it seems likely that she did emigrate. *Regierung zu Potsdam. [Files on the Intended Emigration of Old Lutheran Separatists to America] Vol.II, June 1843 to end of 1845.*

NEITZEL   The farmer Christian Neitzel, from Trechel, Kreis Naugard, wished to emigrate in 1845 with his entire family. He requested a release from citizenship in the middle of March. At the beginning of June he regretted to report that only his oldest son Friedrich Wilhelm Neitzel (27 years) and wife were willing to emigrate. The son and wife were granted exit permits and emigrated to America. In 1846 the father and remaining family members followed them. *Staatsarchiv Stettin. Landratsamt Kammin. Acc.3/1920, Nr. 410, Vol.I, 1843.*

OSSIG   The gardener Gottfried Ossig (58 years), from Polnisch-Peterwitz, Kreis Breslau, was given an exit permit in 1845 to emigrate to Lobethal, Australia, where his coreligionists had settled. Two children of his first marriage, aged 30 and 28 years, remained in Germany, but he took the four children of his second marriage with him. The trip was delayed until 1846, however, as he had difficulty selling his business. *Staatsarchiv Breslau. Rep.207, Acc.2/24, Nr.8 [Files of the Landratsamt Breslau on General Separatist Matters].*

GENNRICH   Fisherman Peter Friedrich Gennrich, from Gross-Benz, Kreis Naugard, emigrated in 1846 with his entire family as a result of letters from America. His daughter Luise appeared before governmental authorities] with her supporters and declared that, since it would be extremely difficult for her to leave Germany, she wished to remain behind; her father and brother, shepherd boy Hermann Gennrich could do what they wished. The father then declared that his daughter could remain in Germany and that he would pay her the sum of 50 Talern as her inheritance. *Staatsarchiv Stettin. Landratsamt Kammin. Acc.3/1920, Nr. 410, Vol.I, 1843.*

LINDNER   Johanna Eleonore Lindner, from Buchwaeldchen, Kreis Lueben, remained in Germany in 1845 to marry. Her parents and siblings emigrated. *Staats-*

archiv Breslau. Rep.201b, Acc.23/24, Nr.39 [Files on Emigration, Etc., from Kreis Lueben] Vol.I, 1836-1849.

ROSENBERG   Similarly, Maria Josefa Rosenberg, from Gruenberg, remained in Germany to marry in 1847, when her family emigrated. *Staatsarchiv Breslau. Rep.201b, Acc.23/24, Nr.10 [Files on Emigration, Etc., from Kreis Gruenberg] Vol.2, 1844-1856.*

MOERBE   Johann Moerbe, of Dauban, the grown son of the widow -- Moerbe, remained behind in 1854. *Regierung zu Potsdam. [Files on the Emigration of Prussian Subjects and Their Naturalization in Foreign Countries in Kreis Rotenburg] Vol. 9/10, 1853/1854.*

LORENTZSCH   The unmarried -- Lorentzsch, from Reichwalde, Kreis Rothenburg, was granted a release from citizenship on 21 Aug 1854 with her daughter Maria Lorentzsch (17 years), whereas two sons, aged 20 and 24 years, remained in Germany. The two women went to Texas. *Ibid.*

MILITARY HARDSHIP CASES

Among the difficulties which occurred for some emigrating families was that of military service or liability to service on the part of young men. The laws promulgated in 1818 and 1842 in Prussia were such that, under ordinary circumstances, young men could usually have their military obligations cancelled and, thus, a hurdle to emigration could be overcome. However, there were numerous officials, both within and without the military establishment, who were much opposed to the Old Lutherans and unsympathetic to their emigration plans. Such persons often made difficulties for Lutheran young men, despite the clear intent of official regulations. For young me in the 17-25 year category an *Attest* (statement) from the *Kreisersatzkommission* (local draft board) was required as a condition of emigration; most frequently this *Attest* was freely granted. A few of the Landraete, as for example Herr v.Voeltz of Kreis Kammin,were uncooperative and would give these *Atteste* only after the would-be emigrant had appealed successfully to the King. Similarly, Landrat v.Stuelpnagel-Dargitz, of Kreis Prenzlau, was so stubborn that the recommendations of military authorities, even that of the commanding general of an army corps, was insufficient to move him. Only after the emigrants had made *Inmediateingaben* (direct appeals) to the King himself would the Landrat grant the *Atteste*, and then only upon direct order of the Minister of War. When he did grant his permission, it was in the form of a *Sammelattest* (group statement) for 21 young men of his Kreis, as follows:

Name	Age	Birthplace
WEGNER, August	17	Falkenwalde
KOEHN, Michael	19	Wollin
KOEHN, Wilhelm	17	Wollin
BETZLAFF, Friedrich	17	Fahrenwalde
HANNEMANN, Gottfried	21	Fahrenwalde
KASSUBE, Friedrich	19	Wallmow
KASSUBE, Johann	17	Wallmow
MUELLER, David	22	Wallmow
MUELLER, Christian	18	Wallmow
MUELLER, Daniel	17	Wallmow
STOLZMANN, Grottfried*	17	Wallmow
HEUER, Friedrich	22	Wallmow
MOLL, Christof Friedrich	18	Wallmow
BUROW, Christof	17	Wallmow

Name	Age	Birthplace
WOLF, August	18	Wallmow
WALK, Johann	21	Wallmow
WALK, Friedrich	18	Wallmow
FLOEGEL, Wilhelm	19	Schwaneberg
BLAUK, Daniel	20	Wetzenow
BARTH, -- (son of a weaver)	17	Prenzlau
GROBENGIESSER, Wilhelm	-	Bruessow

*So spelled.

Regierung zu Potsdam. [Files on the Intended Emigration of Old Lutheran Separatists to America] Vol.II, June 1843 to End of 1845.

SCHULZE The tailor -- Schulze and his family, from Woltersdorf, Kreis Magdeburg, wished to emigrate with Pastor Grabau in 1839. The *Kreisersatzkommission* (local draft board) at Neuhaus refused to grant the necessary *Attest* (statement of release) for a son Peter Schulze on the grounds that his only reason for wanting to emigrate was to avoid military service. Upon appeal, the government stated that the suspicions of the draft board, as given by Landrat v.Muenchhausen, were an insufficient grounds for denial, even though Peter Schulze might be eligible for future service. Exit permits for the entire family, including the son, were granted on 5 Jun 1839. *Staatsarchiv Magdeburg. Regierung zu Magdeburg. [Files on the Emigration Applications of Lutheran Separatists, 1838-1843]. Rep. C 28, Polizeiregistratur.*

SELL, The only known case in which a young man sub-
HOEFS, ject to military service did not eventually
JAEGER lead to an exit permit is that of Christian Friedrich Sell, from Maskow, Kreis Naugard, the illegitimate son of the latter married master tailor -- Hoefs, whose parents had given permission for Sell to emigrate with shepherd Friedrich Jaeger, from Maskow. The *Kreisersatzkommission* (local draft board) refused to grant Sell an *Attest* (release statement) on the grounds that he himself had not applied for it. Despite this refusal, Sell emigrated with the family of Karl Braasch in 1843 without a proper exit permit and without having said goodbye to his mother and stepfather. When the Landrat v.Bismarck sought to obtain an arrest warrant and to open diplomatic negotiations in Hamburg [with the American consulate] the Prussian government thought otherwise, and Sell was allowed to leave the country. That he reached America is verified by an extant letter dated 1844. *Staatsarchiv Stettin. Regierung zu Stettin. Abt.I, Tit.XI, Sekt.1, [Conventicle Affairs in Kreis Naugard].*

GUST Friedrich Gust, son of fisherman Martin Gust, of Berg-Dievenow, Kreis Kammin, was released from Regiment 9, Fusilier Battalion I, Company 10. However, since he did not present a proper statement of release [from military service] to the [Kreis] authorities, his father's passport application was denied on 27 May 1839. The son then requested another release from his regiment and must have received it, since information from Regierung Stettin discloses that the entire family, including the son, were given exit permits on 3 Jun 1839. *Staatsarchiv Stettin. Landratsamt Kammin. [Special Files on the Emigration from Kreis Kammin to America of Dissidents] Vol.II, May-July 1839.*

FRICKMANN An entry, dated 20 Mar 1839, shows that Gottfried Frickmann had been released from the Army Cavalry Reserve in 1837. He was granted an exit permit with his mother in 1839. *Staatsarchiv Magdeburg. [Consistory for Saxony. Separation from the United Evangelical Congregations] Vol.V, to 21 Aug 1839.*

STRASSBURG, The Landrat of Kreis Prenzlau made dif-
WENDT, ficulties not only for the men in ser-
HASELEY vice but also for those who were in the Reserve. He refused to grant exit permits to Wilhelm Strassburg, Christian Wendt, and August Haseley, who then appealed directly to the Minister of War in the following terms:

"The Lord War Minister has been made acquainted with the nature of our emergency through a previous appeal. We are determined to emigrate with our families and have been hindered in this undertaking by the *Kreisersatzkommission* [local draft board]. Since all our people have gone ahead, we are left here alone, and therefore apply to the Lord War Minister to be released from our duties as reservists in accordance with Cabinet Order of 31 Dec 1842, in order that we may travel on a certain Oder [River] barge. [signed] Wilhelm Strassburg, Christian Wendt, August Haseley."

War Minister v. Boyen ordered the Third A[rmy] C[orps] to grant releases to the three petitioners, and they were given these documents by the Potsdam authorities for emigration in 1843. *Regierung zu Potsdam. [Files on the Intended Emigration of Old Lutheran Separatists to America] Vol.II, Jun 1843 to End of 1845.*

BRAASCH The reservist Hermann Braasch, son of Karl Braasch, from Neu-Massow, Kreis Naugard, was denied a release on 21 Feb 1843 from battalion commander Major v. Stargard on the grounds that, until he had completed his period of service, members of the local reserve were not to be granted releases for the purpose of emigration. Nonetheless, the *Kreisersatzkommission* (local draft board) granted the release on 5 May 1843. Here, again, was a case where higher authority was required to correct the erroneous interpretations of law by subordinates. *Staatsarchiv Stettin. Landratsamt Naugard. [Special Files on the Applications for Emigration to America of Persons Who Are Members of Lutheran Separatist Groups, 1842-1846].*

GOETSCH, A certain reservist Friedrich Wilhelm Aug-
KORTH ust Goetsch, from Maskow, Kreis Naugard, was denied a release statement. Neither he nor Karl Friedrich Ludwig Korth, from Braschendorf, Kreis Naugard, are listed in the *Sammelattest* (List of Releases), dated 5 May 1842, and presumably they remained in Germany. *Staatsarchiv Stettin. Regierung zu Stettin. Abt.I, Tit.XI, Sekt.1 [Conventicle Affairs in Kreis Naugard].*

HILLIGENDORF Karl Ludwig Ferdinand Hilligendorf,
or HILGENDORF son of farmer Ernst Friedrich Hilligendorf, from Dresow, Kreis Greifenberg, was on active duty in Pomerania with the Ninth Infantry Regiment and was denied permission to emigrate with the family. Only after the Regierung Stettin had appealed to the general command of the Second Army Corps in Graudenz did General Count Dohna grant a release to this soldier. The exit permit could not be handed to him, because it reached the Landrat's office a day after Hilligendorf had come to get it. The Landrat reported that the family had left Kreis Naugard and that Fusilier Hilligendorf had undoubtedly emigrated with them to America in 1839 [without the exit permit]. *Staatsarchiv Stettin. Regierung zu Stettin. Abt.I, Tit.XI, Sekt.1, Nr.8, Vol.3 [Concerning Conventicle Affairs in Kreis Greifenberg].*

PAECH   Another kind of case is that of Johann Gott-
         fried Paech, son of a farmer, from Kay, Kreis
Zuellichau. He had served nine months in the second
company of the Twelfth Infantry Regiment, but was dismissed because his religious Confirmation had not been
made with a pastor of the State Church. He assumed
that his military service obligation had been ful-
filled thereby, and that his affairs were all in order.
He was given an *Attest* (release statement) from the
Kreisersatzkommission (local draft board) and granted
an exit permit. How he came to have complications is
not clear, but in any event he was unable to emigrate
with his family in 1838. He finally was allowed to
leave the country in 1841 after having gotten permission from his commanding officer and a new exit permit. Apparently, he had been forced to reenter the
service to complete his period of duty. He joined
the group of emigrants under [Pastor?] Fritzsche and
emigrated to Australia in 1841, where he rejoined his
family. *Regierung zu Frankfurt/Oder. [Files on the
Applications of Individuals from Kreis Zuellichau-
Schwiebus for Emigration to Australia] Vol.I, 1838,
and Vol.II, 1840-1857.*

MEISSNER   Johann Karl Meissner was serving with the
            third company of the Thirty-First Infantry
Regiment, when his mother, laundress Johanne Christiane Meissner, from Erfurt, emigrated in 1839. As a
consequence of his active duty status, he could not
emigrate with her; he was instructed to submit an *Attest* (release statement) from military authorities or
to get himself a transfer to the militia, but it is
unknown whether Meissner did so. At any rate, he remained in Germany in 1839. *Staatsarchiv Magdeburg.
Konsistorium der Provinz Sachsen. [Concerning Separations from United Evangelical Congregations] Vol.V,
to 21 Aug 1839.*

KANT,   Johann Friedrich Wilhelm Kant (22 years),
HOFFMEISTER stepson of the master butcher -- Hoff-
             meister, from Hakenwalde, Kreis Naugard,
was on active duty with the Second Artillery Brigade
in Stettin and remained in Germany, when the family
emigrated in 1843. *Staatsarchiv Stettin. Regierung
Stettin. Abt.I, Tit.XI, Sekt.1 [Concerning Conventicle
Affairs in Kreis Naugard].*

HASELEY,   The following young men also remained be-
GLOEGE,   hind on active duty, when their families
PRITZEL,   emigrated: David Haseley, stationed at
HOEPFNER,   Guhrau (probably brother of the farmer's
KRULL?   sons from Wallmow and of August Haseley,
            mentioned *supra*, but whose parents are
not given); -- Gloege, stationed at Garz, from
Schwaneberg, Kreis Prenzlau; Franz Pritzel, stationed
at Schwedt, but whose parents are not recorded;
Friedrich Wilhelm Hoepfner, serving in the Second In-
fantry Regiment at Stettin, son of the invalid --
Hoepfner, from Fiddichow, Kreis Greifenhagen. *Regierung zu Potsdam. [Files on the Intended Emigration of
Old Lutheran Separatists to America] Vol.I, 1843 to
End of May.* The four above-mentioned soldiers were
included in an *Inmediateingabe* (direct appeal) of
Krull/William to the King petitioning for separation
from the armed service on 21 Mar 1843. The appeal
was denied on 25 Apr 1843 under an 1842 law; no ground
for an exception was seen and there was no evidence
that any of them was under any pressure of religious
conscience. In 1844 solder Hoepfner was offered an
opportunity to emigrate free of charge with -- Schroeder, of Fiddichow. Despite the fact that he had only
a few more months of active duty, the Regierung in

Potsdam, on 26 Jun 1844, was unwilling to grant a release, even at the petition of the Landrat. The government did not feel obligated to give a dispensation
to this musketeer. *Ibid; also Staatsarchiv Stettin.
Regierung Stettin, Abt.I, Tit.XI, Sekt.1, Nr.8, Vol.
4 [Concerning Conventicle Affairs in Kreis Greifen-
hagen].*

MARLOW   The following is an unusual case. Johann
          Wilhelm Marlow (23 years), oldest son of
lessor -- Marlow, from Klein-Leistikow, Kreis Naugard,
had completed his military service with the Ninth Infantry Regiment and, without parental permission, had
transferred to the Fourth Ulan Regiment as a recruit.
The father wanted him to be dismissed, because the
father had not given permission for his enlistment.
In October 1844 the Regiment refused to release him
before completion of his period of enlistment and
stated that the father could appeal to higher authority, according to regulations. The outcome of this
case is unknown, because there is nothing further in
the files of Kreis Naugard. It is probable, however,
that further appeal would have been unsuccessful.
*Staatsarchiv Stettin. Regierung Stettin. Abt.I, Tit.
XI, Sekt.1 [Concerning Conventicle Affairs in Kreis
Naugard].*

WACHS,   A most interesting case is that of the peas-
PLAUTZ   ant Johann Christian Wachs, from Neu-Labahn,
          Kreis Regenwalde. In 1844 he was granted
exit permits for his entire family, including his
daughter Albertine Karoline Sophie, and his son Friedrich Johann Ferdinand. The family did not emigrate in
that year, because he was unable to sell his property,
and therefore made no use of the exit permits. In
1846 the father requested new exit permits, without
having reported that the first set of exit permits had
not been used and thereby requesting renaturalization
for the period in which the family remained in Germany.
In the meanwhile the daughter had married musketeer
Wilhelm Plautz of the Ninth Infantry Regiment, and the
son had been called to active duty with the Second Artillery Brigade. Upon Wach's request for a second set
of exit permits, to include his daughter and her husband and his son, it was determined that the daughter
had become renaturalized through her marriage, but
that her husband could not emigrate because he was on
active duty with the Prussian armed forces. The father
then stated that the daughter could not decide between
leaving with her family or remaining with her husband;
the authorities replied that the only recourse was an
appeal to the King on behalf of both the son-in-law
(Plautz) and the son (F.J. Ferdinand Wachs). The son,
it was determined, had been inducted into the Artillery
illegally, since at the time of induction he was no
longer a Prussian subject. An *Inmediateingabe* (direct
appeal) to the King was filed by Regierung zu Stettin.
The King decided, under date of 7 Jul 1846 at San
Souci, as follows:

    "As a consequence of the report of 21 May? I have
    granted a release to canoneer Ferdinand Wachs of
    the Second Artillery Brigade, in order that he may
    emigrate to America with his father and order the
    Regierung so to inform him. As for the son-in-law,
    musketeer [Wilhelm] Plautz, of the Ninth Infantry
    Regiment, the Regierung is to inform [Christian]
    Wachs that Plautz cannot be released from his mili-
    tary obligations."

A further complication to Wach's emigration plan then
occurred, when a legal action was brought against him,
thus causing a withdrawal of the second set of exit

permits. Whether the Wachs family was able eventually to emigrate is not clear from the files, but, if so, the son and his wife would have been able to accompany them, despite his active duty status, but the daughter would have had to remain behind, because of her husband's duty status. *Staatsarchiv Stettin. Regierung Stettin. Abt.I, Tit.XI, Sekt.1, Nr. 8, Vol.4 [Concerning Conventicle Affairs in Kreis Regenwalde].*

HOFFMANN   The two sons of the farmer -- Hoffmann, from Reichenau, Kreis Sagan, were required to remain in Germany, when their parents emigrated in 1847, because of their active duty status in the standing army. The two sons emigrated in 1849, rejoining their family in Australia. *Regierung zu Liegnitz. [Files on the Emigration of Prussian Subjects from Kreis Sagan and Their Naturalization in Foreign States, 1844-1849].*

A FINDING AID TO PLACES OF ORIGIN

At the end of his second volume, Herr Iwan presented hand-sketched maps of the *Kreise* (local administrative districts) from whence the emigrants came. Although these maps are invaluable for pinpointing the locations of very small settlements not on the standard maps, these sketches have been superseded by the new political organizations which took place after the second world war. Thus, it has been thought useful to refer to more recent geographic sources. For locations which are now within the German Democratic Republic (East Germany), the following gazetteer has been used:

U.S. Department of the Interior. Board of Geographic Names. *Germany-Soviet Zone & East Berlin* (Washington, D.C.: Government Printing Office, [1960]).

This gazetteer lists the name and exact geographic location of nearly every village mentioned in Herr Iwan's study, and one is relieved to learn that they still exist as places of human habitation, with the likelihood that their precious church and civil records may have survived. The present administrative region, corresponding to the old *Regierungsbezirk*, to which the villages now belong are listed hereinafter for the convenience of researchers.

Villages in Pomerania and Silesia, Prussian provinces which fell to Poland at the end of the second world war, have been considerably more difficult to account for. The major town in each of the old *Kreise* has been located and its Polish name given, as well as its exact geographic location. Occasionally, other towns in the *Kreise* could also be identified in similar manner. It is likely that many of the Pomeranian and Silesian settlements from which the "Old Lutheran" emigrants came have now entirely disappeared; their remaining German-speaking inhabitants refugees in West Germany; their Polish successors themselves refugees from eastern Poland, now part of the U.S.S.R. When the remaining Germans fled in 1945, the land was completely reorganized. Old farms and estates were consolidated into collective farms. There was a complete break with the past; many of the buildings and other evidences of habitation remained, but the inhabitants themselves were almost entirely new and unfamiliar with local history. The whereabouts of the old

records are unknown. Probably, many remain where they were left when the German inhabitants fled; others may have been destroyed or forwarded to regional archives. Researchers will want first to inquire of the Genealogical Society in Salt Lake City, for, in its on-going project to microfilm Polish records, it is likely to have the most precise information available as to which records have survived a disastrous era.

In determining the locations and names of Pomeranian and Silesian places of origin the following gazetteer has been used:

U.S. Department of the Interior. Board of Geographic Names. *Official Standard Names . . . Poland.* Volumes I and II. (Washington, D.C.: Government Printing Office, 1955).

The table of places of origin hereinafter contains the following information:

Column

A   Name of Kreis and settlement from whence emigrants came

B   Number of emigrants originating in the settlement: 10 = 1 through 10 persons
    30 = 11 through 30 persons
    80 = 31 through 80 persons
    80+ = more than 80 persons

C   Degrees and minutes North of the Equator

D   Degrees and minutes East of Greenwich

E   Present administrative district within the German Democratic Republic (East Germany):
    C = Neubrandenburg
    D = Potsdam
    E = Frankfurt/Oder
    R = Dresden
    Z = Cottbus
The present administrative districts under Polish administration have not been determined.

F   Map in which the settlement can be located:
    01 *Karte des deutschen Reiches*, Reichsamt fuer Landesaufnahme, Berlin, various dates; scale 1:100,000.
    02 *Topographische Uebersichtskarte des deutschen Reiches in 1:200,000*, Reichsamt fuer Landesaufnahme, 1901-36.

Column

F 03 *Uebersichtskarte von Mitteleuropa, 1:300,000*
Reichsamt fuer Landesaufnahme, various dates.

04 *Weltkarte, 1:1,000,000*. Reichsamt fuer
Landesaufnahme, 1940-44.

05 *Mapa Polski*. Wojskowy Instytut Geograficzny,
Warszawa, 1947; scale 1:500,000.

06 *Mapa Polski*. Wojskowy Instytut Geograficzny,
Warszawa, 1947-48; scale 1:1,000,000.

07 *Mapa Administracyjna Rzeczypospolitej Polskiej*. Wydawnictwo Głownego Urzedu Statys-
tycznego Rzeczypospolitej Polskiej, 1937;
scale 1:300,000.

08 [Poland], W.I.G., 1929-38; scale 1:300,000.

09 *Polska: Mapa Administracyjna*, Romer, 1952;
scale 1:800,000.

10 *Michal Janiszewski, Fizyczna Mapa Polski,*
1953; scale 1:750:000.

11 [Poland], W.I.G. [most sheets 1930's];
scale 1:100,000.

G Remarks column (DDR = Deutsche Demokratische
Republik (German Democratic Republic) or East
Germany)

A	B	C	D	E	F	G
Kreis Hoyerswerda						DDR
Zerre	10	51-32	14-23	Z	01	
Spreewitz	10	51-31	14-24	Z	01	
Weiss Collm	10	51-25	14-24	Z	01	Weisskollm
Driewitz	10	-	-		-	Not listed
Colpen	10	51-25	14-28	Z	01	Kolpen; a farm
Geislitz	10	51-26	14-27	Z	01	
Neudorf	10	51-30	14-23	Z	01	Footnote 1
Buchwalde	30	51-15	14-35	Z	01	
Seidewinkel	10	51-27	14-15	Z	01	
Ruhland	10	51-28	13-52	Z	01	
Amtsanbau	30	-	-		-	Footnote 2
Kreis Rothenburg						DDR
Niesky	10	51-18	14-49	R	01	
Neusaerichen	10	51-18	14-50	R	01	Footnote 3
Oedernitz	10	51-17	14-51	R	01	
Neuhof	10	51-18	14-50	R	01	Footnote 1
Dauban	80	51-17	14-38	R	01	
Weigersdorf	30	51-16	14-39	R	01	
Gross Saubernitz	30	51-14	14-39	R	01	
Sand Foerstgen	30	51-14	14-40	R	01	
Gebelzig	30	51-13	14-40	R	01	
Klein Radisch	30	51-21	14-39	R	01	
Oelsa	10	51-06	14-39	R	01	Footnote 1
Muecka	10	51-19	14-42	R	01	
Petershain	10	51-19	14-45	R	01	Footnote 1
Moholz	10	51-18	14-47	R	01	

A	B	C	D	E	F	G
Kreis Rothenburg						
Quitzdorf	10	51-17	14-46	R	01	
Kaschel	30	51-20	14-34	R	01	
Jahmen	30	51-21	14-35	R	01	Footnote 1
Klitten	30	51-21	14-36	R	01	
Duerrbach	80	51-22	14-37	R	01	
Reichwalde	80	51-23	14-40	Z	01	Footnote 1
Creba	10	51-21	14-41	R	01	Kreba
Kringelsdorf	10	51-23	14-37	Z	01	
Wunscha	10	51-24	14-42	Z	01	
Viereichen	10	51-24	14-44	Z	01	
Tzschellen	10	51-27	14-31	Z	01	Tzschelln
Muehlrose	10	51-30	14-31	Z	01	
Nieder-Seiffers-dorf	10	51-13	14-46	R	01	Nieder-Seifersdorf
Thiemendorf	10	51-13	14-49	R	01	Footnote 1
Cunnersdorf	10	51-16	13-40	R	01	Footnote 1
Nieder-Horka	10	51-16	14-15	R	01	Footnote 1
Mueckenhain	10	51-16	14-54	R	01	
Rothenburg	10	51-20	14-56	R	01	Footnote 1
Tormersdorf	10	-	-		-	Footnote 4
Noes	10	51-21	14-58	R	01	
Spree	10	51-21	14-53	R	01	
Neusorge	10	51-23	14-56	R	01	Footnote 1
Saenitz	10	-	-		-	Footnote 5
Leippa	10	51-25	14-04	Z	01	Leippe
Thomaswalde	10	51-21	14-39	R	01	
Kreis Goerlitz						DDR/Poland
Koenigshain	10	51-11	14-52	R	01	
Kreis Sprottau		51-34	15-32	-	01	Poland: Szprotawa
Kunzendorf	10	-	-		-	
Kreis Glogau						Poland:
Glogau	30	51-40	16-06	-	03	Głogów
Brieg	10	- .	-	-	-	Footnote 1
Polwitz	10	-	-		-	
Denkwitz	10	-	-		-	
Kreis Lueben						Poland
Lueben	10	51-24	16-12	-	03	Lubin
Buchwaeldchen	30	-	-	-	-	Footnote 6
Kosslitz	10	-	-		-	
Gugelwitz	10	-	-		-	
Kreis Goldberg						Poland
Goldberg	10	51-07	15-55	-	03	Złotoryja
Polkwitz	10	-	-		-	
Kreis Jauer						Poland
Jauer	10	51-03	16-11	-	03	Jawor

A	B	C	D	E	F	G
Kreis Jauer (continued)						
Skohl	10	-	-	-	-	
Merzdorf	10	-	-	-	-	Mierczyce?
Kreis Liegnitz						Poland
Liegnitz	10	51-12	16-12	-	03	Legnica
Alt Beckern	10	-	-	-	-	
Prinkendorf	10	-	-	-	-	
Neudorf	10	-	-	-	-	
Kroitsch	10	-	-	-	-	
Wildschuetz	10	-	-	-	-	
Rothkirch	10	-	-	-	-	
Pfaffendorf	10	-	-	-	-	
Panten	10	-	-	-	-	
Pohlschildern	10	-	-	-	-	
Merschwitz	10	-	-	-	-	
Amts Altlaest	10	-	-	-	-	
Parchwitz	10	-	-	-	-	
Heidau	10	-	-	-	-	
Wangten	10	-	-	-	-	
Kummernick	30	-	-	-	-	
Royn	10	-	-	-	-	
Gross Tinz	30	-	-	-	-	
Berndorf	10	-	-	-	-	
Klein Jaenowitz	10	-	-	-	-	
Campern	10	-	-	-	-	
Kunitz	10	-	-	-	-	
Kreis Steinau						Poland
Steinau	10	51-25	16-25	-	01	Scinawa
Kreis Breslau						Poland
Breslau	80	51-06	17-02	-	01	Wroclaw
Maria Hoefchen	10	-	-	-	-	
Pilsnitz	10	-	-	-	-	
Polnisch Peter-witz	10	-	-	-	-	
Cammelwitz	10	-	-	-	-	
Rothsuerben	30	-	-	-	-	
Kreis Trebnitz						Poland
Trebnitz	-	51-19	17-03	-	01	Trzebnica
Klein Ujeschuetz	30	-	-	-	-	
Biadauschke	10	-	-	-	-	
Polnisch Hammer	30	-	-	-	-	
Schawoine	10	-	-	-	-	
Lutzine	30	-	-	-	-	
Zantkau	30	-	-	-	-	
Lossen	10	-	-	-	-	
Dockern	10	-	-	-	-	
Schlottau	10	-	-	-	-	

A	B	C	D	E	F	G
Kreis Oels						Poland
Oels	-	51-12	17-23	-	01	Olesnica
Bukowinke	10	-	-	-	-	
Kurzwitz	10	-	-	-	-	
Juliusburg	10	-	-	-	-	
Streblitz	10	-	-	-	-	
Lacumme	30	-	-	-	-	
Gross Graben	10	-	-	-	-	
Nieder-Muehlwitz	10	-	-	-	-	
Galbitz	10	-	-	-	-	
Langenhof	10	-	-	-	-	
Bernstadt	30	-	-	-	-	
Kreis Wartenberg						Poland
Wartenberg	10	-	-	-	-	
Festenberg	30	51-22	17-28	-	01	Twardogóra
Kreis Sagan						Poland
Sagan	-	51-37	15-19	-	02	Zagan
Reichenau	10	-	-	-	-	
Cosel	10	-	-	-	-	
Klein Dobritsch	10	-	-	-	-	
Tschirckau	10	-	-	-	-	
Kottwitz	10	-	-	-	-	
Kreis Freistadt						
Seiffersdorf	30	51-18	16-47	-	01	Seifersdorf
Freistadt	30	-	-	-	-	
Langhermsdorf	30	-	-	-	-	
Ober Siegersdorf	30	-	-	-	-	
Niebusch	10	-	-	-	-	
Steinborn	10	-	-	-	-	
Hartmannsdorf	10	-	-	-	-	
Weichau	10	-	-	-	-	
Brunzelwaldau	10	-	-	-	-	
Lindau	10	-	-	-	-	
Neusalz	10	51-48	15-43	-	02	
Kreis Gruenberg						Poland
Schloin	80	-	-	-	-	
Laettnitz	10	-	-	-	-	
Janny	30	-	-	-	-	
Sawade	80	-	-	-	-	
Prittag	30	-	-	-	-	
Deutsch Kessel	10	-	-	-	-	
Gruenberg	30	51-56	15-30	-	01	Zielona Gora
Kreis Kammin						Poland
Berg Dievenow	10	-	-	-	-	
Raddack	10	-	-	-	-	
Fritzow	10	-	-	-	-	

	A	B	C	D	E	F	G

Kreis Kammin (continued)   Poland

	A	B	C	D	E	F	G
Soltin	10	-	-	-	-		
Granzow	80	-	-	-	-		
Stresow	10	-	-	-	-		
Tribsow	80	-	-	-	-		
Scharchow	30	-	-	-	-		
Revenow	10	-	-	-	-		
Jassow	30	-	-	-	-		
Grambow	80	-	-	-	-		
Morgow	80	-	-	-	-		
Koenigsmuehl	10	-	-	-	-		
Buessenthin	10	-	-	-	-		
Reckow	80	-	-	-	-		
Bandesow	10	-	-	-	-		
Deuthin	10	-	-	-	-		
Benz	30	-	-	-	-		
Duenow	10	-	-	-	-		
Schnatow	80	-	-	-	-		
Pemplow	30	-	-	-	-		
Kopplin	10	-	-	-	-		
Dargow	10	-	-	-	-		
Koeselitz	10	-	-	-	-		
Batzlaff	80	-	-	-	-		
Kretlow	80	-	-	-	-		
Klemmen	10	-	-	-	-		
Baumgarten	10	-	-	-	-		
Gross Justin	30	-	-	-	-		
Knurrbusch	30	-	-	-	-		
Nitznow	30	-	-	-	-		
Brendemuehl	10	-	-	-	-		
Klein Justin	10	-	-	-	-		
Schwirsen	10	-	-	-	-		
Kahlen	10	-	-	-	-		
Buennewitz	10	-	-	-	-		
Grisow	10	-	-	-	-		
Kuchlow	10	-	-	-	-		
Polchow	10	-	-	-	-		
Hagen	10	-	-	-	-		
Neu Tessin	10	-	-	-	-		
Staewen	10	-	-	-	-		
Wietstock	10	-	-	-	-		
Moratz	10	-	-	-	-		
Drewitz	10	-	-	-	-		
Kloetzin	10	-	-	-	-		
Langendorf	10	-	-	-	-		
Dieschenhagen	10	-	-	-	-		
Rakitt	10	-	-	-	-		
Luisenhof	30	-	-	-	-		

Kreis Kammin (continued)

	A	B	C	D	E	F	G
Pribbernow	30	53-45	14-46	-	01	Przybiernow	
Medewitz	30	-	-	-	-		
Hermannsthal	10	-	-	-	-		
Weistenthin	10	-	-	-	-		
Tonnebuhr	80	-	-	-	-		
Kammin	80	53-58	14-47	-	01	Kamień Po-morskie	
Platchow	10	-	-	-	-		
Scheffin	10	-	-	-	-		

Kreis Usedom-Wollin   Poland

	A	B	C	D	E	F	G
Wollin	10	53-51	14-37	-	02	Wolin	
Schwantus	80	-	-	-	-		
Kolzow	10	-	-	-	-	Kolczewo	
Wartlow	10	-	-	-	-		
Dannenberg	30	-	-	-	-		
Fernowsfelde	80	-	-	-	-		
Warnow	80	-	-	-	-		
Kodram	30	-	-	-	-		
Dargebanz	10	-	-	-	-		
Lebbin	10	-	-	-	-	Lubin	
Vietzig	10	-	-	-	-	Footnote 7	
Rehberg	80	-	-	-	-		
Swinemuende	?	53-55	14-15	-	02	Swinoujscie	

Kreis Greifenberg   Poland

	A	B	C	D	E	F	G
Greifenberg	10	53-54	15-12	-	03	Gryfice	
Treptow	30	54-04	15-16	-	03	Trzebiatów	
Zitzmar	10	-	-	-	-		
Trieglaff	10	-	-	-	-		
Neides	10	-	-	-	-		
Arnsberg	30	-	-	-	-	Bieczyno?	
Prust	10	-	-	-	-		
Schwessow	80	-	-	-	-		
Dorphagen	10	-	-	-	-		
Dresow	30	-	-	-	-		
Mittelhagen	10	-	-	-	-		
Horst	10	-	-	-	-		
Holm	30	-	-	-	-		
Pribbernow	10	53-55	15-10	-	01	Przybier-nowka	
Wittenfelde	10	-	-	-	-		
Gruchow	30	-	-	-	-		
Zimdarse	10	-	-	-	-		
Darsow	30	-	-	-	-		

Kreis Regenwalde   Poland

	A	B	C	D	E	F	G
Muddelmow	10	-	-	-	-		
Plathe	80	53-48	15-16	-	03	Płoty	

A	B	C	D	E	F	G
Kreis Regenwalde (continued)						
Wisbu	30	–	–	–	–	
Labuhn	30	54-27	17-48	–	01	Łabun or Labunia
Ruebenhagen	10	–	–	–	–	
Ornshagen	10	–	–	–	–	
Zimmershausen	10	–	–	–	–	
Geiglitz	10	–	–	–	–	
Zowen	10	–	–	–	–	
Natelfitz	80	–	–	–	–	
Neu Gabbuhn	10	–	–	–	–	
Kreis Naugard						Poland
Naugard	–	53-39	15-07	–	03	Nowogard
Braschendorf	10	–	–	–	–	
Wangeritz	10	–	–	–	–	
Pflugrade	80	–	–	–	–	
Wismar	10	–	–	–	–	
Langkafel	10	–	–	–	–	
Bernhagen	10	–	–	–	–	
Gross Benz	30	–	–	–	–	
Kniephof	10	–	–	–	–	
Maskow	30	–	–	–	–	
Gross & Klein Sabor	10	–	–	–	–	
Ottendorf	10	–	–	–	–	
Klein Leistikow	10	–	–	–	–	
Graewenhagen	10	–	–	–	–	
Friedrichsberg	10	–	–	–	–	
Trechel	30	–	–	–	–	
Rothenfier	10	–	–	–	–	
Alt & Neu Fanger	30	–	–	–	–	
Parlin	10	–	–	–	–	
Massow	10	53-29	15-03	–	03	Maszewo
Falkenberg	30	–	–	–	–	
Hakenwalde	30	–	–	–	–	
Gollnow	80	53-34	14-49	–	02	Goleniów
Ibenhorst	30	–	–	–	–	
Kreis Saatzig						Poland
Stargard	–	53-20	15-03	–	03	Starogrod-Szczeciński
Lenz	10	–	–	–	–	
Alt Damerow	30	–	–	–	–	
Uchtenhagen	10	–	–	–	–	
Kreis Randow						DDR
Gartz	?	53-12	14-23	E	01	Gartz/Oder
Book	80	53-29	14-16	C	01	Boock
Ploewen	80	53-28	14-16	C	01	
Mewegen	80	53-31	14-15	C	01	

A	B	C	D	E	F	G
Kreis Randow (continued)						
Rothen Klempenow	10	53-31	14-12	C	01	
Loecknitz	10	53-27	14-13	C	01	Footnote 1
Salzow	10	53-26	14-15	C	01	
Zedlitzfelde	10	–	–	–	–	Not listed
Hagen	10	–	–	–	–	Not listed Footnote 1
Stornow	10	–	–	–	–	Not listed
Stettin	?	53-25	14-35	–	02	Szczecin, Poland
Kurow	?	–	–	–	–	Footnote 8
Kreis Prenzlau						DDR
Prenzlau	–	53-20	13-55	C	03	
Falkenwalde	80	53-16	14-00	C	01	
Kleinow	10	53-16	14-02	C	01	Footnote 1
Wollin	30	53-17	14-04	C	01	Footnote 1
Eichstedt	10	–	–	–	–	Not listed
Woddow	10	53-23	14-11	C	01	
Menkin	30	53-25	14-12	C	01	
Bruessow	80	53-24	14-08	C	01	
Grimme	80	53-26	14-09	C	01	Footnote 1
Bergholz	80	53-27	14-10	C	01	Footnote 1
Kaselow	10	53-27	14-08	C	01	Caselow
Rossow	10	53-28	14-08	C	01	Footnote 1
Weitzenow	10	–	–	–	–	Not listed
Roggow	10	53-29	14-03	C	01	Footnote 1
Zerenthin	10	–	–	–	–	Not listed
Fahrenwalde	80	53-26	14-04	C	01	
Bagemuehl	10	53-22	14-12	C	01	
Schwaneberg	30	53-19	14-07	C	01	
Wallmow	80	53-21	14-05	C	01	
Hammelstall	10	53-23	14-07	C	01	A farm; Footnote 1
Rollberg	10	53-19	14-04	C	01	
Damme	10	53-18	14-01	C	01	
Gruenow	10	53-19	13-57	C	01	Footnote 1
Prenzlau	80	53-19	13-52	C	01	
Schenkenberg	30	53-22	13-57	C	01	
Kremzow	10	–	–	–	–	Not listed
Tornow	10	53-24	13-58	C	01	Footnote 1
Nieden	10	53-26	13-55	E	01	
Fuerstenwerder	10	53-24	13-36	C	01	
Strasburg	10	53-31	13-45	C	01	
Wismar	10	53-31	13-47	C	01	
Kreis Angermuende						DDR
Greiffenberg	10	53-05	13-57	E	01	
Guenterberg	30	53-06	13-58	E	01	
Wedellsberg	10	53-09	13-56	C	01	Wedelsberg; Gruenheide

A	B	C	D	E	F	G
Kreis Angermuende (continued)						
Polssen	10	53-10	13-59	C	01	
Bruchhagen	10	53-05	13-58	E	01	
Welsow	30	53-04	14-00	E	01	
Gruenow	10	53-08	14-04	E	01	Footnote 1
Frauenhagen	30	53-05	14-02	E	01	
Meichow	30	53-11	13-59	C	01	
Gramzow	10	-	-	-	-	Footnote 1
Guestow	10	-	-	-	-	Footnote 1
Luetzlow	30	53-15	14-03	C	01	Footnote 1
Schwedt	10	53-04	14-18	E	01	
Lunow	30	52-55	14-07	E	01	
Liepe	30	52-52	13-58	E	01	Footnote 1
Chorinchen	10	-	-	-	-	Not listed
Angermuende	80	53-02	14-00	E	01	
Oderberg	?	-	-	-	-	Not listed
Kreis Greifenhagen						Poland
Greifenhagen	-	53-15	14-29	-	03	Gryfino
Schulzendorf	10	-	-	-	-	
Fiddichow	30	53-07	14-23	-	01	Widuchowo
Wilhelmshoehe	10	-	-	-	-	
Nipperwiese	80+	53-05	14-23	-	01	
Kranzfelde	10	-	-	-	-	
Bayershoehe	10	-	-	-	-	
Roderbeck	10	-	-	-	-	
Jaegersfelde	10	-	-	-	-	
Wildenbruch	10	-	-	-	-	
Uchtdorf	10	-	-	-	-	Lisie Pole
Kreis Koenigsberg						Poland
Koenigsberg	-	52-58	14-26	-	01	Chojna
Gross Wubiser	10	-	-	-	-	
Lietzegoericke	80	-	-	-	-	
Kreis Ober-Barnim						DDR
Alt Wriezen	10	52-44	14-12	E	01	
Neu Medewitz	10	-	-	-	-	Not listed
Neu Kietz	30	52-44	14-10	E	01	Footnote 1
Beauregard	10	52-44	14-12	E	01	Altwriezen-Beauregard Commune
Alt Lewin	10	52-42	14-16	E	01	
Gross Barnim	10	52-41	14-16	E	01	
Neu Trebbin	10	52-40	14-14	E	01	
Wuschewier	10	52-39	14-16	E	01	
Stetzing	30	-	-	-	-	Not listed
Alt Friedland	10	52-38	14-13	E	01	
Kreis Lebus						DDR (Seelow)
Sophienthal	10	52-39	14-27	E	01	

A	B	C	D	E	F	G
Kreis Lebus (continued)						
Neu Langsow	10	52-34	14-24	E	01	
Ortwig	10	52-42	14-21	E	01	
Leischin	10	-	-	-	-	Not listed
Rehfeld	10	52-38	14-26	E	01	
Kreis West Sternberg						Poland
Zielenzig	10	52-26	15-06	-	01	Sulecin
Kreis Zuellichau						Poland
Zuellichau	80	52-05	15-37	-	03	Sulechów
Padligar	30	-	-	-	-	
Ostritz	10	-	-	-	-	
Schmoellen	30	-	-	-	-	
Krauschow	10	-	-	-	-	
Krummendorf	30	-	-	-	-	
Langmeil	30	-	-	-	-	
Kay	80	-	-	-	-	
Guthren	30	-	-	-	-	
Lochow	30	-	-	-	-	
Klemzig	80+	-	-	-	-	
Goltzen	30	-	-	-	-	
Langheinersdorf	30	-	-	-	-	
Harthe	30	-	-	-	-	
Nickern	80	-	-	-	-	
Schoenborn	30	-	-	-	-	
Friedrichsfelde	10	-	-	-	-	
Rissen	10	-	-	-	-	
Rackau	30	-	-	-	-	
Klippendorf	10	-	-	-	-	
Kutschlau	10	-	-	-	-	
Rentschen	10	-	-	-	-	
Skampe	30	-	-	-	-	
Jehser	10	-	-	-	-	
Schwiebus	30	52-15	15-32	-	03	Świebodzin
Salkau	10	-	-	-	-	
Graeditz	10	-	-	-	-	
Muschten	30	-	-	-	-	
Keitschen	30	-	-	-	-	
Klein Dammer	30	-	-	-	-	
Moestchen	30	-	-	-	-	
Niedewitz	10	-	-	-	-	
Friedrichs Laesgen	10	-	-	-	-	
Tschicherzig	?	-	-	-	-	
PROVINCE POSEN						
Kreis Meseritz						Poland
Meseritz	80	52-26	15-35	-	02	Miedzyrzecz
Gross Dammer	80	-	-	-	-	

A	B	C	D	E	F	G
Kreis Meseritz (continued)						
Chlastawe	80	-	-	-	-	
Kuschten	10	-	-	-	-	
Tirschtigel	80	52-22	15-52	-	01	Trzciel
Ziegelscheuner Hauland	30	-	-	-	-	
Kreis Bomst						Poland
Bomst	10	52-10	15-49	-	03	
Brausendorf	10	-	-	-	-	
Kramzig	10	-	-	-	-	
Unruhstadt	10	52-04	15-51	-	01	Kargowa
Karge	30	-	-	-	-	Kargowa?
Chwalim	10	-	-	-	-	
Schwenten	10	-	-	-	-	
Wollstein	10	52-07	16-08	-	08	Wolsztyn
Tuchorze	10	52-11	16-03	-	05	Tuchorza
Scharker Hauland	10	-	-	-	-	
Borui	80	-	-	-	-	
Kuelpin	10	-	-	-	-	
Ruden	10	-	-	-	-	
Kreis Buk						Poland
Buk	-	52-21	16-32	-	05	Buk
Cichagora	10	52-18	16-12	-	08	Cicha Gora
Sontop	10	-	-	-	-	
Tomysl	10	52-21	16-10	-	05	Nowy or Stary Tomysl
Kreis Samter						Poland
Samter	-	52-37	16-35	-	05	Szamotuły
Turowo	10	52-28	16-19	-	05	
Pinne	10	-	-	-	-	
Kreis Birnbaum						Poland; footnote 9
Birnbaum	10	52-29	15-52	-	08	Swiechocin?
Prittisch	80	-	-	-	-	
Kreis Kosten						Poland
Rensko	30	52-06	16-26	-	08	
Pruchzkowo	10	-	-	-	-	
Prauschwitz	10	-	-	-	-	
Stadt Posen						Poznań
Kreis Krossen (Crossen)						Poland
Krossen	80	52-03	15-05	-	03	Krosno Odrzanskie
Deutsch Nettkau	10	-	-	-	-	Nietkow
Blumberg	30	-	-	-	-	
Plau	80	-	-	-	-	
Merzwiese	30	-	-	-	-	
Boberstag	10	-	-	-	-	
Treppeln	30	-	-	-	-	
Kreis Guben						Poland
Guben	10	51-56	14-43	-	01	Gubin
Kreis Sorau						Poland
Sorau	10	51-38	15-09	-	01	Zary
Christianstadt	30	51-47	15-15	-	01	Krystowice
Niemenau	10	-	-	-	-	
Friedersdorf	10	-	-	-	-	
Rodstock	10	-	-	-	-	
Guschau	10	-	-	-	-	
Tielitz	10	-	-	-	-	
Kreis Kottbus (Cottbus)						DDR
Kottbus	30	51-46	14-20	Z	01	

FOOTNOTES:

1. Many villages of this name.
2. Directly south of Seidewinkel; might be in Hoyerswerda itself.
3. Do not confuse with the village of Neusaerchen.
4. East of Noes; now in Poland.
5. Northeast of Neusorge.
6. Four kilometers from Pohlschildern; 38 inhabitants in 1913.
7. Township government merged with Lebbin (Lubin=Polish) in 1937.
8. On Polish side of the border.
9. Area now called Puszcza Notecka, between the Warta (Warthe] and Notec Rivers.

INDEX OF PLACE NAMES

Place names mentioned in the text have been indexed to include not only the page number but also position on the page. For example, a reference to page 34c indicates that the place name will be found in the lower third of the left-hand column of page 34; page 34e indicates that the place name will be found in the middle third of the right-hand column of page 34.

```
: a   .   d :
:     .     :
:     .     :
: b   .   e :
:     .     :
:     .     :
: c   .   f :
```

In addition, some abbreviations have been used, as follows: Pr. = province (*Land; Regierung*)
  Bez. = *Bezirk* (governmental region)
  Kr. = *Kreis* (governmental district, about the size of a township in the U.S.A.)

When not otherwise indicated, the place name is a village, parish, or farm. The modern-day Polish equivalents for larger entities has been included, when these could be determined.

New Bergholz, New York 2e; 47c
New York, state of 2c
Nickern, Kr. Zuellichau 5d; 5e; 58f; 72e
Niebusch, Kr. Freistadt 7b; 34a; 69e
Nieden, Kr. Prenzlau 32d; 43a; 71f
Nieder-Finow, Kr. not given, Brandenburg Pr. 45d
Nieder-Horka, Kr. Rothenburg 48a; 68e
Nieder-Muehlwitz, Kr. Oels 17b; 69d
Nieder-Seiffersdorf, Kr. Rothenburg 48d; 51d; 68d
Niedewitz, Kr. Zuellichau 36c; 72f
Niemenau, Kr. Sorau 34f; 73e
Niesky, Kr. Rothenburg 48d; 51d; 68c
Nietkow = *Polish for* Deutsch-Nettkau, Kr. Krossen
Nipperwiese, Kr. Greifenhagen 27c; 27d; 33c; 33d;
  53c; 55e; 60b; 63a; 63c; 72b
Nismenau, Kr. Sorau 34f; 73e
Nitznow, Kr. Kammin 24e; 40f; 70b
Noes, Kr. Rothenburg 48c; 68e
Nordhausen, Kr. Erfurt 12f
North America 3b
Nowogard = *Polish for* Naugard, Kr. Naugard
Nowy-Tomysl, Kr. Buk 3b
Ober-Siegersdorf, Kr. Freistadt 34a; 69e
Oderberg, Kr. Angermuende 72b
Oedernitz, Kr. Rothenburg 49b; 68c
Oels Kreis 69d
Oels, Kr. Oels 69d
Oelsa, Kr. Rothenburg 51b; 68c
Olesnica = *Polish for* Oels, Kr. Oels
Ornshagen, Kr. Regenwalde 29e; 71a
Ortwig, Kr. Lebus 33c; 72d
Oshkosh, Wisconsin 2d
Osterwieck, Bez. Magdeburg 52f
Osterwieck, Kr. Osterwieck 13e
Ostritz, Kr. Zuellichau 6d; 72d
Ottendorf, Kr. Naugard 26e; 71b
Padligar, Kr. Zuellichau 45b; 72d
Panten, Kr. Liegnitz 45e; 69a
Parchwitz, Kr. Liegnitz 19c; 36e; 45f; 69b
Parlin, Kr. Naugard 42a; 71c
Pemplow, Kr. Kammin 11d; 70b
Perleberg, Kr. West-Priegnitz 43d; 43e
Petershain, Kr. Rothenburg 49b; 68c
Peterwitz, Kr. Breslau 43f
Pfaffendorf, Kr. Liegnitz 19c; 69a
Pflugrade, Kr. Naugard 38c; 38d; 71b
Pilsnitz, Kr. Breslau 15a; 69c
Pinne, Kr. Samter 19b; 73b
Pittsburgh, Pennsylvania 13f

Platchow, Kr. Kammin 3c; 70d
Plathe, Kr. Regenwalde 10a; 29d; 38d; 70f
Plau, Kr. Crossen (Krossen) 14d; 62b; 73d
Ploewen, Kr. Randow 26b; 31b; 38f; 39f;
  40a; 44b; 71c
Ploty = *Polish for* Plathe, Kr. Regenwalde
Poessen Kolonie, Kr. Angermuende 43c
Pohlschildern, Kr. Liegnitz 36c; 69a
Polchow, Kr. Kammin 3e; 11e; 70c
Polkwitz, Kr. Glogau 16d
Polkwitz, Kr. Goldberg 68f
Polnisch-Hammer, Kr. Trebnitz 15e; 52e; 55e; 69c
Polnisch-Peterwitz, Kr. Breslau 64b
Polnisch-Wartenberg, Kr. Wartenberg 16a
Polssen, Kr. Angermuende 72a
Polwitz, Kr. Glogau 16d; 68f
Pomerania Pr. 19b
Pomerania Pr., Bez. Coeslin 12a; 30e
Pomerania Pr., Kr. Fuerstentumer [Duchies] 30e
Pomerania Pr., Kr. Greifenberg 9e; 28c; 33e
Pomerania Pr., Kr. Greifenhagen 10c; 27c; 33c
Pomerania Pr., Kr. Kammin 3b; 3d; 10d; 23e;
  31b; 38f; 40e
Pomerania Pr., Kr. Naugard 3d; 10d; 26b; 38a
Pomerania Pr., Kr. Neu-Stettin 12a
Pomerania Pr., Kr. Prenzlau 30e
Pomerania Pr., Kr. Randow 26b; 38f; 39f
Pomerania Pr., Kr. Regenwalde 10a; 29b; 38d
Pomerania Pr., Kr. Saatzig 30d; 38e
Pomerania Pr., Kr. Usedom-Wollin 3d; 9a; 29f; 39d
Port Adelaide, Australia 2f
Posen, Kr. Posen 45c; 47a; 73d
Posen Pr. 7d; 19a
Posen Pr., Bentschen 8a
Posen Pr., Kr. Birnbaum 8d
Posen Pr., Kr. Bomst 8f
Posen Pr., Kr. Buk 37b
Posen Pr., Kr. Kosten 37c
Posen Pr., Kr. Meseritz 35c
Poznan = *Polish for* Posen
Prauschwitz, Kr. Kosten 45c; 73d
Prenzlau Kreis 64e; 65d
Prenzlau, Kr. Prenzlau 22a; 32a; 42c; 42d;
  53d; 71d; 71f
Pribbernow bei Stepenitz, Kr. Kammin 61a
Pribbernow, Kr. Greifenberg 10a; 70f
Pribbernow, Kr. Kammin 24b; 70d
Prinkendorf, Kr. Liegnitz 44f; 69a
Prittag, Kr. Gruenberg 18f; 19a; 69f
Prittisch, Kr. Birnbaum 8d; 73d

SURNAME INDEX

Surnames mentioned in the text have been indexed to include not only the page number but also their position on the page. For example, a reference to page 34c indicates that the surname will be found in the lower third of the left-hand column of page 34; page 34e indicates that the surname will be found in the middle third of the right-hand column of page 34.

```
: a . d :
:   .   :
: b . e :
:   .   :
: c . f :
```

Hoppe	28e
Horn	29d
Hottas	47f; 49e; 50e
Houdelette	38f
Hourtienne	32c; 56c
Huck	23c; 42c
Huebner	23a; 45d
Huebsch	15b
Hueller	42f
Igel	16a
Ike	37f
Ilgner	4a; 19c
Illies	11f
Irmler	18d
Irrgang	34a; 34f
Iselt	50b; 50f; 51c
Jachning	5e
Jacob	36a
Jacobi	12e
Jaeckel	15c; 16c
Jaeger	11d; 25c; 25d; 26d; 40f; 59b; 63a; 65b
Jaensch	4c; 5b
Jaeschke	9a
Jageritz	37f
Jagow	39f; 43a
Jahn	20c
Jahncke	11e
Jandke	6b
Janetz	50f
Janetzky	5f
Janke	25a; 25b
Jannack	51c
Jenke	48e
Jennrich	41f
Jennrich. See also Gennrich	
Jentsch	34b; 36b
Jochmann	16c
John	36d; 37a
Joppich	45f
Jordan	15f; 52e
Judisch	42e; 42f
Juedes	29e
Junge	23a
Jungfer	36f; 37a
Jurack	49d
Jureck	37b
Juritz	51b
Jurz	50f; 51a
Jurz. See also Goers	

Just	11b
Kaergel	18f
Kaestner	7b
Kaethner	34d
Kahl	46e
Kahle	34c
Kahn	41f
Kaiser	48e; 51c
Kaleske	7e; 8c
Kallies. See Callies	
Kalm	45c
Kamann. See Camann	
Kammer	17a
Kammrade	41e
Kannenberg	25e; 38f; 39c
Kant	26f; 58c; 66b
Kanther	17a
Kanuth	20c
Kaplik. See Caplik	
Kapp	25d
Kappler	8b
Karg	8d
Karge	27d
Karl	14c
Kasparick. See Casparick	
Kasper	48b; 48e; 49c; 50e
Kasper. See also Casper	
Kassner	3c
Kassube	64f
Kassube. See also Cassube	
Kasten	3c
Kauffung	13e
Kavel	8f
Keibler	41f
Keil	3a; 15f; 17a
Keller	15d
Kempfe	13b; 13d
Kempfert	42a
Kiank	48e
Kieckhoefel	19e; 64a
Kieckhoefer	24b; 24c
Kieschnik	50a
Kiesetz	50a
Kiesling, Kiessling	47f; 49a
Kilian, Pastor	49a; 53e
Kindermann, Pastor	2e; 23e; 55c; 61b
Kintzel	8d
Kirsch	5d; 5e
Kirschke	6c; 44d

Kist	11f
Kittlau	3b
Klamp	24c
Klant	36f
Klar	19a; 58a
Kleber	18e
Klee	20d; 21b
Kleemann	2f; 3d
Klemm	35c
Klemtke	52b
Klenke	5b; 5c
Kletzke	51f
Kliche	18e
Kliese	23f
Klimke	18c
Klinkhard	10e
Klitschke	47e
Klohn	25e
Klose	15f; 16c; 34c; 34d; 61d; 62a
Kluck	12a; 33d
Kluetz	53f
Klug	10a; 10c; 12b; 25b; 38e
Kluge	5f; 6a; 18b; 58f
Kluth	30c; 30d
Knall	41a
Knauerhase	44d
Kneiske	30a
Knipper	51e
Knispel	6a
Knobel	17c
Knoll	11e; 23e; 41a
Knopf	43a
Knorr	27c
Knuschke	36f
Knuth	9e; 10c; 54c
Koatny	50f
Koch	6a; 22b; 26a; 61b
Kockejoy	5a
Kockul	50e
Koebel	49c
Koehler	4c; 11c; 12a; 13e; 35f
Koehn	21f; 22a; 42e; 64f
Koeller	10c
Koenig	5a; 5f; 31d
Koepke	25f; 38f; 39a; 40f; 62f
Koeppen	23a
Koepsel, Koepsell	10e; 28f; 29a; 29d; 41a; 41b; 62c
Koerber	4e; 6c
Koerk	49f

Mackenzie	34c
Maerten	42f
Magnitz	30a; 30e
Mahn	6d
Maidorn	49b
Maillefert	32b
Maire	22d
Maltick	49c
Manke	42b
Manthey	10c; 30e
Mantke	43c
Markhoff	21e
Marlow	26e; 26f; 63b; 66d
Marten, Martin	13c; 25d; 32d
Martschink	50c
Marx	11a
Mashop, Pastor	2e
Masur	47c
Mathias	15c; 17b
Mathiske	4f
Matjetz	48a
Matter	28f
Mattner	8b; 18e; 45a; 47b
Matuck	49d
Matusch	51f
Matz	50c
Matzanke	17e; 18e
Matzdorff	20b
Matzke	15e
Mauer	13e
Mehle	51b
Mehls	21f
Meinke	36a
Meissner	5f; 12e; 14f; 23b; 31d; 47d; 66b
Meister	25c
Mengert	27a
Mente	17d
Merkel	42f
Mersch	18d
Merten, Mertens	22a; 40e
Merting	50c; 50f
Mesicke	33b
Messner	35b

Messner. *See also* Meissner

Metzenthin	35e
Metzner	16b; 17b

Metzner. *See also* Miesner, Mietzner

Mewes	42e

Meyer	14d; 17f; 20d; 32d; 42; 42f; 43a

Meyer. *See also* Maire

Michalk	48a; 51b
Michler	51a
Mickan	49a
Miegel	4c
Miehle	23a
Mielenz	22c
Miersch	49a
Miesner	50b
Mietzner	42d

Mietzner. *See also* Metzner

Milbrath	9b; 30c
Mildebrath	11a; 11b; 11c
Milius	23b
Milleville	42d
Mitschke	51a
Mitzlaff	24d; 24e; 40f
Modisdach	35d
Moegenburg	39b
Moerbe	50a; 64d
Moesch	38c
Moldenhauer	22c; 22e; 23e; 28d; 33b; 63f
Moll	26b; 31a; 40b; 40c; 40d; 42d; 44c; 56d; 57a; 57b; 57c; 57d; 64f
Molz	39a
Mros	49f
Mrosk, Mroske	14d; 50d; 50e
Muechling	15b
Muecke	43d
Mueggenburg	45d

Mueggenburg. *See also* Moegenburg

Muehlenbeck	41e
Mueller	12c; 12d; 13b; 16d; 19b; 20c; 21b; 21e; 24c; 25a; 25f; 28b; 32c; 40d; 41c; 42f; 43c; 45e; 46e; 48e; 50f; 55e; 64f
Mueller, Pastor	2e
Muenchenberg	8a
Muenchhausen, von	65a
Muesch	39d
Mullak	8d
Mummert	37b
Muster	37c
Nasch	45a
Nass	30d; 38e
Natzke	9e
Naumann	60c

Nebe	13e
Nehrlich	19a
Neimann	13b
Neitzel	38a; 41e; 64b
Nell	25a; 33e
Nettenberg	18e
Neubauer	13c
Neumann	5b; 5c; 5e; 10a; 10e; 17f; 20d; 24a; 36f; 37e; 39d; 42f; 43c; 48a; 49a; 53e
Neumoeth	28d
Nicolai	18f
Nicolaus	28d; 59c
Nippe	34e; 44e
Nitschke	5b; 5c; 5d; 6e; 17a; 18c; 18d; 18f
Noack, Noak	35f; 48f; 46d; 50a; 51c
Nocke	49b
Nofke	25a
Nowke	49d
Obst	31d; 36d; 36e; 37a
Oelgarte	56e; 57d
Oertwig	27f; 33c
Ohm	24a
Ossig	43f; 64b
Oster	45c
Oster, Pastor	47a
Ott, Otte	9e; 36d; 39d
Otterstein	27a; 33a
Otto	13b; 23f; 32b; 39d; 40f
Paech	5b; 5d; 5e; 6e; 17e; 36b; 36c; 54c; 58c; 66a
Page	28b; 60d
Pagel	29b; 42f
Pagenkopf	9e
Pahlow	30a

Pahlow. *See also* Bahlow, Behlow

Palm	43e
Pankow	22d; 25b; 31e; 37c; 37d; 39c
Pankow, Pastor	64a
Papke	33d; 33e
Parlow	9d; 54f
Paschke	8e
Pasewalk	38c; 38d
Passau	13a
Patratz	23e
Patschke	51f
Paulick	50b; 50d